THE FUN REVOLUTION

OTHER WORKS BY THE WIZARD

My Life as a Miracle (Canterbury University Press, 1998)

The Wizard's harmless, sensational, original, all-embracing,. up-to-date and thoroughly uplifting Nonsense Almanac for 1974.
(The Union of Melbourne University, 1974.)

Copyright 2021 The Wizard of New Zealand Ltd

Acknowledgments: Photos: John McCombe (cover photos), Kurt Langer and Karl Filipov and various untraceable newspapers, magazines and individuals over the past 50 years.

Collaboration on design: Alice, Phill Simmonds, Tania and Mark from Blueprint Media, and Martin Taylor from Digital Strategies.

THE FUN REVOLUTION

JACK'S ADVENTURES
IN IDEOLOGYLAND

THE WIZARD OF NEW ZEALAND QSM

This book is dedicated to Jacinta Price, Candace Owens and Charles, Prince of Wales, individuals with 'dragon energy' who stand up for truth, beauty and goodness in spite of great pressure from conformists.

*The best lack all conviction,
while the worst are full of passionate intensity.
Surely some revelation is at hand.*

This book is an 'ideological meme-complex' created in the fun-revolutionary warfare laboratory of the Wizard of NZ, who is a shaman in the virtual global village. This meme-complex is a metaphysical virus that has been sequenced over fifty years and has been carefully spliced together from extracts from various physical, psychological, social and cultural ideologies. It has the ability to penetrate ideological cell walls to create comical cognitive dissonance through intellectual reductio ad absurdum. It also provides symbolic-verbal support for the deep organic 'mimetic reaction' to his personal Road Runner-like public behaviour in Australasia. This has been taking place for over fifty years and is now embedded in the collective unconscious. Exposure to both his ideodynamic, mythodynamic and psychodynamic reflexivity can weaken or destroy those repressive and non-existential ideologies that are based on the fear of life and playfulness. Many of these ideological bogeymen are spawned by the egoistic desire for spiritual immortality or by the desire for material immortality through personal reputation after death.

Psychological addiction to coercive power over others is becoming increasingly common. This 'Will to Power' is justified in order to bring about a future perfect society resembling an environmentally destructive and inhuman ant heap. This can be halted by fun revolutionary action designed to reveal the absurdity and dysfunctionality of their penny-wise and pound-foolish concern with trivialities.

A SANE REVOLUTION

If you make a revolution, make it for fun,
don't make it in ghastly seriousness,
don't do it in deadly earnest, do it for fun.
Don't do it because you hate people,
do it just to spit in their eye.
Don't do it for the money,
do it and be damned to the money.
Don't do it for equality,
do it because we've got too much equality
and it would be fun to upset the apple-cart
and see which way the apples would go a-rolling.
- DH Lawrence

The Beatles song "Revolution" made a big impact in 1968 but upset the serious revolutionaries who objected to the lines shown underneath: it has not been heard much since then.

You say you'll change the constitution
Well, you know
We all want to change your head
You tell me it's the institution
Well, you know
You better free you mind instead
But if you go carrying pictures of chairman Mao
You ain't going to make it with anyone anyhow
Don't you know it's gonna be
All right, all right, all right

CONTENTS

Introduction: A View From The Ivory Tower	11
Foreword: The Fun Revolution – Theory and Practice	13
The Funpowder Plot and Real Avant Garde Theatre	33
Roles - The Missing Link	55
Hunting The Boojum	97
Opening The Great Portal	117
Sex And The Heavenly Singularity	135
What's The Matter Of Britain?	167
The Great Leap Backward	185
World Systems in Collision	211
The Wizard's Great Reset	225
Discombobulating The Blob	271
The End	281
Decoding The Wizard's Process Cosmology	291

PRIME MINISTER

PROCLAMATION

Be it known by all and singular that the Wizard of Christchurch, Living Work of Art at the National Gallery of Victoria and the Robert MacDougall Art Gallery in Christchurch, and Cosmologer of the University of Melbourne, formerly known as Ian Brackenbury Channell; is hereby appointed the first Wizard of New Zealand, entitled to wear the appropriate regalia and be required to carry out the duties of national Wizard, namely to protect the Government, to bless new enterprises, cast out evil spirits, upset fanatics, cheer up the population, attract tourists and in particular to design and promote a new and improved universe which puts New Zealand on top of the world both physically and metaphysically.

Given under my hand, this Sixth Day of October, in the Year of Our Lord 1990, Sesquicentennial year of the Dominion of New Zealand.

The Right Honourable Mike Moore
Member of Parliament
Prime Minister of New Zealand

Once upon a time in New Zealand

Putting the fear of God into the Government Statistician (Photo: Evening Post)

A VIEW FROM THE IVORY TOWER

- Jeff Malpas, Emeritus Distinguished Professor, University of Tasmania, Feb 2020.

It is commonplace to regard wizards as fictional characters – and by fictional, I mean non-existent outside of the pages of story books, films, comics and other entertainments. But wizards are not fictional – they are not the stuff merely of 'entertainment' – and one of the great achievements, perhaps the greatest achievement of the Wizard of New Zealand, has been to demonstrate that this is the case. One might even say that, through his own self-creation, the Wizard has made wizards real – and that surely is a feat of genuine magic.

Yet magic does not come about accidentally – it is achieved only through enormous effort, skill, and learning. The Wizard's own path to wizardry has been a long one, and it has been pursued, not only practically, but also theoretically. What this book contains is both an account of aspects of that practice, including some of its history, *and* an exposition of the ideas that underpin it, and with which it is embedded.

What becomes evident here is the extent to which the task of wizardly creation is based is itself based in a well-worked out set of ideas that make use of spells and charms learned first in the 'groves of academe'; a body of thinking that is indebted to Weber, Jung, Nietzsche, Vaihinger, Whitehead, Turner, and many others – who can perhaps themselves be seen as precursors to, or prophets of, contemporary wizardry.

True Wizards are both of their time and yet apart from their time – they act, to some extent, as time-turners, shifting their time, even though this can be done only through the shifting of the elements of both time and space as these are present in their own places. These essays contribute, just a little, to that task of time-turning, but they also provide entry to a way of understanding the nature of this time, this 'present age', in relation to the long past that precedes it and the wide cosmos in which it is set, that is critical and yet also strangely optimistic. Perhaps that is the way of wizards – to be fierce in their diagnosis of our ills but gentle in their hope for something better.

*The method employed I would gladly explain
While I have it so clear in my head.
If I had but the time and you had but the brain –
But much yet remains to be said.* – Lewis Carroll

FOREWORD

FOREWARNED IS FOREARMED

THE FUN REVOLUTION IN THEORY AND PRACTICE

I originally titled this first collection of my short essays *Mein Kopf* since they have been buzzing round in my head for many years. The book is designed primarily for those widely-read individuals disillusioned by their experiences in higher education but who have not yet lost their native curiosity, scepticism, and sense of humour.

In peppering a wide range of targets like a scatter gun, one of my aims is to show my view of some of the connections between the different values embedded in cultural belief systems, their adaptations to their main technological environmental ecosystems, the different institutionalised roles that enact them, and the unique mimetic human behavioural system they are all based upon.

For example, the religious-fertility ideologies and institutions of rural agricultural societies can be compared and contrasted with the secular-economic ideologies and institutions of urbanised mercantile and manufacturing societies. Both of these can be compared and contrasted with the emerging values and institutions of the suburban conglomerates of the ideology of consumerism. The latter is based on the recent exploitation of electricity for power and communication. Since 'history is written in iron' we have come to the end of history and are entering virtual reality. Individuals like the Boy Scouts who have spent time camping together like hunter gatherers, exploring the natural environment and developing hunter gatherer skills and like the lone backpackers who have also explored different cultural environments, are less likely to be embedded in the contemporary cultural world and can imagine alternatives. Without such a detached overall view it is difficult to decide on the best course of action to take to remain safe, sane, emotionally stable and consistent.

I have been a cultural activist since 1968 and those who appreciate the subtlety of my fun revolutionary provocations might want to know why I act as I do and even to copy me through magical mimesis. So I put together a collection of independently written essays and not a well-structured dissertation: I apologise for the repetition of ideas and descriptions that has thereby resulted and for my writing style. I am essentially an actor, not a writer. Although I am full of ideas I express myself in print with some difficulty.

WHAT SHALL WE DO TO BE SAVED?

The common narrative running through most cultures since the agricultural revolution is that of some sort of fall into original sin, followed by alienation and the need for redemption. The resultant self-loathing distorts perception and inhibits the selection of what Joseph Campbell called *Myths to Live By*. However successful they may prove in experimental practice certain working hypotheses or what I refer to as 'useful fictions', may be rejected for psychological, social or political-economic reasons. This is what persuades me to urge the solution provided by my proposed Fun Revolution. I fully realise that having fun is against the grain of the onward rush of history which is still based on the sin of feeling compelled to seek future redemption. Fun is existential, promising no future reward, even though this may happen unintentionally. All determinism demands great effort and suffering, promising futures that in practice are rarely reached. What should happen often doesn't, and what shouldn't happen often does. 'Sufficient unto the day is the evil thereof.' Projecting one's own guilt onto others and punishing them brings no redemption. Only through continuously forgiving ourselves and others of bad actions and showing our repentance by not repeating them, can we return to the Garden. Once we have returned we will have to cut down the Tree of Knowledge of Good and Evil that gives the gods their supernatural power and feast on the fruit of the neglected Tree of Life and continue to evolve again like playful children.

A HIERARCHY OF USEFUL FICTIONS

What can we do to solve the problem of what happens when our cherished beliefs are confounded and the goals we pursue are revealed to be based on fictions? Can human beings live without ideological determinism based on the assumption that we are in possession of the absolute truth? Over time many of what were once believed to be absolute truths cease being valued solely for their truthfulness and instead become traditions valued for such intrinsic qualities as beauty and love through community integration. My solution is to rank truth from 'least true' to 'most true' and then to link these relative truths in a hierarchy of usefulness ranging from 'very useful' (where we encounter reason) to 'very harmful' (where we encounter ethics) whilst allowing 'useless but harmless' (where we enter the realm of art). Even usefulness is not absolute since it is always relative to the decisions of rulers and the different life-styles of societies and groups within societies.

Since they are not located outside the universe, neither verbal nor mathematical statements can be assumed to be absolutely true, only more or less true. The highest truth is that which acknowledges that all human truths created through cultural evolution are ultimately subjective. The most truthful belief systems are those based on this so-called 'postmodern' relativistic assumption. Human beings cannot live orderly and meaningful lives without useful fictions or working hypotheses which cannot be proved to be objectively true. Useful fictions can only function effectively when arranged hierarchically and are based on the fundamental useful fiction that the universe is ordered and ultimately comprehensible. A consensual cosmological paradigm is needed to do this. Only then can other essential aspects of reality, such as the transcendental validation of essential laws, forms of government, family and other institutions, currency systems etcetera, function effectively.

Science as a discipline is based on falsifiable hypotheses and has proved very successful in rejecting or modifying hypotheses by considering them useful fictions open to being progressively improved or completely disproved. The same approach can be taken to all belief systems. Useful fictions or hypotheses for a scientist making weapons for the military industrial complex, are not the same as those chosen by a biochemist seeking medical cures or a psychotherapist concerned with the mental health in a globalised consumer society. An economist charged with increasing the national GDP will chose different useful fictions from those of an ecological scientist specialising in the state of the land and the oceans. They may be completely disconnected and may even contradict each other.

A task that urgently needs to be undertaken is the ordering of useful fictions in terms of an evolving process or inclusive cosmological ecosystem. Using information theory, a cosmology can be constructed with feedback and control loops which prioritises which useful fictions are the most useful for the whole. This is needed to bring together the fragments of the mechanistic enlightenment cosmology shattered by relativity theory, quantum mechanics, and the theory of evolution. Particularly needed is the end of the irrational belief in the possibility of semi-divine objective 'observers'. In his dramatic poetry William Blake expressed his conviction that malevolent secular scientists replaced the love-driven act of understanding and appreciation with the power-driven act of naming and measuring. Adopting process theories to examine evolving inter-related ecosystems rather than measuring isolated 'things' in specific 'locations' in linear sequential space, is proving the only truly rational approach today.

TRUTH BEAUTY AND GOODNESS

These fundamental cultural values are traditionally linked in eventuality ecosystems and mutually support human experiential meaning. When they are politicised they may split up, lose meaning and begin to turn into their opposites. Politicised truth in the public universities may turn into meaningless lies maintained by the persecution or marginalisation of academic dissidents. Politicised art in public art galleries and public places chosen and funded by certificated managers is likely to 'cancel' the representation of their own traditional history, and transcendental religious values. Public art then becomes repetitive politically correct ugliness or empty abstract novelties. Politicised virtue in the governments becomes petty control by meaningless and stupefyingly boring bureaucrats justifying their authoritarian control through fake social science, psychobabble, exaggerated health and safety risks and self-righteous puritanical moralising. Committees then multiply like a cancerous growth and any personal responsibility for the increasing incompetence disappears down a maze of rabbit holes accompanied by mission statements promising spectacular improvements that never occur. This is a rather exaggerated picture of the current state of our values but I am trying to penetrate the fog of justification pouring out of the commercial mass media now forming a monopoly meshed together with the state controlled mass education system.

Since the Second World War there has been a major psychological shift in our civilization from insensitive neurotic goal-achieving to over-sensitive narcissistic virtue signalling. At the same time there has been a social shift from risk-taking entrepreneurial mercantile meritocracy to conformist socialist bureaucratic 'mediocracy', and politically from the cultural cohesion provided by national identity to the multicultural confusion created by coercive attempts to create a supranational egalitarian identity based on inherited biological characteristics. Currently the accumulated values of over two-thousand years of Western civilization may not be taught, endorsed, praised or even described in public without condemnation by fanatics, fools and thugs as 'white male supremacy' which is a largely fictional fear combining racist and sexist ideology as crazy and fanatical as that of the German National Socialists. When free speech is used to criticise this state of affairs it is sometimes silenced by being renamed 'hate speech' and freed from traditional legal protection. Fear of losing one's job and income without debate or appeal is a much more common deterrent used to maintain this absurd and evil fiction. There are some dangerous beasts in Ideologyland.

Another dangerous ideological monster is being sheltered in many modern laboratories. Mechanistic scientists are trying to succeed in their plans for artificial intelligence to replace 'irrational' organic life forms to rule the Earth. At the present time all cultures are being stripped of their diverse values by belief in the unquestionable historical inevitability of selective, bottom-line-measured, bureaucratic globalisation. History has been deified and the superordinate prioritisation of economic-technological progress must not be questioned since it has replaced God's will. This requires no subtle discrimination involving genuine fundamental values. The new power elite are enforcing superficial identity politics as fake new moral absolutes, replacing traditional values of truth, beauty and goodness as the basis for discrimination. Nietzsche's 'will to power' is triumphing over 'the will to love'. As George Orwell prophesied in 1984 the brutal socialist boot has begun stamping on our faces? How close is the Lord of The Rings to finding and putting on the missing master ring of power?

LOVE LOGIC AND LEVITY

Naked power unrestrained by any meaningful values may eat away at the foundations of a civilized culture as a river may undermine the underwater foundations of the piers of a bridge over a fast flowing river. To demystify and counter the compelling force of determinism, both religious and secular, transcendental and reductionist, I have found that only a fun revolution based on a conflation of the motivating forces of love, logic and levity is truly effective. Alfred North Whitehead refined American pragmatism into process philosophy which satisfies most of my requirements for logical analysis. Religious mystics from all cultures have been my guide in appreciating the power of love to stand firm against the love of power. This is not a particularly unusual approach. What I consider to be my greatest strength, which others may perceive as my greatest weakness, is my unusual adoption of levity to balance too much emphasis on logic and love which may cancel each other out. Whilst researching into the nature of aesthetics for my PhD in the Sociology of Art, I had come across a book written in the 1930s by Johan Huizinga, an historian and philologist, called *Homo Ludens, a study of the play element in culture.* He was disturbed by the puritanical elements in the rising totalitarian communist and fascist 'welfare-warfare' states. He surveyed a whole range of different cultures, past and present, pre-literate and literate, rural and urbanised, which successfully functioned largely free from totalitarian forms of government through creative playful elements in their cultural institutions. He found the Anglo-Saxon word 'fun' indispensable in understanding the essence of creative play. This provided the key I had been looking for and opened a door for me to escape from all ideologies placing too much reliance on future reward or punishment for their motivating power. I started the Fun Revolution as a way of life, an existential expression of the trinity of love, logic and levity and began my adventures in ideologyland.

This happened early in 1968, a tipping point in Western civilization when the new 'sensational' paradigms created by the Electric Age technology, heralded by the electronic prophet, Marshall McLuhan, were increasingly melting down the 'sensate' but rigid mechanistic Enlightenment meaning systems. Beatlemania struck and young and well-educated hippies began to experiment with 'sensational' life styles base on love, ecstatic music, sex and mystical religions. At this time Michael Murphy of the Esalin Institute in California brought together many original thinkers whose interaction began the task of providing the foundations of a new civilization. As Wordsworth put it during the heady romantic upheaval that preceded the French Revolution, 'Bliss was it in that dawn to be alive, but to be young was very heaven!'

The French revolution, like the Russian revolution a century later, had begun as an outburst of romantic self-expression against the decadent aristocracy and fossilised Christian Church. Tragically it had been hijacked by resentful intellectuals and the ambitious lawyers and bureaucrats of the rising nouveau riche bourgeoisie to become 'The Terror' of the Jacobins. The playful trusting optimism of the late nineteen sixties was similarly hijacked by the neo-Marxist Parisian intellectuals who were apparently disappointed at the failure of communism to take over all of Europe. The neo-Jacobin celebrity intellectuals of the Ecole Nationale d'Administration, established by the French government to train their public servants, and independent Marxist philosophers were being worshipped like gods in university arts departments and their converts were already seizing administrative control of the burgeoning sociology schools in the universities. During the short failed uprising in Paris in 1968 thousands of students became infected with demonic power and, inspired by the neo-Marxist Gramsci's theory of cultural hegemony, began their 'Long March through the institutions'. Love and trust were soon replaced by fear, distrust and hate. 'Love is all you need' and the flower symbol of the hippies suddenly disappeared, to be replaced by 'empowerment' as the meaning of life and the new symbol was the clenched fist of the socialists. 1968 became 1984. It is becoming clear to me that psychologically and socially our civilization as a whole is currently going through what first happened in the universities in the USA and Western Europe fifty years ago.

Learning to fly in the RAF 1951-53

Attempting to fly: Sunbury Rock Festival 1974

Rain Dance Kid: Waimate 1988

With Mater: Christchurch 1975

Burning money: offering up secular banknotes and replacing them with Heavenly Credits

The Domain, Sydney 1968: pretending to be a serious revolutionary

DEFYING POLITICISATION THROUGH FUN

The rationale for this shift to left wing extremism was clearly provided by the sudden establishment of social science in the arts faculties in Europe and North America. At the age of 35 as the first lecturer in theoretical sociology in the first school of sociology in Australasia I found myself in a pivotal position. Like Peter Berger, author of *Adventures of an Accidental Sociologist*, I became a sociology academic by pure chance. My own theoretical orientation was in the tradition of Max Weber who, influenced by Goethe, was interested in the non-mechanistic tradition of subjective elective affinities. Like Carl Jung in the same alchemical tradition I was passionate about the subjective co-evolution of male and female consciousness. This however was certainly not the view of the Prussians like Hegel and Bismarck who regarded human beings as things to be bureaucratically manipulated for the sake of the evolution of the state as the ultimate expression of God's will or Divine Providence. This deterministic assumption was shared by Marx who added to it class struggle as a

Darwinian evolutionary necessity and revolutionary millenarianism from his priestly Judaeo-Christian background. A toxic mixture.

My past experience in the early 1960s as a pioneer in administering artistic events on behalf of university authorities and my earlier years of wandering among the ruins of past civilizations had given me a sceptical view of the ethnocentric social engineering expected of sociologists employed by the state. In early 1968, inspired by the hippies' deep radicalism which was based on defying both economic determinism and sex-based original sin, I started my Fun Revolution based on sensational creative play to act as a fire break to halt the spread of the approaching grim millenarianism of the student power movement. I did not share the hippies' enthusiasm for antinomian sexual promiscuity which desensitises and exploits vulnerable young women, nor was I attracted to experimenting with chemical boosts to consciousness. In the many counter cultural events I appeared in at the time as the weird and wonderful wizard, I was still partly an outsider.

By 1970 I realised that traditional values of truth, beauty and goodness were being politicised, inverted, and brought under puritanical political control as prophesied in Orwell's 1984. I decided to move fast and using my knowledge and past experience in the fields of aesthetic performance, psychology, sociology, religion and magical persuasion, I set about destroying my old roles and acquiring authentic new roles which being processual and liminal could not be easily controlled by power-driven bureaucrats in the future I saw coming. I had already begun this process by being appointed official Wizard of the University of NSW as part of the initial success of the Fun Revolution which had achieved reforms in teaching and conditions there. To free my consciousness from unconscious determinism by the political controls of the welfare state by 1972 I had allowed most such legal documents to lapse. Instead I had been appointed by the Union of Melbourne University as their official but unpaid Cosmologer, Shaman-prophet and Living Work of Art. The latter title and manifested role action was also recognised by the National Gallery of Victoria and confirmed later by the NZ Art Gallery Directors Council. A few years later the puritanical politicisation of state institutions and their distrust of playful non-socialist and non-capitalist ideologies had reached a point where this would have been absolutely impossible.

THE PLUG PULLED ON THE FUN REVOLUTION

The annual conference of the World University Service held in Hamburg in 1969 backed the Fun Revolution I was leading at the time as their Wizard. I left my base at the University of NSW and my 1970 tour of Australian campuses was proceeding with great success when suddenly the head office in Melbourne ceased communicating and relocated with no forwarding address. I was now marooned in Melbourne. The Fun Revolution had been brutally terminated without explanation by orders from above. At the same time the Student Unions and their newspaper monopolies in the major universities were taken over by deadly-earnest left-wing extremists whose only skill was bureaucratic manipulation. By 1970 dissenting free speech was now described as hate speech on the campuses and was already being censored and forcibly supressed supported by student newspaper monopolies paid for by compulsory fees. My delight in using humour to upset bullies and my special interest in millenarian movements both religious and secular and the collective psychoses that accompany them, inspired me to carry on. I was eventually reduced to circulating roneoed samizdats making fun of the crude ideological justifications and the rather amateurish bureaucratic power games of the student leaders. They claimed to be Maoists or Trotskyites, but they were more like neo-Jacobins and Pol Pot. I have kept records hoping that the ridiculous events of that time would one day come to light to provide an entertaining farce and have written a detailed and documented account of those events in the form of a dialogue between myself as an academic sociologist and myself as a wizard entitled *Channelling the Wizard*.

Summing up; I assume that the cosmos is not a machine driven by chance which bureaucratically organised individuals manipulate to enrich or empower themselves. It is an evolving 'being' subject to emotion where sometimes trust and love is in the ascendant and sometimes fear and hate. In 1968 the latter and the associated pursuit of power rose suddenly as it did in the social disorder that led to Communism in Russia and Nazism in Germany. Happily the reverse may also happen, as it did in the British Empire in 1940 which unfortunately lost most of its power and wealth as a consequence of standing alone to preserve its values against both forms of culture-destroying bureaucratic socialism.

Is there a way to avoid hating hate, fearing fear, and using power to oppose power which only multiplies the evil? As Jesus and other spiritual masters taught, it can be done by loving love, courageously defying fear and, having resisted destruction, forgiving our enemies. What is it that drives us to hate and fear others? It can be seen as original sin which hides like a poisonous serpent in the garden of our hearts tempting us to internalise good and evil and then to project this forbidden supernatural knowledge on to others to gain power over them. The Tree of Life is also growing in the garden and if we internalise its vital force, the love of being alive, we can outgrow our baser instincts.

Bringing playful and all-inclusive and sensational fun to bear on deep behavioural levels in all our attempts to reach deeper truths, more delight in art, and more resilient ethical systems, has not been tried like this before. I believe it has been demonstrated that the only way to proceed in this age of fear and panic and increasingly absurd political programmes is that we have to laugh at it all to stay sane. To support this contention I can do no better than to quote what Merlin Donald says about the neglected phenomenon of mimesis in *A Mind so Rare*, his recent book about the subjective 'involution' and objective 'evolution' of consciousness.

> "The first humanlike culture was associated with a new species, Homo. This was a culture of public action, without languages or symbols but equipped with mimetic expressive skills. This was the birth of the actor, the tribe and the gesture. Given its evolutionary proximity to primate social styles, it must have been dominated by direct expressions of emotion, and indeed, the control of emotion by public action and gesture would have been one of its first priorities. Thus public displays, public competition for control, and a great deal of deception, would have been the rule. It would also have been possible to share attention and knowledge, albeit indirectly, by means of gesture, body language and mime, any of which can communicate an intention quite effectively, without words or grammars. Mimesis must have come quite early in hominoid prehistory because it was a necessary preadaptation for the later evolution of language."

Communicating the truth in the form of linguistic expression may be difficult if we are up against the skilled use of deceit through mimesis. This is what characterises narcissists in particular. There is a long tradition of wise sayings dramatising this use of distracting deceit. Pointing out the hypocrisy of criticising another for having a mote in their eye whilst having a beam in one's own exemplifies the psychological phenomenon of passive-aggressive projection. Another piece of practical advice from the Gospels is, 'By their fruit shall ye know them', which helps us to penetrate the verbal and mimetic screens deceitfully erected to prevent us from 'walking away' and investigating what is actually happening.

Is there a better way to reveal a falsehood than by *reductio ad absurdum* which is also deeply funny? Moral earnestness is often malevolence masked in puritanical self-righteous hypocrisy. What fun it can be when the masks slip. Pure playfulness drives the creation of beautiful things and performances. Shakespeare, like Moliére, knew we are not just slot-machines in a deterministic commercial scenario nor are we Kafka's soulless 'things' to be controlled by bureaucrats empowered by the state who act like artificial intelligence automata. We are not even autonomous individual organisms. We are all social actors playing our parts, well or badly, even in mime. Whatever the scenario, 'The Play's the thing'.

WHAT IS TRUTH?

Truth for humans can be described as a verbally-expressed and interrelated set of concepts used for communicating fundamental values concerning veracity. Creating and sustaining truth values depends on mutual trust, reliability and the belief that individual experiences can be mutually communicated in order to describe the physical, behavioural and socio-cultural environment in order to design rules for living. Although they are mainly communicated in linguistic-verbal or mathematical form, Merlin Donald has clearly shown that these are related through control and feedback to organic mimesis at a deeper level. Although connected to them, truth can be distinguished from other fundamental values such as beauty, and goodness. Truth values are indissolubly linked to virtue values. Bad actors may deliberately lie to harm others, good actors may lie to help others, and foolish actors may lie to avoid admitting their ignorance. Truth values are also linked to aesthetic values which may arouse powerful organic feelings that may be sensed as dangerous and create a need to be rationalised.

'Useful fictions' is another way of describing what scientists call 'working hypotheses'. The term was first used by Hans Vaihinger in his 1911 book As If?, referring to creating intellectual fictions (i.e. 'pretending' can be reaching forward). He distinguishes between those which lead to useful scientific/mathematical discoveries, those that fall apart through internal and external contradictions, dead ends which may be imaginative and entertaining but which have no apparent usefulness, and fictions that if acted on are very destructive of the psychological, social and/or cultural ecosystems.

LIVING IN VIRTUAL REALITY

We cannot escape the conclusion that there is no objective, absolute truth in verbally expressed religious and secular ideologies, or even in mathematical operating systems which validate scientific theories, as Gödel's incompleteness theorem demonstrates. We must assume we cannot avoid living in virtual reality and can only try to get as close to the truth as we can, whilst openly acknowledging our imperfection. One of my favourite science fiction novellas, *Mindswap* by Robert Sheckley, illustrates my point with great sophistication. My own postmodern approach, which differs fundamentally from the fake postmodernism of puritanical believers in millenarian Jacobin nihilism, is to rate our useful fictions in order of relative truthfulness, goodness, beauty and usefulness. Mature personalities who are both mentally balanced and intelligent can openly and honestly debate truth and other value systems. We must be vigilant, since people whose power, wealth or reputational ego is threatened by others being truthful, can lie skilfully or threaten to use force to silence debate. We cannot do better than copy the sages and mystics who regard the divine as indescribable and unnameable, and hence have no belief in determinism or historical inevitability. Such individuals are found in most conservative religions and ideologies, especially in Daoism or the Way.

LOVE LOGIC AND LEVITY DIVIDED

Love without Logic is barren;

Love without Levity is suffocating;

Logic without Love is meaningless;

Logic without Levity is obsessional;

Levity without Love is vindictive;

Levity without Logic is asinine;

Love without Logic or Levity is juvenile;

Levity without Love or Logic is suicidal;

Logic without Love or Levity is Dr Frankenstein's monster of AI sparked into life by electricity.

THE FUNPOWDER PLOT

THE ORIGINS

My involvement with radical university politics began in April 1968 at the University of New South Wales in Sydney. This was when student power was on the rise. As a junior academic, I organised a meeting of staff and students to debate the issues of university reform. As things began to take off on other campuses and with the cooperation of concerned students and staff I put together a list of proposed reforms which I called the ALF Charter, harking back to the populist Chartist movement. The acronym ALF stood for Action for Love and Freedom. I was well aware that in choosing it so early I had spiked the guns of any communist group attempting to found an Australian Liberation Front.

At the same time, I was influenced by the surprisingly non-violent and humorous responses shown by Dubcek and the Czechs to the Soviet led Warsaw Pact invasion of their communist country. Their sin seemed to be that the Czech government was showing signs of 'socialism with a human face' and were tolerating colourful popular music and fun. At the time, the editorial of the Czech official communist newspaper *Rude Pravo* ironically welcomed their Russian 'visitors' but politely asked them why they had come. It was signed Josef Schweik, the hero of that wonderful novel *Good Soldier Schweik*.

I am unaware of any use of the word 'funpowder' or 'funpowder plot' as a revolutionary strategy before I coined the term during the student power upheavals of the late 1960s. Must all revolutions be deadly serious affairs? Later I came across D.H. Lawrence's poem *A Sane Revolution* expressing similar sentiments to my own. The Fun Revolution was how I described the techniques I adopted to break down the rigid structures of both the increasingly bureaucratic university administration and the radical student movement which opposed reform as they needed oppression to increase in order to generate the hatred required for a violent revolution. During 1968 I travelled around many other university campuses in Australia with great success as a missionary for the Fun Revolution.

FINDING THE BALANCE: AN ACTION PHILOSOPHY CALLED ALF

Action for Love and Freedom was a synthesis of the two different radical youth movements which broke away from the conventions of the time; the life-style hippies and what had begun as the New Left politics. The hippies were a unique element rejecting consumerism and a regular job for life in an office, preferring colour, music, free love and communal living with no private property. They also rejected self-righteous intolerant monotheism and were attracted instead by Eastern religions, various forms of drug induced enlightenment, and New Age magic.

At the time, I was giving lectures in the School of Sociology on the various antinomian religious movements in Europe that had broken out during the Middle Ages and was able to use the hippies, who were living free from their parents' moral values, as contemporary examples. It was all too clear to me that their attempts would soon fail. Unlike the political Left they showed little interest in gaining power over others, being essentially escapists who chose love rather than freedom. Being powerless they soon lost freedom in the process. Choosing rebellious political freedom rather than rebellious sexuality and love, the political student radicals were more likely to succeed in their aims but they were destined to become more and more intolerant and consumed with hatred.

My solution in founding ALF was to combine reformist ideas from those who saw capitalism as greatly destructive of both humanitarian community values and the natural environment as well as making use of the informal romantic bohemianism of the youth movement of the time. The idea of a revolution mainly for fun, where both means and ends were the same, appealed to me. Success or failure were not the most important thing. This echoes the lines in Kipling's poem *'If'*, *'and treat those twin imposters just the same'*. Brutal means are frequently adopted to achieve noble ends, but supposing the brutality was always unconsciously intended and the justification of good intentions merely a verbal rationalisation to avoid confronting one's dark side?

Freedom without love had been the result of the Whig revolutions of the industrialising 18th century. Love without freedom characterised the previous agricultural Tory religious monarchy that they replaced. I concluded that the British Constitutional Monarchy was about the best balance that had been achieved so far. Unfortunately, this balance was fast being lost. Since the Great War educational employees of the secular state had been making systematic attacks on the 'wickedness' and/or historical 'irrelevance' of the religious monarchy. Their aim was the replacement of voluntary charitable institutions based on Judaeo-Christian love of one's community by a socialist welfare state based on individualistic human rights and administered by a state managerial elite with great powers of enforcement. The result was dissolving the glue of love that binds a community together without coercion. The amazing demonstration of mass affection for the Monarchy shown at coronations, royal weddings and the birth of heirs to the throne, regardless of class or ideology made no sense to 'weird' (western, educated, industrialised, rich, democrat) sociologists.

THE TACTICS OF THE FUN REVOLUTION

Fortunately, in Paul Comrie-Thompson we had a supportive editor of the student newspaper *Tharunka* who came from a traditional Christian Catholic background. He was initially puzzled by our new political approach. Following publication of an article I wrote for him in early 1968 entitled *Soul Power and Funpowder versus Will Power andGunpowder*, he was prepared to collaborate with our plans. We declared war on the administration and a photo of our cardboard cannon facing the registry building appeared on the front page of *Tharunka*. Positive feedback in the form of loving one's enemies was an essential part of ALF. We offered to let academic staff use the student toilets. When Sir Philip Baxter the Vice Chancellor left Sydney for a meeting we went to the airport with balloons and banners begging him not to leave us. Other universities were beginning to dissolve in chaos as buildings were forcibly occupied by violent Red Guard inspired student groups.

I was now writing articles for various student newspapers on the topic of 'guerrilla warfare of the mind'. The enemy was not just the student-despising administrators and academics but anyone who overused their power over other people, including authoritarian student radicals who were ruining the good relations we were building up in order to get more humane treatment for the students.

On one memorable occasion the students at Sydney University, led by their student executive, occupied their VC's office in the admin building over a minor admissions technicality. I led a small band of students to occupy the empty Student President's office in their admin building at the same time as a protest against a protest. When they returned from occupying the offices of the university executives, the furious student administrators threw us out by force. Single-handedly I occupied occupations, sat in sit-ins and with others demonstrated inside demonstrations. These were some examples of transgressing against transgressing for love, logic and levity.

I became more hated than Nixon and rumours circulated that I had been driven insane by drug use or was a paid stooge for the CIA. To put the record straight I am a drug user as I smoke cigars, occasionally drink whisky, and am addicted to coffee. I have never tried pot or any hallucinatory drugs. I don't need to, I am high most of the time anyway and my imagination runs riot without any prompting. Somehow, I don't think the CIA would recruit someone like me. Sometimes I think I must be 'enlightened' but I enjoy playful self-deprecating ego-tripping too much and find the prospect of becoming an adored guru a very boring ego-trip.

The political radicals endorsed the Soviet-supported communist Viet Cong, who were invading the South, against their own government's backing of the capitalist South Vietnamese government. In Australia conscription had been foolishly introduced so that more troops could be sent to help the Americans, presumably in the hope of better trade deals with the USA. This naturally enough inflamed the students who were now in the firing line. The various student groups, some of whom were devoted to overthrowing their own government, were fortunately influenced by the mass marches and rallies of the highly successful and well administered Civil Rights movement of the time and mostly chose democratic means, though a few Trotskyite infiltrators tried hard to get students to resort to violence.

THE RISE OF THE PURITANS

I soon found the intolerance of the Left was even greater than that of the authorities they wanted to replace. They believed that anyone who was not with them heart and soul must be against them. As a revolutionary using fun to modify rigid authoritarian behaviour in both the establishment and anti-establishment, I was seen by them as a counter-revolutionary, distracting people from 'the real issues'; meaning of course their own antiquated ideas about capitalism and socialism. Their shallowness, lack of experience of political activism and aping of their counterparts in America well fits the description given them of being 'radical chic'. I was also giving lectures at the

Free University on Marshall McLuhan and the institutions of industrial society and pointing out that successful socialist revolutions, although 'well intentioned', inevitably led to authoritarian tyranny by fanatical intellectuals, an increase in the size of the state bureaucracy, and overall impoverishment.

The other radical student leaders were also middle class 'weirds' and had very little experience of living amongst people who did not share their values. They were also convinced that they alone knew what was good for other people and wanted to impose their own values on others by force. No wonder my group of ALF fun revolutionaries were treated like pariahs by the radicals who soon took over the Student Unions and student newspapers. The academic career bureaucrats also saw our fun revolutionary activities as having no meaning and considered they were lowering the tone of the university. I began to call my deadly serious opponents Puritans; the label fitted perfectly.

Diving into lemonade at Mad Mel's Giant Stir, Bondi Beach.

THE ALFS

I have described some of the events that took place at UNSW in Sydney in my short memoir published by Canterbury University Press in 1998. A summary of the most significant as far as I am concerned should be made here. The ALFs had no formal structure but were prepared to act as a pressure group and to speak at formal meetings. The members of our tiny band were not just students and junior academics but even office workers from the administration. We felt the whole university community needed to be 'remoralised' before any significant reforms along the lines of the ALF Charter which we had put together could take place. We assumed that laughter and openly expressed good will would heal the apathy produced by physical separation, automatic rejection of alternative viewpoints and fear of academic failure.

We simply gathered at lunchtimes to swap ideas and to plan our activities. Unlike the other radical activist groups, we had no bureaucratic structure. At this time, radical student groups were forming at other universities, but as they were only concerned with power they lacked any interest in love which they saw as weakness. They regarded university administrations as the capitalist enemy to be opposed by direct confrontation and mob action. As I prophesied regularly at the time, many of these ambitious radicals soon ended up as senior academics, education department bureaucrats, or in their fathers' wealthy businesses.

THE UNIVERSITY MEETINGS

The Round House on the UNSW campus was an unusual building which was ideal for gatherings of all kinds. I organised a series of what I called University Meetings and produced pamphlets on the theme 'What Shall We Do to Be Saved?' I had persuaded the VC to attend and this was announced as 'The Deity will be in attendance accompanied by a chorus of Admin Angels'. A rock group played in between speeches, which were preceded by a drum roll. To encourage lively performances there were 16mm cameras rolling (empty, for reasons of economy) and anyone could express their feelings and propose and pass any motions they liked since it would make no difference anyway. Instead they were urged to 'pass emotions'. The result was a great upsurge of feeling in the packed building rather like an evangelical church service. The high point was when the VC himself got up and announced that he too was bored and that universities were the most bureaucratic institutions he had ever come across in his long career as an administrator. After consultation with students, staff, and administrators I drew up a document for university reform I called this the ALF Charter and it was adopted overwhelmingly at one of these mass meetings. The headline in the *Sydney Morning Herald* next day was 'Students Stage Happening and Launch Power Drive'. A succinct summing up of this unique synthesis.

CONFRONTATION AT LAST

Alfs were given the use of a spare room in one of the temporary academic departments where we used to make signs, banners and costumes etc. The Administration needed us to vacate the room for a meeting; this had happened before without any trouble. Unfortunately, this time the message was not passed on to us and the university saw our innocently remaining in the room as an occupation and we were ordered to leave. It looked like confrontation and puritanical hatred would triumph over freedom, love and fun. The Student Union leaders of that early time did not want us to come into conflict over the issue but the Left radicals waiting in the wings saw this as a great opportunity to demonstrate the inherent violence of the system and to publicise their cause. We put our heads together and came up with a solution based on our own principles. We made large banners announcing, 'We Shall Not Be Moved', and then moved out proudly singing this traditional trade union song. To our delight, choosing love, rather than freedom, was rewarded. The VC responded on his own initiative shortly afterwards by giving us the sole use of a small hut he erected for us on the campus that we named 'The Alf House'.

I was not surprised that in 1968 my wife, a school teacher who had been a good friend and travelling companion for several years, was distressed by my behaviour and made it clear that I had changed too much for her to cope with and that either we left Sydney to carry on our world travelling or we must separate. Luckily, we had no children. It was hard and I hated the suffering that I was causing her but I had found my calling. She thought I was going insane, but I was not only more active socially than usual but was teaching very successfully and reading more than ever. My rather unusual double honours degree in psychological and social theory enabled me to resist pressure from others to believe that I was going mad. I suppose that living for love, logic, and levity can be seen as mad in a mad world.

THE TIPPING POINT

Then, late in 1968 just when my marriage had come to an abrupt end my professor, trained not as sociologist but as a political scientist, cancelled my PhD Thesis in the Sociology of Art on the grounds of 'insufficient progress'. He had not even replied to my requests for a meeting to discuss it. My contract as a teaching fellow and my academic career were both terminated. This was a particularly vicious thing to do as I was well qualified and had given up a tenured lectureship at the University of Western Australia to join the staff of this first sociology department in Australasia. This was on the basis of his promise that I could take as long as I liked on my thesis since I was appointed to design courses and carry much of the teaching load. Before I left WA he had also promised in writing that I would be given a lectureship at UNSW as soon as one became available. My last progress report made earlier in the year had been fulsome in its praise of my teaching ability.

The University Staff Association advised me to sue the university, but that is not my way. The VC was shocked at my treatment by the Professorial Board and the broken promises made and had a similarly sceptical view to my own about the teaching standards and practices of the recently formed Arts Faculty. Above all, I wanted to remain on campus to continue my experiments in a new form of political agitation which had so far proved successful in getting reforms whilst at the same time provided much needed community therapy. He offered financial compensation but instead we

Lone champion of the oppressed peasants.

came to a gentleman's agreement, not a contract. If the Student Union was in favour, then they and the University Administration would jointly provide a small honorarium and I could continue as before. I needed an informal role free from contractual control by the Professorial Board and that could not be seen as either secular (politically righteous) or religious (spiritually righteous). I believe that pure fun is easily corrupted by serious self-righteous moral posturing. I saw the solution in taking on the role of official university Wizard. Not only was *Lord of the Rings* enjoying a massive revival at the time but wizards (wise men and/or tricksters) although not seen by priests or secular humanists as particularly moral people, are believed to have mysterious abilities.

Of course students are bound to be very suspicious of unusual initiatives coming from the administration. I had also incurred the wrath of the serious revolutionaries for making fun of their juvenile attempts to start a violent Paris style confrontational revolution. It would not be easy to persuade the Student Union to join the Administration in appointing a university wizard and providing an honorarium, even though it was even smaller than the salary I received as a mere teaching fellow.

HAVE YOUR WORST SUSPICIONS CONFIRMED

I called a meeting in the Union which I titled 'Have your worst suspicions confirmed'. In order to forestall my enemies I put on my radical student power costume (black leather jacket and peaked denim cap) to denounce the appointment as 'a cunning plan by the Vice Chancellor to divert attention from the genuine issues and to conceal the real violence inherent in the system'. Then I put on my white robe and silly hat and spoke of the humourless violence that was being openly shown by the puritanical left-wing radicals who admired dictators like Mao Tse Tung, promoted his Little Red Book, and could only maintain their humourless authority by entangling students in meaningless bureaucratic procedures.

At the meeting I gave the students questionnaires and asked them to tick which of alternative statements they thought were true. Examples were 'Channell is the VC's stooge *or* The VC is Channell's stooge'; 'Channell is destroying himself *or* Channell is destroying the University'; 'Channell is a fool *or* Channell is making fools of us all'; 'Channell is sexually frustrated *or* Channell is a sexual libertine'; 'Channell was dismissed for academic incompetence' *or* 'Channell was dismissed for no academic reason at all'.

I was delighted and amazed when following this event the Student Union executive agreed to the joint appointment. I foolishly imagined that the appointment of an official wizard with an honorarium by the administration of a major university in association with a Student Union would be newsworthy and might even attract the attention of sociologists and psychologists. All that happened was a short paragraph in the Sydney papers, and dead silence from all academics but one, a political scientist who accused me in the pages of *Tharunka* of wrecking the university as a community of scholars. This silence has continued ever since. Surely such a radical and unusual departure from conventional ideas and lifestyle is worthy of some sort of intellectual recognition, even if negative? The first proto-scientists who initiated the new consciousness were monks who stayed within the Church for institutional support and I had been careful to stay within the ethical rules of academia. Then I remembered that it was mechanists and Pythagorean number worshippers like Newton, a numerologist and one of the last great magicians, who had founded modern materialistic science. Other magicians like Kepler, who regarded Western religion, magic and aesthetics as inextricable aspects of reality, were demonised by the materialistic mechanists. I am not stupid nor am I closed minded. I must represent some sort of indescribable threat. Could I be a one-eyed man in a country of the blind? Since reading Huizinga's *Homo Ludens* I have chosen creative fun as my ultimate *raison d'etre* rather than intellectual superiority or moral righteousness. I have caused considerable disruptions to normal cultural life in New Zealand and earlier in Australia. The deafening silence and lack of reflexivity from leading political, artistic, moral and intellectual authorities was unexpected but has not put me off my strange calling.

Before the essays which apply love, logic and levity to my understanding of the involution of consciousness as exemplified in the evolution of human culture, I provide an account here of my personal use of this new fun revolutionary tool at the University of NSW between 1968 and 1970.

REAL AVANT GARDE THEATRE

AT LAST THE 1848 STUDENT POWER SHOW

Towards the end of 1969, before leaving for the World University Service Conference in Europe, as actor-manager I designed, produced and acted as Magister Ludi in an interactive ritual drama assisted by my partner Adele. I did this on behalf of the Student Union entertainments programme; it took place in the ideal setting of the UNSW Roundhouse, the venue for the ritualised mass meetings run by ALF the previous year which had endorsed the ALF Charter. The stars of the show were Super VC, played by the Vice Chancellor himself, Ape (Anti-Puritan Electro-man) was played by myself as The Wizard, and the part of Ross Clarke the radical Sydney University Labour Club leader was played by Ross Clarke. The UNSW Student Union president, the conservative engineering students' president etc. also played themselves. Unlike traditional bourgeois theatre the actors were not 'representing' other characters. On the contrary, it was the audience or chorus who were doing so, as designated student power groups. It was a sacred ritual, both sublime and ridiculous.

The show was in three parts. As the students entered the Roundhouse they were met by student cheer leaders wearing hats labelled with the names of the common student power groups of the time who gave them arm bands at random and directed them to the relevant sections of the audience/crowd. As in TV shows, during the action the cheer leaders held up signs reading 'Cheer!' 'Boo! 'Groan'! and so on. In Act One, the action, which was not scripted or rehearsed but conducted by the Magister Ludi, was the gradual growth of dissatisfaction amongst the student crowd. Super VC watched as the various stars of the student power groups, both radical and conservative, argued and struggled to a backdrop of student roars urging them on. There were cardboard boxes in the centre and strobe lights flickered as the main actors eventually fought and smashed the boxes. Then there was a flash of light, everything stopped and a junior academic was transformed into a wizard.

The shouting mobs of the first act, together with the main performers, now became an audience. To soft hippy music, with strobes and dimmed coloured lights, sinuous dancers writhed to perform Act Two.

For Act Three, the lights came up and the master of ceremonies pointed out that the person to blame for all the conflict was up above them. There, suspended in the dome of the roof, was a huge transparent figure. 'Eat the Body of God!' he cried out and the figure was lowered to the floor where it was torn apart by the audience who had left their seats. Inside the figure were sweets and plastic instruments; the rock band started playing and everyone danced and danced.

TARRING AND FEATHERING

Hearing of a smear campaign being organised against the Wizard as 'the VC's stooge', (a common complaint), I anticipated my enemies' malevolent intent. Accordingly, I organised my friends (dressed in black Klu Klux Klan style costumes), to bind my wrists and attired in a white sacrificial robe, I was dragged from the Student Union up to the top campus where I was tarred and feathered below the Chancellery. My desperate appeals for rescue made to my father figure somewhere in the brutalist concrete palace towering over me, went unanswered.

THE DICTATORSHIP

A COUP D'ETAT

A few days later I left for Europe. However, having travelled to Hamburg for the World University Service Conference, I found myself stranded in London, where I was staying with my sister. My return ticket which was being organised by the UNSW branch of WUS, had not been cleared by the Student Union. For over a week I received no replies to the anxious telegrams sent to my partner Adele who was also my 'Hon Sec'. Eventually the ticket was cleared and I returned to UNSW to find chaos in the Student Union. No wonder I had been stranded. During my absence a surprise Special General Meeting had voted to abolish it!

The transgressive revolutionaries took up residence in the building and followed the usual romantic narrative of polishing off the drinks etc. Being amateurs, they didn't occupy the premises immediately and the old Union Committee had time to remove essential equipment and files so they could continue administering the student services from another location. The libertarians even left the building early in the evening and consequently the rest of the equipment could be removed for safe keeping and the phones cut off for fear

In the city of London on my way to Hamburg.

of long distance calls being made. This was a professional bureaucratic counter-coup against an amateur bureaucratic coup! Nevertheless, the staff were demoralised and some left, and students seeking help were turned away by the revolutionary heroes. Fortunately, emergency student services were operated with some difficulty by the *ancien régime* from temporary premises, but serious disruption and unnecessary expenses had been incurred.

TAKING ADVANTAGE OF A TEMPORARY SOCIAL ANTI-STRUCTURE

Another SGM was held soon after I returned, and the motion to abolish the SUC was rescinded by a large majority. I addressed the meeting and to the horror of the revolutionaries I proposed that I be elected Dictator of the Student Union until the end of the term in three weeks' time. I promised to restore student and staff morale and raise funds to replace those wasted on this foolish and destructive exercise in 'radical chic'. At this the puritan heroes who had staged the coup exploded in fury which persuaded the other students to enthusiastically support the idea. I had become the first dictator ever to be voted into office as such by a union, and a Student Union at that! I must admit that Kurt Vonnegut's *Cat's Cradle* was in the back of my mind; this was a wonderful opportunity to realise his fantasy.

T shirts carrying the university logo modified by the words *Dictatorship of the University of New South Wales* were quickly silk-screened and sold fast. Friends from ALF made up some khaki uniforms with red trims and formed a bodyguard known as the dictator's 'henchmen' and we held daily Kensington Rallies. Buttons reading 'Loyal Peasant

The power beside the throne.

Alf' were sold to raise funds. Any student caught without a button could be summarily executed by 'pie kill' (shaving cream in the face like a traditional custard pie). At the daily Rallies I addressed the peasant masses from places high enough to be out of reach of most of the barrage of flour and water bombs. My henchmen had already made large shields. Some of them, disguised in civvies, circulated amongst the crowd selling ripe tomatoes and rotten fruit. More income for the Union. I ranted and raved each lunchtime and read poems of praise of my enlightened leadership, composed by myself. Finding the Latin term 'dictator' rather wimpish, I insisted on being called 'tyrant' from the Greek. For a few days I appointed a well-endowed 'tyrantess' who also modelled the T shirts whilst I stood beside the improvised throne whispering in her ear like Rasputin. Female students lined up so that I could select my Wench for The Day.

THE HEROIC ENEMY OF THE DICTATOR ARISES

The daily Rallies soon moved to the upper campus to a ledge jutting out from the library which was located amongst the main administrative buildings. The ledge was directly above a courtyard where, attracted by the din, the student masses gathered. One day I found my bicycle tyres had been let down and a note was attached from 'The Black Spider', claiming responsibility. This was my chance to create an attractive and dramatic enemy since the existing ones were only juvenile intellectuals gaining reflected glory with their colleagues by talking and writing about me as a dangerous, counter-revolutionary, bourgeois deviationist, distracting the students from the real issues, etc. etc. etc. I gathered my henchmen together and we made a kind of spider costume with lots of arms and gave this together with some flares to the Black Spider himself. I did not wish to spoil my fun by meeting him and discovering his identity. I did meet him many years later when he came up and introduced himself in Tamworth just after I had performed one of my famous successful rain dances in the drought-stricken outback. We also quickly silk-screened some T shirts with the slogan 'Death to All Tyrants' above the image of a hairy black spider which we sold to raise funds along with the popular University Dictatorship T shirts which bore a superficial resemblance to the official ones. During my raving monologues the enemy appeared on the roof of a nearby tall departmental building waving his multiple arms and letting off a flare. Becoming incoherent with rage I sent some henchmen off to seize him, unsuccessfully of course. For a variation on the theme a large stuffed black spider was gradually lowered down from the library roof which could be seen by everybody except me and my henchmen until it reached us.

THE ASSASSINATION

The next act in the therapeutic psychodrama began when a student unknown to me and wearing a beret with a scarf in his open necked shirt, was allowed to approach me to read a poem of praise for my enlightened rule. After several verses of fulsome praise, the tone suddenly changed and crying out 'and so foul tyrant, thou shalt die', he reached into his shirt and brought out a custard pie which he planted full in my face. I accepted this as a suitably imaginative and theatrically appealing assassination and left the dais to join the crowd below.

The assassin, as could be expected, had no further action planned and stood wondering what to do next. It was beginning to get boring and since no-one had paid for their seats and it was not morally uplifting political propaganda nor an intellectually challenging piece of avant garde theatre, I had to act fast.

I shouted to him that if he was not willing to become the next dictator he should appoint someone else to fill the vacuum. 'Who?' he said. 'Anyone!' I replied. He pointed to a student standing nearby with a clip file clutched to his chest and told him he was the new dictator. The youth turned pale and tried to escape, but his treacherous friends forced him up onto the platform. My henchmen did not even pause to ask him his name but immediately extended their arms in the Alf salute and cried out 'Hail Whatshisname!' He gave a few half-hearted commands but the show was going flat and I cried out 'Boring!' in the traditional sing-song manner. The crowd realised that I was the key and urged me to return to my lofty platform. I declined, claiming almost in tears that they didn't love me, since they never returned my Alf salute or cried out 'Hail Alf!' as was expected when I appeared. The mob roared back 'We *do* love you', and proved it by crying out 'Hail Alf' in a single voice. Overjoyed I hurried back to my old post, relieved the worried usurper and, chest puffed out like Mussolini, I gave the salute accompanied by an expectant 'Hail Alf'. The reply was a deafening 'Boo!' Such is life.

CORRUPTION AMONGST THE HENCHMEN

On another occasion, I cooperated with the Student Union to book one of the best folk-rock bands in Sydney to perform in the Roundhouse just for me as Tyrant. This was for my ears only and no riff raff were to be admitted so I posted my loyal henchmen on the doors to keep them out. Alas I had not reckoned on their venal nature and they accepted bribes. To my obvious fury, the Roundhouse was soon full and the Union coffers were headed the same way.

THE CLIMAX, A FAILED PUTSCH

The Dictatorship climaxed and ended on the last day of term. A Kensington Rally was held outside the Student Union building at the lower end of the campus and culminated in one of my megalomaniacal raves. I was no longer content to be merely the Dictator of the Student Union; I was going to carry out a Munich-style putsch and become Dictator of the University of NSW. Followed by a mob of students and led by a small brass group playing the march from *Aida*, my henchmen and I proceeded up the long stairway to the Chancellery on the Acropolis. Max Merritt and the Meteors were playing nearby as I stood and shouted that I had come to seize power. At this point Sir Rupert the Vice Chancellor came out on his balcony and ordered me to come up to his rooms. My henchmen went pale and refused to follow me. I had gone too far this time! Courageously I entered the Chancellery and soon appeared beside the VC on the balcony carrying a copy of the ALF Charter of University Reform. He quickly tied me up in red tape, stepped forward and opened his suit jacket to reveal that he was wearing a UNSW Dictatorship T shirt! My henchmen cried out lustily 'Hail Rupert' and the crowd dispersed to listen to Max Merritt. It was all over! But not quite. Years later Sir Rupert informed me that he was due to meet the Australian Prime Minister in his office and hurriedly buttoned up his suit jacket before he went back inside.

ALF'S LIVING THEATRE IS CRAP

My studies for my doctoral thesis in the Sociology of Art had acquainted me with Beck's Living Theatre and Grotowski's Theatre Lab which I considered to be over-planned by elitist individuals with inflated egos, and which were still politically and financially controlled by traditional cultural institutions. In 1969 during my short rule as Dictator I wrote a short article making these points for the student newspaper, entitled *ALF Living Theatre is Crap* (Cultural Revolution against Puritanism). The Dictatorship was taking place in real life and real time, not in a small pond called the 'Counter Culture' with its own protected and introverted institutions like Dada and its imitators. The Fun Revolution was too avant garde and as such was largely incomprehensible to the conformist and very serious avant garde theatre producers. To prove my point, to date no one has written anything about these unique events, whist reams have been written and published about other more conventional performances. I was also solving real organisational problems whilst revitalising and providing community therapy for a student community that had been deliberately damaged by elitist radicals during my absence abroad. Having no ego invested in any 'serious' social institutions with hidden agendas and having the support of the Vice Chancellor who represented the interests of the wider community, I was protected from my enemies on campus desperate to stop my 'counter-revolutionary' influence over the students.

THE PSYCHOANALYTIC HISTORY DISSERTATION

The last performance I put on before leaving to go on tour was in the Science Lecture Theatre, with music by Extradition, an excellent folk-rock group (unfortunately short lived). It was based largely on Norman Brown's sociological reinterpretation of Freud, *Life Against Death*. My farewell to the academic life was a kind of postmodern conflation of a mystery play and medieval thesis where a scholar stood before his masters to be orally tested. *The Four Ages of Man and Fool's Paradise Regained* took place over three nights and the programme notes presented my early rough thoughts about cultural evolution. It began on the theme of immortality and concluded with my leaving the stage (and university) to commence an 'immorality show' in the real world. I was not personally satisfied with this as it was too preachy, lacked spontaneity and there was a traditional audience. It would have better as a planned interactive pantomime/thesis.

I continued this form of avant-garde theatre in New Zealand. Examples are the struggle to be allowed to speak in Cathedral Square; the aesthetic war to persuade the Council to consider my proposal that I could make an exhibition of myself as part of the activities of their art gallery; and the widely publicised situationist dramas I designed and starred in to avoid being normalised by the compulsory national Census. Such dramas are so avant-garde that no state bureaucrat would ever give me a grant and no wealthy individual could improve their status in the community by underwriting them. They were such radical stands against real oppression that even self-righteous revolutionaries gave me no support. But the love I got from the Christchurch 'hobbits' made my day.

ROLES - THE MISSING LINK

> Society and society's laws
> Lay hid in night,
> God said, "Let Parsons be!"
> And all was light.
> It did not last,
> The devil, crying "Ho!
> Let Foucault be,"
> Restored the Status Quo.

WHY HAS THE CONCEPT OF ROLES LARGELY DISAPPEARED FROM RECENT SOCIOLOGICAL WRITINGS?

This would only be explicable if social science has developed a new paradigm which renders the concept redundant. The authoritative statement on the nature of roles accepted by leading social scientists until the end of the 1960s, when the newly recruited army of sociology academics led the left wing march through the institutions, can be seen in Ralf Dahrendorf's *Homo Sociologicus* written in the 1950s and translated into English later. This should not be confused with Bourdieu's very different *Homo Academicus* of 1988. I can see no major theoretical breakthrough to replace the 'grand' Social Action Theory synthesised from a wide variety of psychological, sociological and cultural theories by Talcott Parsons and his colleagues in

Chicago in the 1940s and 1950s. Essential to the overall synthesis is role interaction, which progressively defines and redefines the social situation which is embedded in cultural value complexes. To the disappointment of secular millenarians, voluntaristic social action theory, although based on dynamic equilibrium, is not driven by any revolutionary social Darwinist need to overthrow capitalism. Nor is it a version of recent socio-biological genetic determinism. It was non-ethnocentric, non-deterministic, non-reductionistic and fundamentally an open-ended form of evolution. The influence of George Mead's symbolic interactionism and sophisticated psychological insight into role dynamics, now called reflexivity, underlay its theoretical foundations.

Parsons wasn't looking for a fight and had a good reputation for standing up to both left and right wing political bullies. Having undergone Freudian analysis himself, Parsons adopted much of his psychological dynamic from the theories of Freud which centred too much on the need for libidinal repression to preserve the 'reality principle' of industrial societies, both capitalist and socialist. It should be borne in mind that Freud was aware that he himself was an hysteric.

The psychodynamic aspects of the Social Action Theory need to be revised in light of connections now being found between ethology and Jung's less culturally specific psychodynamic approach. Between 1970 and 1972 I myself put together the bare bones of a similar multi-level evolutionary, non-deterministic, non-reductionist synthesis. Unlike Marxists then and now, I did not irrationally reject Social Action Theory but I wanted to reform it and make connections with physical science by introducing process thinking and making use of new theories including non-equilibrium thermodynamics, together with advances in neuroscience, depth psychology, ethology, and ecosystem analysis.

IRRESPONSIBILITY THEORY

The only way human beings can be held to be responsible for their own actions and protected from the irresponsible actions of others is through carefully specified rights and obligations. These are embodied in cultural prescriptions of meaning and value and linked to their fundamental nature as organisms by their positions in social institutions as role actors embedded in the rule of law. There is no exception to this process which has its roots in animal roles linking parent and offspring, male with female, group members with group leaders etc. Only psychopaths, extreme narcissists or ressentiment-fuelled 'sociopathic' true believers in self-righteous ideologies, can avoid taking responsibility for their own actions.

Those who claim they are not role-acting but 'serious' are demonstrating that their beliefs are held so inflexibly that there is no element of free choice in their actions and hence like madmen they cannot take personal accountability for any anti-social consequences. There is also much irrational animosity towards the exercise of responsible and essential forms of power by legitimate authorities. I am being led to the conclusion that social scientists have been swept along by the contemporary tide of personal irresponsibility and infantile transgression like so many people in a civilization now increasingly driven by little more than the unconscious desire for career advancement or fame and fortune regardless of long term consequences.

WHERE HAVE ALL THE ROLES GONE? DECONSTRUCTED, EVERY ONE.

There must be an explanation for the disappearance of the concept of roles and role complexes which are surely as important for analysing social systems as the concept of atoms and molecules are for physics. I shall try and explain what I believe happened. Searching the index sections in recent sociological writings, reference to roles seems to vanish at the same time as the writings of French deconstructionist philosophers became *de rigeur*. With their roots in traditional French revolutionary anti-clericalism they have flourished like cancer cells in the host of academic bodies even outside France. Most of these philosophers seem to be either overt or covert Marxists and their interest is pathologically focussed on the distribution of power in social systems to the neglect of all other stratifying principles.

A normal human being does not live by power alone unless neurotically driven by hatred of any form of authority, other than their own of course. I can heartily recommend a study of Max Scheler's *Ressentiment* to show how values such as love, honour and truth can be actually inverted and their opposites pursued with highly contagious enthusiasm. Lynch mobs and riots come to mind. For the deconstructionist school, the 1968 student riots in Paris have become a kind of revolutionary paradise lost and since the fall they have been yearning for a return to those few days of glory, much as the early Marxists looked back at the rather less ephemeral days of the 1870 Paris Commune, who no doubt looked back to the blissful time of the French Revolution when the landed aristocracy and religious monarchy were driven out or guillotined.

The glory days for me are quite different: the Restoration of the Monarchy after the military dictatorship of Cromwell the puritan, Dubcek's playful response to the brutal Russian invasion to stop 'socialism with a human face', not the juvenile events in Paris that same year. Highly significant to me were the hilarious reformist actions of the philosopher Antanas Mockus who in 1993 abandoned his position as university chancellor in disgust, after 'mooning' the university community, to become the creative, fun-loving reformist 'Eco-Mayor' of Bogota.

POWER WITHOUT RESPONSIBILITY

Since roles are acted out by human beings as organisms of the species Homo sapiens, any psychological deformation will affect their performances. My assessment of the psychological origins of this 'role repression' is that we are now dealing with the rapidly growing psychological phenomena of narcissism and schizophrenia. Psychiatrists are reporting that they are at present seeing fewer anxiety-ridden neurotics and a great increase in narcissists and schizophrenics who feel their lives are empty and meaningless. Neurotics were ideally suited for success in the previous mechanistic goal-driven industrial age, since neurotics take their instrumental roles very seriously, even to the point of violence and self-destruction. Sixty years ago the sociologist David Riesman, as part of the national debate on the connections between character and social structure, drew attention to a change in personality taking place in the USA just after the Second World War. I was greatly influenced at the time by *The Lonely Crowd*, his witty psycho-social evolutionary theory. He noted that the personality types, which he labelled 'inner directed', were being replaced by 'other directed' personalities whose identification was no longer with an internalised conscience or super ego but with their popularity with their peer groups.

This matches with what we know about narcissism. In spite of popular misconceptions, this form of dysfunctional psychodynamics is based on fundamental self-loathing and is the polar opposite to egotism since the authentic personal self is severely repressed and is replaced by a need for reassurance by others that they are significant. Narcissists flourish in the hysteria of a consumer society of short-lived political, religious and artistic fads and fashions and are greatly attracted to self-improvement gurus. They live in the present and show little interest or understanding of history and their notion of the future is usually some vague irrational utopia. Successful narcissists make talented spin doctors who can charm the birds off the trees, but they often have psychopathic tendencies which render them unable to feel empathy for others. However, they can 'fake' such feelings superbly well. Such people cannot feel deep guilt and cannot therefore accept responsibility for any unpleasant consequences of their own actions. Since roles involve both rights and responsibilities the concept of roles is anathema to them. Ideologies like deconstructionism and relativistic morality attract this personality type who only respond deeply to the acquisition of fame, money or power, since no thought of any future consequences for others bothers them. If they can be anchored to anything it is to a significant sexual partner who alone makes them feel real. Neurotics on the other hand prefer puritanical left or right wing ideologies requiring self-sacrifice and devotion to duty.

SOCIALISTS NEED CAPITALISTS

Adherents of the various forms of the ideology of socialism are attracted to careers as school teachers and arts faculty academics but they set little store on traditional family values. Social mobility is a much more important value emphasised in the curricula of the compulsory secondary, (and increasingly obligatory) tertiary educational institutions. The alternative offered to compulsory socialist egalitarianism is self-enrichment through personal effort. Both ideologies gain their meaning through unquestioned belief in the paradigm of economic development at almost any price. Anthony Giddens the social theorist claims that the pursuit of power is the most powerful form of addiction he is aware of and like all forms of an obsession its addicts are prepared to lie and cheat. How can anyone take socialism seriously? The symbiotic relationship between socialists and capitalists is so obvious. They are both obsessed with power and money and they both lie to hide their addiction. The socialists attempt to use the power of the secular state to reduce everyone to egalitarian slaves educated by the state and controlled by bureaucratic bullies, and the capitalists use cunning, guile, and bribery to corrupt them in order to enrich themselves whilst ruining the environment.

Similar patterns may occur in religious societies. Religious beliefs are the major structuring social forces in agricultural civilizations. Money and power are no longer associated so closely. Instead, in these cultures sin and power are related in much the same way as debt and power in mercantile civilizations. The established priesthood claims a monopoly of holiness and controls the relief of sin through their ecclesiastical institutions. Fear of damnation, of living in delusion, or being reincarnated in a lower caste or as a woman or animal, provides the stick. In the West the carrot is heavenly salvation. In Asia it is more likely to be reincarnation into a higher caste or, for a woman, reincarnation as a man, and for a tiny number, reaching enlightenment. Belief in equality, if found at all, is a belief in the importance of each individual soul and even animals may sometimes be assumed to have souls. Religious families are not broken down like secularists living in cities as bourgeois individualists bound together into contractually-united nuclear families. They are social units bonded by religious obligation into extended families which are largely economically self-supporting welfare institutions. Their prime motivation is 'more holy and more caring than thou', unlike materialists who strive to be 'more radical and more intelligent than thou'.

Religious radicals may appear claiming God's mandate to overthrow the corrupt priesthood. They usually fail and are burned at the stake or suffer some other gruesome fate. Sometimes they succeed, but only if they have the backing of powerful groups who share the religious revolutionaries' desire to throw off the yoke of the established professional priesthood. As the Latin Church as a political force grew weak, Luther obtained the backing of the German princes to oppose the Vatican, and soon afterwards King Henry VIII in his desperate need to divorce his wife and beget a legitimate male heir, allied himself with Protestant reformers to create a schismatic new English Reformed Catholic Church.

RESSENTIMENT

As I mentioned earlier, a hundred years ago Max Scheler came up with a currently neglected theory which throws light on the motivation of all revolutionaries who have no time for reformers. Scheler criticised and modified Nietzsche's theory of 'the will to power' which underlies not only socialism and capitalism but postmodern deconstructionism. Scheler suggested that instead social scientists should be concentrating on 'the will to love' which requires power to be truly effective. Instead of self-love inspired and encouraged by the admiration and imitation of others one respects, self-hatred may develop out of negative envy and resentment which leads to uncontrollable hatred and the desire to destroy one's betters. Traditional human values are inverted. Spiritual values like selfless love and ethical integrity are at the bottom of the value hierarchy and the least esteemed, then comes living vitalistic values like health, then mental values, now deformed by rationalised hatred, and finally and the most valued of all, power over others through naked force leading to control of material resources.

Once this inversion of values has occurred it can spread like a contagion through mimesis. Only a strong-minded individual with a well worked out political or religious ideology can resist the intellectual rationalisations of revolutionary spindoctors who can justify almost any actions no matter how brutal. This psychological phenomenon is more commonly found amongst Riesman's inner-directed neurotics. Other-directed narcissists are more likely to be paralysed by fear and, if present, will find themselves being carried away by others and lost in mindless revolutionary mob action. Psychopaths and sociopaths, who are born rather than made, occurring in about one percent of any population, soon take over and the rule of terror begins.

LOST IN THE CULTURAL MAZE.
A MYTHIC METAPHOR.

Lifting our gaze from the deforming psychological aspects of ressentiment up to the mapping functions of culture which provides us with cognitive symbolic explanations of reality we find an amazing sight. The deconstructionists who are masters of word play have built a brilliant magical maze from which no one can escape. It is constructed from words whose meaning is ambivalent to say the least. All over the academic world there are intellectuals wandering through the deconstructionist maze getting more confused and desperate. They are all seeking the centre where they will find the Minotaur so that they can slay it. As a wily maze-runner I have secured the help of an Ariadne whose self-empowerment freed her from having to use 'embowerment', as Camille Paglia puts it, to secure a mate. As I skip along the pathways using her feminine memory thread to retrace my steps whenever I come to a dead end, I realise that, jumping for joy as I go, I can catch glimpses of the pathways on the other side of the impenetrable walls or hedges. The higher I jump the more I can see of the maze and its dead ends. For those whose obsessional relativistic reasoning has caused them to paint themselves into a corner, the only way out is up. Without a leap of faith, they are paralysed, cannot jump to any conclusion and comfort themselves by retreating into irony. I reached the centre a long time ago and, as others have intuited, the Minotaur turned out to be myself. A narcissist would be unable to take his eyes off the mirror believing it to be his true self. A neurotic cannot raise his eyes to look in the face of what he believes is his feared superego. Only a self-deprecating egotistical show-off can destroy his own image for fun.

MODERNISM AS FASHION DICTATOR. THE CREATIVE ARTS AND THE AVANT-GARDE.

The transition from the mechanistic enlightenment paradigm to that of the present 'other directed' postmodern consumerism was extremely fast but not as extreme as the dialectical shift from 'tradition-directed' religious agricultural civilizations to the rapidly expanding industrialised mercantile civilizations. Modernist ideology, which picked up speed, particularly after the prophet Nietzsche described it so accurately, was more like slippage. By the end of the 19th century most of the world was linked in a global industrial civilization as producers, manufacturers, raw material suppliers, labourers or consumers. Increasing leisure for the rapidly growing middle classes and greater specialisation of labour especially in the service sector led to a greater demand for surplus value in the form of artistic products and entertainments. No longer needing to please aristocratic patrons the rapidly increasing number of artists, playwrights, novelists, film makers etc. began to specialise in providing artistic products targeting different groups in the community from the vulgar to the sophisticated. Competition between artists varied from those trying to reach the widest consumer group and enrich themselves, to others with less vulgar aspirations competing with each other to be more original. This had the effect of transforming much art into fashion statements. I am trying here to be as dismissive of modernism and abusive to its proponents as they have been towards traditional practitioners but I fear it is impossible. The best criticism of most modernism is that it is the world view of a schizophrenic. Of course I find some modern creations exciting and moving but I shall ignore these since this a polemic not an objective appreciation.

Out of this competition to be 'more original, shocking and innovative than thou' arose the cult of modernism. It is best seen as a cult since it has god-like cult leaders, and those who are not impressed are seen as lost souls, ridiculed as ignorant, or shunned as evil. Modernist architects found new patrons in the powerful bureaucrats now multiplying as a result of the compulsory taxes raised to fund the new welfare states. Most of the early modern architects were communists who, like similar puritans in the past, insist on providing people with what they think is good for them, whether they like it or not. Like all puritanical utilitarians they are obsessed with physical health, hygienic sterility and cleanliness, with bare 'honest' concrete walls, 'clean' geometrical forms, uncomfortable utilitarian fittings and furniture and environmentally wasteful amounts of plain glass. The bare, windswept, flat surfaces surrounding their plain towers were studded with odd bits of meaningless abstract art. The tower blocks which deconstructed the communal life of the old terraces quickly became the only architectural forms approved of by the cult leaders whose devotees exercised a totalitarian monopoly of the architectural schools, journals, and magazines. In their personal lives however many architects lived like members of the Soviet Comintern in a comfortable bohemian fashion in beautiful traditional houses surrounded by gardens and leafy trees.

Widespread morbid introspection and fascination with transgression, self-loathing, and self-destruction could not be institutionally enforced in much modern literature, and electronic media since they are within the means of private individuals. Even magic and fantasy narratives, regarded by soulless moral guardians as mere escapism, are flourishing. However, the indirect but influential state control of the curricula of secondary education and the increasing need for certification as a requirement for paid employment continues to direct the consciousness of those studying the humanities.

THE PLAY'S THE THING

At the time of writing this essay I was rehearsing for a small part in a musical comedy called *Spamalot*. I played the part of a wizard narrator and commentator, which interestingly reflects the role I am playing in the world outside the theatre. I was reminded of the fruitful metaphor that social life is like a theatrical performance, based on a quasi-sacred script and directed by a master of ceremonies. Allowing for the cultural relevance of the scenario and the competence of the director, the satisfaction derived from acting out roles, which usually have no foundation in the world outside, is considerable for performers and audience alike. The strength and appeal of Confucianism lies in such a satisfaction. Imagine the result if deconstructionists staged plays without roles and with scenarios based on post-modern undermining of meaning and with authoritarian directors who don't allow their actors to project their genuine feelings because like all puritanical cult leaders they regard passionate 'acting' as insincere. Actually some avant-garde theatre is rather like this and only exists because its directors are skilled at persuading bureaucrats to part with subsidies from compulsory taxes and who can find actors who enjoy being bullied in the name of a higher cause, such as the genius of the playwright or director.

ROLES AS LEVERS

I am convinced that the concept of role is the critical link between up-to-date neuroscience, psychological states, social action based on narratives and ideological world views as expressed in mimesis-based symbol systems. Symbolic interaction without role action to implement it, is like changing gears without engaging the motor. This is a surprisingly common practice amongst social science academics. As a fun revolutionary without any predetermined agenda other than avoiding reactionary determinism, I regard roles and role-complexes as Archimedean levers that can move the social world. This is of course provided a role actor has the right scenario to provide them with a firm enough place to stand, and a long enough lever to reach the world. This is an unusual and targeted form of what is now being referred to as reflexivity. The place I chose to stand was upon my own process cosmology which provides me with a firm subjective location in the neural communication network of the electronic mass media, or global village.

A fourth century Christian philosopher described God as *"an intelligible sphere whose centre is everywhere and whose circumference is nowhere"*. Later, Renaissance philosophers replaced 'God' with 'Nature' or 'the Cosmos'. Disliking the idea that the universe was deconstructed in this way and influenced by Teilhard de Chardin I was driven by a desire to bring about a temporary convergence of time, space and identity in the form of an imagination experiment that was 'embodied' and not abstract.

By 1972 I had completed the scenario for my performances in the form of a shamanistic tree of life cosmology. I stand as best I can where I have stood since 1968, at the subjective centre of my own cosmology and my levers are provided by my roles as communicated in the cultural matrix or simulacrum now being transformed by the electronic mass media. Of course I have to go through the motions of being a law-abiding member of the welfare-warfare state and its mechanical soul. Acting without conviction is essential.

Victor Turner's theory of liminal transformations and what he calls 'communitas' and 'social anti-structures', which I have only recently come across, clarified what I was instinctively trying to do. I was deliberately provoking harmless but sensational crises in order to create temporary 'social anti-structures' which could facilitate the later emergence of more flexible social role structures that created 'communitas'. At the time I saw this as a kind of dialectic to increase tension playfully in order to resolve it. Reducing tension by confrontational aggression merely repressed the problem which might reappear later in a more extreme form. I saw my rather disturbing liminal actions as an unpredictable open-ended process of psycho-socio-cultural evolution. It is now appropriate to demonstrate my theory by providing case histories. The first step is to explain why I chose the office and status of a wizard to implement my socio-cultural engineering.

THE MASTER ROLE COMPLEX OF THE WIZARD

Nel mezzo del cammin di nostra vita, mi ritrovai per una selva oscura, che la diritta via era smarrita. These opening words of Dante's *Divine Comedy*, which I had learned as a schoolboy for a part in a play, were ringing in my head in 1968 when, at the half way point in my own life's path, I found I too had wandered off the main road and had found myself in a dark wood. With nothing to lose except my sense of humour and trusting my intuition, I chose to push on into the thorny unknown. Not being a Catholic Italian, neither Virgil nor any beautiful young woman appeared to guide me. Instead, as an Anglican Englishman, it was the wizard Merlin in his recent incarnation as Gandalf who became my guiding spirit or daemon. In order to find my way out I took the difficult and dangerous course of using my psychological and sociological skills to engineer a new identity. As I have recounted elsewhere I became the official wizard of a large modern university. I realised I was not only risking being diagnosed as insane but I would be courting notoriety and poverty rather than fame and fortune. However, such a course of action was becoming a little more culturally acceptable in that remarkable year of 1968. Tolkien's *Lord of The Rings* trilogy had become a best seller and was leading to the reappearance in the mass media of the wizard archetype in heroic epics and fantasy. At the same time the counter-culture hippies were not only rediscovering but living out other forms of cultural reality than our own decadent consumer capitalism. Romantic revolution was also in the air as the politically ambitious young left wing radicals were getting increasingly fired up by the example of the Chinese Red Guards and the student-led riots in Paris.

I was an enthusiastic participant in the late 1960s revolution in consciousness which rejected Cartesian subject/object dualism, reductionism, (which is mistakenly seen as causation), and the obvious take-over of tertiary education by the mechanistic utilitarian values of militarism and managerial capitalism. The initial success of my Fun Revolution revealed to me that play was the only way to calm down and reform this tsunami of self-destructive stupidity. Experience and social interaction could replace arrogant god-like observation. I saw my appointment as an official university wizard as a unique opportunity to establish a less self-righteous, less closed-minded, and more playful way of interacting with others. In the absence of any previous official wizards in Western Civilization I was free to construct my own job specifications deriving from my own cultural scenario. In my new area of academic competence, I was no longer obliged to confine my discourse to merely critiquing the interactive activities of others like an anthropologist looking down from his rational high table observing the antics of the ignorant savages below. I could now get my hands dirty by experimenting.

The sociologist Anthony Giddens is now recognising the importance of 'reflexive modernity'. His argument is that over time society is becoming increasingly more self-aware, reflective and hence reflexive. I have accordingly adopted the concept of reflexivity to describe my role interactions with other role actors.

The advantages of the wizard role-complex are not just those of having no master to control my behaviour and restrict my thinking, the title can be interpreted so widely. It can be used to describe a practitioner who combines art, religion, and science, like the alchemists, astrologers and other magicians who provided the bridge between the religious decline and growing secular scientific beliefs in 17th century Europe. A brilliant technological inventor is frequently called a wizard. Showmen who can perform magic tricks to amuse the masses often adopt the title. Such nomenclature can also be used to describe a spell-casting sorcerer like a spin doctor in the fields of political propaganda, advertising, or self-improvement. It can also be taken to mean a provocative wise man as opposed to a conformist educated fool. Best of all it indicates cultural autonomy, being relatively free from control by both moral and rational enforcers. Traditionally the greatest threat to wizards comes from being 'embowered' by female magic. My personal preference is to see wizards as the world's oldest profession who can trace themselves back to the hunter-gatherer shamans thereby antedating by thousands of years the prostitutes and priests who first appear in the much later religious agricultural civilizations.

EXAMPLES OF SOCIO-CULTURAL LEVERAGE

THE ROLE OF COSMOLOGER OF MELBOURNE UNIVERSITY UNION

What better place to create and publish a new subjective process cosmology than in an experimental inter-disciplinary department at a reputable university? Between 1971 and 1974 the Department of Levity at Melbourne University, also known as the Wizard's Cosmological Research and Development Centre, was housed in a charming Neo-gothic building in the centre of the campus. My lectures and workshops were open to all who registered with the Union Council. I acted out the role on the right stage and according to the traditional scenario of the university as a community of scholars. As a consequence of the increasing specialisation and bureaucratic organisation of academic teaching and research, I was not hopeful that any academics would be able to respond to my overtures. How could I apply pressure even with such a carefully designed scientific lever if cosmology as an academic subject did not exist other than as historical descriptions of outdated models or as simple reductionist astro-physics? Aquinas saw, to his horror, that a split was already developing between natural philosophy and theology. Theology has now become moral philosophies such as sociology and political science and the split has become permanent, except amongst process thinkers.

I struck at the heart of irrational 'belief' in the objective reality of current scientific models of the physical universe by rejecting the absolute frame of Newton the Unitarian deist that was still assumed by astrophysicists. We need to break the spellbound 'gaze' of the alienated scientific observer. By applying my principles of Love, Logic and Levity I made a conformal inversion of the coordinates of the current model, where the Earth is believed to be a sphere surrounded by the rest of the universe, to produce a model where the Earth is hypothesised to be a huge hollow space with the rest of the universe inside it. As there is no absolute frame, neither model could be seen as true, both models are essentially useful fictions. But what happens once we realise this? By bravely exploring inner space I had found a powerful lever that could not only move the Earth but turn it upside down and even inside out. What would Archimedes have made of this thought experiment!

"*The cloud-capped towers, the gorgeous places, the solemn temples, the great globe itself, yea all which it inherit, shall dissolve and, like this insubstantial pageant faded, leave not a wrack behind. We are such stuff as dreams are made on, and our little life is rounded with a sleep.*" These words of Shakespeare were carved on the plinth of his statue overlooking the Sydney Domain where I started my career as a public orator amongst the other Sunday soap box orators in the days before that particular insubstantial pageant finally faded after almost a century.

RELIGION AND ROLE REFLEXIVITY; THE ROLE OF PROPHET OF THE CHURCH OF ENGLAND

In 1970 the Union Council of Melbourne University had acceded to my request to be appointed their official wizard combining the roles of shaman and prophet as well as their cosmologer and artistic exhibitionist. I saw the role of prophet to be of the exemplary variety, rather than the exhortatory and thus more shamanic and reflexive than political. In 1973, before leaving for New Zealand, I wrote to the Primate of the Anglican Church in Australia pointing out that I had a background of lecturing in the sociology of religion and felt that I now had a calling to act out the role of a prophet in the Anglican Church. My mission was to stimulate open debate I felt was badly needed between subtle modern theology and crude fundamentalist certainty. In a playful way I asked if the Church would examine me to test me and my motives. I did not expect a reply and did not receive one.

On arrival in Christchurch in 1974, and dressed in a costume resembling that of John the Baptist the wild man in his camel skin, I stood on a ladder in Cathedral Square outside the Anglican Cathedral and acted out the role of an ironic false prophet. I was soon known as the 'Hammer of the Heretics'. My mission was to save the souls of those excited fundamentalists who were thronging outside the Cathedral doors insisting that such conventional churchgoers that they called religious people were doomed to go to hell. I claimed they themselves were possessed by demons and should go to qualified priests to be exorcised. City councillors and bureaucrats, scared of the fury of their fundamentalist colleagues, did all in their power to have me arrested but my antics and verbal acrobatics were attracting large crowds of well-wishers and the local newspapers regarded me as a harmless entertaining eccentric. In the end the City Council ceased trying to arrest and prosecute me for 'speaking out loud in Cathedral Square', made the area into a speaker's corner, and promoted me as a tourist attraction.

Cathedral Square began to become a place of entertainment. I designed and printed Heavenly Credits which were watermarked 'Bank of Heaven', numbered, and signed by myself personally as the Chief Cashier. The Governor of the Bank of Heaven was the Head of the Anglican Church, Her Majesty Queen Elizabeth the Second. Pictures of us in our salad days adorned the banknotes. Stating my concern that the NZ Prime Minister was printing money to fix his financial problems I generously sold my heavenly credits for a dollar each and, as a sacrifice to God, regularly burned the New Zealand banknotes I received in Cathedral Square in an elaborate ritual. No criminal charge was laid and, as I pointed out, I was helping the NZ economy by making the remaining banknotes more valuable. Not long afterwards, in spite of a well-publicised protest by myself and my royalist followers, the government removed the

Queen's image from all but one of their banknote denominations.

In 1976 as Prophet of Christchurch I designed and published a board game I called *Salvation* which appeared identical to *Monopoly* but with Heavenly Credits, marked 'not genuine' of course, in place of money. I meant this as an educational aid to help people realise that both money and salvation were useful fictions for ruling elites. The game began with Unmerited Grace in the form of two hundred heavenly credits and each circuit of the board was similarly rewarded. Divine Providence cards replaced Chance, and Temptation cards replaced Community Chest. Instead of properties for rental, the sets were 'good works' with the exact amount of heavenly credits due printed on each card. The cards could be 'disgraced' by being turned over in exchange for credits from the Bank of Heaven, and 'redeemed' by repayment. Religious professionals could be placed on the good works provided a complete mission was owned. Paralleling the houses in Monopoly, these ranged from priest to canon to bishop, to archbishop to saint (a hotel). If a pilgrim landed on one of the good works he or she was 'helped' and was required to gratefully hand over the specified amount of heavenly credits which varied with the quality of the ecclesiastical functionaries involved. They were expected to say 'thank you brother' or be fined as they handed over their credits which encouraged healthy self-discipline. The Penitentiary was the only square that retained its meaning in Monopoly. The railway sta-

The Salvation Game.

tions became the Roman Catholic, Orthodox, Anglican and Lutheran Churches and the Services became Monastic Houses. The lowest-rated good works involved simple healing; helping families to stay together was rated higher, as was setting up orphanages, schools and hospitals. Campaigns against pagans and conversions of kings and their people were rated as even more important. Finally, confounding psychiatrists, demolishing scientific materialism in the popular press and getting bankers to confess to the sin of usury and giving all their money to the Church was only inferior to the Reconversion of Russia to Orthodox Christianity and the Reconversion of America to the established Anglican Faith. This was the highest good work possible.

Art work for the game was done by Alice, my then girlfriend and present fiancée, with metal pilgrims, boards, religious, dice, fake heavenly credits etc. and sold for a dollar in Cathedral Square. The City Council leapt to the attack, attempting to prosecute me for hawking without a licence. Since I could prove that even with voluntary labour the game cost two dollars to produce, the expert lawyer the Council employed quietly let the case lapse.

Over the years many attempts were made by fundamentalist parents to prevent me from making state school visits and a few pusillanimous principals capitulated. On one memorable occasion in Cathedral Square a beefy fundamentalist seized my wooden ladder, raised it above his head and smashed it to pieces on the cobbles. Later I burst into tears for the news cameras. I donated the remains of the ladder to the city museum where it was displayed for years. I cunningly affixed small pieces of 'the true ladder' to postcards of myself as Hammer of the Heretics, which I signed and sold as genuine relics to locals and tourists. A ladder-making company publicised themselves by presenting me with a new aluminium ladder but it looked too modern and squeaked unpleasantly so I eventually went back to a traditional wooden one.

The Postmodern Prophet: Hammer of the Heretics in 1974

DECLARATION OF WAR

Be it known throughout the Canterbury Region
THAT
having declined even to attempt to fulfil the conditions clearly put forward in the ULTIMATUM of October 31st 1975 of the Christian Era
A STATE OF WAR
now exists between The Peoples' Representatives known as
THE CHRISTCHURCH CITY COUNCIL
and The Peoples' champion against the gloom and bureaucracy deliberately produced by The Peoples' Representatives, known as The WIZARD

This state of war shall exist UNTIL: either The City Council shows signs of responding to popular opinion and to informed advice concerning the matters raised in The Wizard's correspondence by appointing him
ARCHWIZARD OF CANTERBURY
OR
The Wizard, who is rapidly becoming a major tourist attraction in addition to his functions as raiser of community morale, provoker of ideas and defuser of fanatics,
IS
finally forced to submit to the ignorant ill-mannered enmity of the Christchurch City Councillors
BY
giving up his last ditch stand in Cathedral Square and abandoning the city to the ravages of The Peoples' Representatives who are ignorantly destroying the very people who elected them.

Ian B Channell

Cosmologer by Appointment to Melbourne University Union
Wizard by Appointment to the World University Service (Australia) & Canterbury Council of Calligraphers
Prophet by Appointment to Christchurch Technical Institute Students' Association
Founder and Leader of the Imperial British Conservative Party
Generalissimo of Alf's Imperial Army
Chairman of the Home Rule for The West Coast movement.

Still going strong in the Square in the 1980s (postcard)

The Wizmobile

Official plaque in the Square

ART AND ROLE REFLEXIVITY; THE ROLE OF THE LIVING WORK OF ART

Doubtful of being able to provoke any symbolic interaction or reflexivity with other academic process thinkers (who at that time were very thin on the ground), I designed an aesthetic lever to produce role reactions amongst the artistic avant garde. As I have already described, whilst at the University of NSW I had developed new forms of avant garde theatre which took place in the real world, rather than in specialist entertainment venues, or predictable anti-establishment political agitprop in the street. My early career as the first cultural affairs officer in an English university and my experiences as the cultural facilitator for the University of WA, together with my doctoral studies in the Sociology of Art at UNSW, had led me to question the covert values frequently informing Renaissance, Enlightenment and Modern art forms and fashions. In the early 20th century the very nature of paintings and sculptures as collectable art objects in a market economy was being questioned by modern conceptual artists. However, although transgressive in their approach to the traditional values of public art, they were still embedded in the specialist bourgeois aesthetic institutions such as art galleries, concert halls and theatres. Their puritanical moral intensity and elitist disdain of people who held traditional values such as good and evil and beautiful versus repulsive, meant that their work attracted few people. Educational institutions saw it as their duty to alter public taste towards appreciation of these new art forms by emphasising ideological and rational understanding over intuitive emotional responses of disgust or alienation. State funding from compulsory taxes enabled the elitist artistic institutions and the new artists to survive and gradually gain acceptance. The point was reached where spin and marketing gurus were able to build up a modern art market amongst the fast growing nouveaux riches of the consumer society. Those arts which only function through voluntary public participation still needed tax-payer support. I must emphasise that significant and popular theatrical, musical, literary and especially cinematic art works were still being produced by major talents without the need for state sponsorship, though the thinning of the ranks of entrepreneurial capitalists and their replacement by unimaginative and conformist managerial administrators meant the loss of wealthy private sponsors with good taste.

It was with these considerations in mind that I decided to create an even more avant garde role for myself in the art world than that of the conceptual artists who exhibited in art galleries and who were sponsored by state bureaucrats with their educational moral agendas. Some had changed their names and life-styles but not their fundamental identities or world views. It seemed to me that, as their name implied, their creations were designed to draw attention to their superior psychological or political awareness since few showed signs of great ability as craftspeople. As I saw it, the first half of the century was a period bursting with new ideas and new artistic techniques but that period was now over. The manufactured media celebrity cult of the artist as self-destructive Dionysian genius could not disguise the fact that in most cases the emperor had no clothes. My new liminal role as University Wizard, an obviously fictional character, enabled me to playfully extricate myself as much as I could from my previous dependency roles in the welfare state. With my interest in role interaction or reflexivity and seeing art as process, my attention was caught in 1970 by James Lee Byars, a young performer who displayed himself in colourful clothes around the Metropolitan Museum in New York. I had earlier been intrigued by the Fool in Vancouver and most of all by Emperor Norton in 19th century San Francisco whose instinctive role interaction with the locals and the media was carried out with great skill.

My first step was to propose a motion at the Annual General Meeting of the Australian Branch of the World University Service in 1970. At the meeting a motion was passed unanimously donating my living body to the National Gallery of Victoria to be acquisitioned as a living work of art. The living work of art was created as a shamanic synthesis of artist, art work, performer, orator and art critic that could not be bought or sold and was not just posing as an art object in art galleries but exhibiting itself everywhere by acting out various roles and making suitable reference to learned writings. Sir Eric Westbrook, the director, contacted James Pilgrim the assistant curator-in-chief of the Metropolitan Museum in New York who wrote back saying he had already heard of me and commenting that although such a 'fascinating' project could not be not be undertaken by such a large and complex institution as MMA, it might be attempted by the Melbourne gallery. He emphasised the unprecedented process elements involved. *"I think that an investigation of provenance, physical condition, condition checking, cataloguing, record photography etc. should prove interesting feedback to the Museum and its traditionally accepted processes. It should certainly give those people who participate a fuller understanding of what a work of art may be, what their relationship to it might be, and at the very least that a living work of art can be."*

Westbrook was asked by the press why he had given me the title and what it all signified. I quote here his prescient comments about the Living Work of Art in *The Australian* newspaper of January 1972. Referring to acquisitioning, cataloguing etc., he said; *"It would be a kind of happening, which in the current structure, is becoming more and more important. The visual arts are much closer to the theatre. The distinction between ballet, music, painting, sculpture is becoming narrower"* ... *"His general attitude is to make life fuller, richer more interesting and more fun for people."*

Westbrook met with me and Alice who, with her art history interests, could act as the curator of the Living Work of Art. Full acquisitioning, although a tempting prospect emphasising process, rather than exhibiting an object or a room redecoration as a conceptual art work as a thing, would unfortunately mean my incarceration in the gallery as this was the form for all new art works added to their collection. I did not fancy the prospect of being a gallery slave. The solution was for the gallery to accept the World University Service offer 'on extended loan'.

On arrival in New Zealand in 1974 I offered my services free to the Christchurch City Council who simply ignored my letters. Any response is better than the stony disapproving silence I usually receive to my friendly offers of service. Finally, and informing the mass media, I issued an Ultimatum in the form of a calligraphic document finely crafted by Alice my curator. If the Cultural Committee of the Council continued to ignore my letters offering my skilled and experienced services, I would declare artistic war on them. I still received no acknowledgement so I sent them a Declaration of War in the form of another fine example of calligraphy. I made an exhibition of myself outside their offices, and they eventually responded with rude and uneducated comments about my character and recommending with loud guffaws that I should be hung.

In 1980 the title was transferred to the Christchurch Art Gallery and finally in 1982, with the encouragement of Rodney Wilson, an outstandingly creative gallery director, the title was endorsed independently by the NZ Art Gallery Directors Council. I was issued with an artistic licence, and acquisitioning could begin.

My identity as a living work of art had faced its first crisis in 1975 when confronted by the Department of Statistics. During the 1970s and 1980s I was required by the government to complete the five-yearly census questionnaires and I was driven to use my performing skills to successfully preserve my hard-won identity as a living work of art. Since 1968 I had not been registered with the income tax authorities, received no state benefits, and had no driving licence or passport. This was not a criminal act, only a thought crime, and was only done in order to reach a state of independence from non-aesthetic political-economic control of my identity. I was trying to establish the validity of my identity as the first Living Work of Art which had the aesthetic backing of art gallery directors. I was prepared to supply essential information such as my gender and age, which would provide a base for further demographic calculation. In my role as a process scientist, I wrote to newspapers explaining that properly conducted random sampling was a far more accurate and economic way to proceed than massive data collecting since, in reaction to the bullying tactics adopted, many people deliberately misled their enumerators. Nor could I resist quoting the wise saying that 'there are lies, damned lies and statistics'.

Acting out another of my roles, that of an exemplary prophet, I also pointed out that anyone who took the Bible seriously as a guide to morality should be aware that one of the few occasions when Satan appears in the Biblical narrative is when he tempts King David to hold a census. The result was that Israel and its king suffered God's wrath for this heinous sin. The hypocritical religious fundamentalists who dutifully filled in their forms gave me no credit for my principled stand and continued their venomous campaign to stop me speaking in the Square and making school visits on the simplistic grounds that wizards are evil. Similarly, anarchists and socialist extremists keen to overthrow the state accorded me no credit for my radical opposition to the secular welfare state, no doubt because they felt guilty for being bought off by the financial benefits offered them if they dutifully registered themselves with the authorities. I became a folk hero for my successful avoidance of the census on several occasions.

CHRISTCHURCH: The dark-robed Wizard of Christchurch and two members of his imperial army landed at the New Zealand port of Lyttelton last Wednesday after a voyage to beat the census.
The Wizard, a sort of one-man Hyde Park corner, had sailed the day before to be out of New Zealand on census night.
The* he reckoned without the tenacity of the bureaucrats.
Waiting for him at the dock were two officers from the Statistics Department, heavily armed with census forms.
The Wizard was prosecuted after the last census in 1976 for refusing to fill out the forms, but got off on a technicality.
This time officialdom may win the day.

* LONDON AUSTRALASIAN MAGAZINE

My analogue escapes from being 'brought into line' and digitalised by bean-counting philistines took the form of truly avant garde dramas in which I starred and which were acted out on the pages of newspapers, in the courtrooms and on the screens of television sets. The first escape took place after I cast a spell in the Chief Statistician's office which caused all the lights to go out for several hours. In the consequent panic he must have forgotten to start the prosecution process within the statutory time and after some years the charges were finally dismissed by the Court of Appeal and the Census Act was amended. I paid my lawyer in Heavenly Credits. The second involved my going out to sea beyond the twelve-mile limit on census night with a radio reporter and members of Alf's Imperial Army. This was a war-mongering performance art group I had founded in 1971 at Melbourne University to draw attention away from peace-loving demonstrators against the Vietnam War whose activities usually erupted in violence. Attempts by government officials to prosecute me failed ignominiously since they did not realise that their political jurisdiction did not apply beyond the twelve-mile limit.

My favourite piece of census-inspired avant garde theatre was *The Vanishing*. I notified the government and newspapers that I intended to call on my powers as a wizard to vanish at midnight on census night and would reappear at noon the next day. I stated that I did not believe that the state had the authority to judge whether or not wizards could vanish and reappear, in the same way as they had no authority to decide whether or not Christians go to Heaven or Hell when they die. 'I believe the Wizard vanished' stickers were circulated all over the country and I put forms in the main newspapers which people could fill in, sign, and send in to the Promotions Officer of the Christchurch City Council. They were asked whether or not they believed I vanished. If a witness appeared who had seen me at the time of the count or if there was preponderance of disbelief in my powers, I would resign as the of-

ficial city wizard and go back to my previous occupation as a sociology academic. The response was overwhelming. I can only assume that wizards were more popular with the general public than sociologists. When I reappeared I felt rejuvenated and realised that my beard was slightly darker.

Shortly after my appointment by the NZ Art Gallery Directors Council in 1983 I was invited to Australia to appear in the Adelaide Arts Festival. This would have been a refreshing change for me as only a few years before I had been the chief executive officer of their rival, the long established Perth Arts Festival. My lack of documentation as a 'real person', as defined by the secular state, required ingenuity. In addition to the art gallery directors and arts festival organisers I enlisted the help of 'Aussie' Malcolm, the NZ Minister of Immigration whose cooperation was beyond the call of duty. Telexes between the immigration ministers and their departments on both sides of the Tasman were exchanged. These make interesting and amusing reading as creative attempts by 'Aussie' Malcom to classify me in ingenious ways as a non-person met with grim, unimaginative and negative responses from the Australian minister. Even though I had been packaged and despatched by air by the city art gallery in Christchurch to the city art gallery in Auckland ready for the trip, I was denied entry and not even allowed on the aircraft. At the end of it all I appointed the NZ minister 'Wizard Third Class'. He was thrilled and proudly affixed the certificate to his office wall.

A final attempt to save us all the bother of yet another battle over the census was made in 1986 by the Minister of Tourism, Mike Moore, who wrote to his ministerial colleague in Australia urging him to accept the art gallery directors' authority that I was indeed a Living Work of Art. Sadly his appeal fell upon deaf ears. A few years later, when he unexpectedly found himself Prime Minister for a few weeks, he issued a proclamation from his office appointing me official Wizard of New Zealand for which heroic act he earned my undying gratitude. During the 1990s the Police Department issued me with a certificate authorising me (as Wizard, The) to drive a 'horseless carriage', and shortly afterwards the British High Commissioner issued me with a passport made out to 'The Wizard of New Zealand'. This was admittedly a compromise but a small one, and I was able at last to travel more freely and could head across the Tasman Sea at the approach of the dreaded census.

The only occasion when I made an exhibition of myself in an art gallery was in 1995 when, with the whole-hearted support of Neil Roberts the Acting Director and friend, the city council sponsored *Wizards Week*, including an exhibition with Alice as the curator, to celebrate 21 years of my performing in the city. Unfortunately for me at this time the gallery acquired a new director from Australia who did his best to sabotage the exhibition. The Mayor intervened to save the day, although he did manage to limit the exhibition to only a few days. Newspaper and magazine stories, photographs and cosmological diagrams adorned the walls of the charming Robert McDougall Art Gallery. The opening involved me breaking out of a large egg in a bird costume with the help of 'midwives' who included the current mayor, an ex-prime minister, a senior lecturer in fine arts, and a previous gallery director. *The Hatching* took place surrounded by members of a wizards' conclave, several of whom had come from Australia. The catalogue was published in the form of two editions of a newspaper called *The McDougall Times*, one published before and one immediately after the opening. The empty cracked egg was carried by six wizards down Christchurch's equivalent of a sacred way from the art gallery to Cathedral Square where crowds gathered to watch the ceremonies which culminated in the wizards entering the egg which rocked to and fro and then exploded in a cloud of smoke. Excited wizards beat each other over the head with the polystyrene fragments and then offered them to the spectators as pieces of magic egg shell that would bring good luck. During *Wizards Week*, with the help of the School of Fine Arts, the wizards built a large nest on top of the eleven storey library tower at Canterbury University. This was constructed of cardboard tubes and resembled a stork's nest. As part of a *Day of Rage*, a protest against unnotified commercial exploitation of the Wizard's image by a travel firm in Australia, they tore the nest apart.

The wizards went jet boating, made sandcastles, and attended a Mad Hatters Tea Party. The week culminated with my skydiving into Lancaster Park whilst casting a spell for the Canterbury Crusaders in an important rugby match against Auckland. When the smoke cleared at the Wizard's Disco in the old town hall building, we danced the night away to the recorded music of Pentangle.

Wizards Week 1991

ROLES - THE MISSING LINK   87

REFLEXIVITY IN THE MICROCOSM; A POST-FEMINIST MARRIAGE FORM.

Whilst participating in these complex role interactions I was continually testing out a new psychological and social way of relating to the opposite sex to form a social bond that encouraged the evolution of cultural and spiritual values, both masculine animus and female anima. It would need to be strong enough to withstand the attacks of anti-religious, androphobic feminists legally enforcing political egalitarianism as an absolute value, as well as pressure from the traditional misogynistic religious patriarchy based on fertility as an absolute value. My identification since childhood with pre-agricultural hunter gatherers led me to concentrate on the pre-patriarchal hunter gatherer marriage form, which separated roles based on romantic love and sexual intercourse, from roles based on reproduction and parental love.

In constructing my cosmology I had assumed the process paradigm that the universe was not a mechanism driven by incomprehensible objective forces and shaped by chance, but a growing organism where learning modifies the control exercised by chance. The subjective intention that I assumed to be 'involving' was being expressed through various more complex forms of love. Arising from *electro magnetism* and *chemical bonding* into *bios* (or chi) and *philia* (psyche) to *storge* (parental love), *eros* (sexual love) and ultimately into *agape* (love of cultural identity). I theorised that each of these forms of self-expression is ranked in a hierarchy where control and feedback encourages qualitative upgrading in the form of evolution. Ideally agape controls eros, which controls storge, and so on.

Freud, an outspoken antitheist, was nevertheless committed to patriarchy and reproductive determinism. He concluded that storge and eros could never be reconciled due to what he believed to be the universal Oedipus complex. Patriarchy is founded on the idea of biological fatherhood as the base for personal immortality not only in the afterlife but in posthumous fame and property ownership. Women as wives and mothers are therefore more likely to be valued as the means by which this is achieved than as sexual partners. Wives are often expected to continue their storge roles for their husbands as housewives. Men are valued more as economic providers than as lovers. Before the emergence of romantic love, which causes major disruptions to the patriarchy, most marriages were arranged by parents.

This is true of agricultural cultures but it is not the case with the hunter gatherers for whom sexual relationships are more existential, and male parenting is based on storge and hence not dependent on any erotic relationship with the mother. Like most male animals it is the mature male who is the sex object and the young females are sexually attracted by their beauty, ritual display, and dominance ranking. Young males may confuse unresolved storge need for maternal dominance and approval and become attracted anti-socially to young females as magical sex objects. This would lead them to be resentful of mature males and allow their storge dependency roles to overrule their unreadiness for eros roles, which involve responsibility for the cultural development of their dependent loved ones. Unless controlled by the mature males and females young males may cause the weakening or collapse of the social structure. This is I believe the essence of what Freud described as the Oedipus complex which occurs in patriarchal cultures and hence the need for repression to maintain his ethnocentric 'reality principle'.

To prevent this happening in hunter gatherer cultures male children around the age of seven leave their mothers to bond with and join the males living away from the matriarchal settlements, Since there is no concept of male biological fatherhood, important early male parenting may be carried out by any relative of the mother.

This is an ideal type description of the essential socio-cultural differences between hunter gatherers and agriculturalists. It is therefore an heuristic device. In the real world things are more fuzzy and complex. The reason I was so interested in alternatives to patriarchy was that my mother and her mother were early examples of feminism in action rather than in political agitation and both carefully pursued and married their husbands driven by romantic passion rather than for traditional economic reasons and family pressures.

My revitalisation by the Boy Scout movement as a youth during the postwar austerity and my identification with Tarzan and Red Indian braves meant I found the prospect of ending up married with children with a mortgage and 9-5 job quite terrifying. In my late teens I met a young woman from a dysfunctional family who was similarly frightened of the same fate and we compromised by forming a companionate egalitarian marriage based on alternatively teaching and travelling for extended periods. After 15 years of courtship and marriage, changes in my career path, which involved moving to Australia and becoming an academic in adult education and then in sociology, gradually led to the stressful break-up of the marriage. I was forced to consider the nature of egalitarian companionate marriage as a kind of folie à deux.

The 1960s were a time of great confusion over the new roles for young women who were freed by the contraceptive pill from any existential concern with reproductive consequences and who were abandoning their traditional reticence in approaching males. The female capacity for deep orgasm was also being recognised. Most important of all the fundamental nature of patriarchy, heterosexual marriage, the nuclear family and even monogamy were all being questioned. My dream as a youth of living like a hunter gatherer might now be possible without abandoning mankind's cultural advances in religion, science and art.

In other essays I have described the efforts I made with the cooperation of a number of romantic young women to create a truly post patriarchal and enduring marriage form. Nowhere was my gift of intuitive reflexivity needed more than in this enterprise.

This introduction to my new role complex in relation to the opposite sex is necessarily complex as it is the most radical of my cultural engineering projects. It freed me from being bound by the social control that inevitably follows more traditional sexual bonding but without any loss of deep and powerful biological, psychological, social, cultural and spiritual reflexive interaction. I believe that only this 'great work' of the spiritual alchemists seeking the *rebis* or elective affinity of the *coniunctio oppositorum* has the potential to create a more evolved post-patriarchal marriage form in a world clearly reaching out for it.

REFLEXIVITY WITH THE COSMOS; THE MIRACULOUS RAIN DANCES

Another form of ritual avant garde theatre aimed at provoking reflexivity were the four rain dances I performed to break serious droughts in Waimate, Nelson and Auckland in New Zealand and in Tamworth in the Australian outback.

I may not have been successful in my attempts to relate reflexively with the ruling elites of our civilization at the socio-cultural level but I succeeded beyond everyone's expectations when I entered into this potentially very reflexive relationship with the macrocosm at all levels from the physical and biological to the psychological, social, and cultural. Like the 17th century magicians I assume that microcosm and macrocosm are in a *coniunctio oppositorum* relationship. I also share the opinion of the process philosopher Whitehead that the universe is best understood by us as being an inclusive super-organism or ecosystem which evolves by growing since it is curious and emotional, loves beauty and is capable of learning and self-improvement.

I accepted invitations to attempt to bring much needed rain to drought stricken regions as a form of avant garde ritual theatre rain dances. I regarded doing this as both therapy and entertainment. All the rain dances were initiated by invitation from reputable local authorities made several weeks beforehand. To ensure that it was the rain dance that produced any precipitation, the rain had to fall in reasonable quantities within three days of my performance. This happened in all cases.

In 1988 I received a letter from the Mayor of Waimate, a small and rather remote agricultural town in South Canterbury, requesting that I perform a rain dance to break their serious drought. The public announcement of my imminent arrival provoked considerable reflexivity in the local populations. The Assembly of God, who had failed to break their shocking drought with their prayers, were furious with their mayor for inviting me and cancelled all their advertising in the Agricultural and Pastoralists Show that was the venue for the rain dance. He defied them and the farmers were delighted when a few hours after my rain dance a dense black cloud ap-

The shaman at work in Waimate

peared (only over the Waimate region) and the skies opened, rendering the show a muddy morass. A full page was devoted to this event in the *New York Times*. Another rain dance in laid-back Nelson a year later aroused less controversy but also broke their drought so thoroughly that I received many complaints. My reputation grew in spite of the strenuous efforts of all those who believed in either scientific or divine causation to stop it.

Water Services in Auckland contacted the Mayor of Christchurch in 1994 to request the services of their wizard to break a drought in Auckland. This was so severe that plans were being made to drill a tunnel through to the Waikato River. Vicki Buck was happy to oblige and I began my preparations. Then the news came through that a storm of protest had broken out in all the separate councils that then made up the city. The radio talkbacks were deluged, but not with rain but with righteous fury that an evil wizard was coming to Auckland to perform a rain dance. There such an explosion of wrath that Water Services withdrew their invitation and each of the separate councils backed down and made it clear that I was not welcome. Shades of Salem! A wizard hunt was in full swing. This is what I call negative reflexivity! Then I received a letter from the media-savvy Mayor of Silverdale, a small factory town just north of Auckland, inviting me to perform a rain dance in the shopping precinct. This would be in the presence of the school children who were keen to see a wizard in action. A local shop keeper had offered his services as an assistant wizard and would publicise the visit. When I arrived with my large drum and magic horn I found I was offered the services of a helicopter and the local radio station so I was able fly over Auckland whilst broadcasting to those below. I urged them to wave as I passed overhead if wizard friendly, or shake their fists if not. This was real avant garde theatre and truly populist at the same time. But the drama was not over yet. Having performed my ritual which as usual included buckets of water being thrown over me from the four magic directions, I returned home exhausted. Within the allotted three days the rains came, but it was more like the Indian monsoon. For almost a year it was so heavy and continuous that I received many letters begging me to stop the rain. I replied that I would attempt do so if I received a word of thanks for the rain from at least one of the councils who had rudely rejected me. 'But answer came there none'.

This was high drama, but even better was to follow. The Auckland saga, showing how such a liminal figure as a prophet is often unrecognised and unwelcome in his own country, must have touched the hearts of Australians. A major radio station in Sydney, 2GB, invited me to come over the Tasman and perform a ritual rain dance in Tamworth in outback New South Wales, well known for hosting Country and Western music festivals. It had not rained there in any quantity for seven years and many farmers had been bankrupted. Whether or not I could break the local drought I could at least break some of the local spiritual depression. I was lucky that TV3, a Christchurch TV station which had contacts in Australia, agreed to send a cameraman and journalist with me to cover the story. There is therefore a good film record of the drama. The radio station set up a press conference at the famous Rocks in Sydney where I boasted and bragged and 'skited' in true Aussie fashion about my past achievements which no one else in the world could match etc. etc. I carried an umbrella as a symbol with which I could punctuate my speech. My confidence that I could bring the rain knew no bounds. I leave it to the reader to imagine the effect this had on the assembled Australian TV and newspaper journalists crowding around who are not known for their trust in people like me, and especially a 'pommie bastard'. Through a nun friend who had worked for years with the Aboriginal people of NSW, I had already informed their elders that I was going to revive one of their ancient magical practices and that I would be pleased if they were to attend. I flew in and was met by the Mayor and a few dispirited farmers and performed the rain dance near fields where the wheat was only about six inches high. The Aboriginal tribal leaders who attended congratulated me afterwards for having retained belief in the interweaving of human and natural forces. What was said about the rain dance in the mysterious Aboriginal subculture about what transpired I will never know, but that's what I call 'deep play' and 'cross-cultural reflexivity'!

As I was leaving for home two days later I heard that storm clouds were gathering round Tamworth. That night on TV3 news an astonished weather man showed scenes of thunder and lightning and downpour over Tamworth. People there were interviewed but most ascribed it to chance or divine intervention. I received little credit and no official thanks. But for me 'The Play's the Thing'. My genius as a dramatist and leading actor has never been recognised or even mentioned by the unimaginative and self-promoting theatrical avant garde. I hope that I am not condemned like Nietzsche to be a 'posthumous man'. Fearful that I might have great healing powers ascribed to me as a result of my clearly demonstrated magical prowess and cause a major disruption in the smug self-satisfied welfare state, I faced the possibility of crucifixion modern style by being given psychotherapy by the authorities. I gave up my unrewarded and thankless career as 'the rain dance kid' and quit whilst I was ahead. A few years later my horn and bass drum were both destroyed when the large wooden house that Alice and I lived in was set on fire in the middle of the night. Luckily we awoke and made our escape, but the house and most of our possessions were destroyed.

Since that time there have been few opportunities for the Living Work of Art to interact. The art galleries have gone the way of so many modern institutions. Now unimaginative bureaucratic managers, who are easily impressed by the shallow spin of conceptual artists, seem to be horrified at any signs of playfulness and originality and they refuse to consider the Living Work of Art as worth a moment's thought. Perhaps I am not obscene or blasphemous enough for their taste. My rather Pollyanna-like approach to the avant garde can be a bit unnerving. But I also know deep down that, paradoxically, the ridiculous and the sublime cannot be disentangled.

An impenetrable wall has appeared around me in Christchurch. I am no longer invited to speak anywhere even though I have been the most famous speaker in NZ since 1974. My letters to the City Council are unanswered. The legendary Wizard is not even mentioned in the pamphlets or on websites produced by the national or even Canterbury tourist authorities. The local press and TV have lost their independence and are now monopolies that avoid controversies and lack curiosity in original events happening in Christchurch (unless they are bad news). They are convinced that overseas, and occasionally Auckland, is 'where it's all at'. I have therefore concentrated on mixing and mingling with the locals and tourists who are delighted to interact briefly with me as I proceed around the earthquake-devastated city centre.

Realising the importance of mimetic communication through image projection I wear my pointy black hat and robe and carry a staff. This is to encourage the emergence of the wizard archetype as a specific brand image which I control. Heaven help any poor unfortunate who sets himself up as an independent rival. Distinguishing 'wizards' from 'wankers' is important to avoid bringing the new profession into disrepute in these early stages. I have also capped three other wizards in NZ of reasonably mature years and independent life-styles who are apprentices learning by example. In particular a love of music and the realisation of its fundamental importance to the unique human brain and consciousness unites us.

THE KINEMATICS OF THE ANDROGYNE

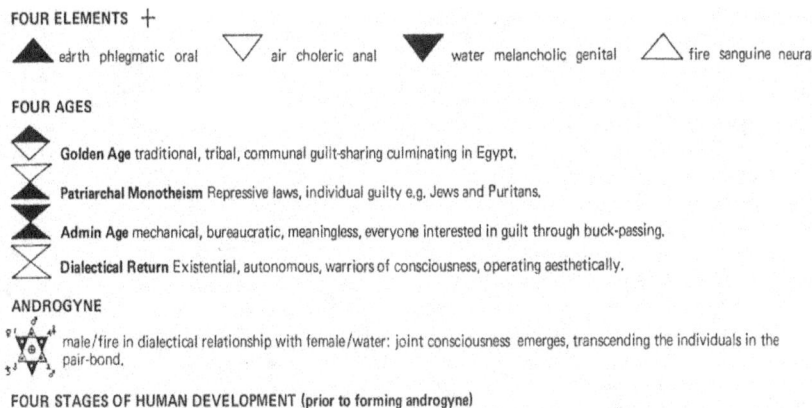

HUNTING THE BOOJUM

INSPIRED BY DANTE AND LEWIS CARROLL

*"Ah! But a man's reach should exceed his grasp
or what's a heaven for!"* – Browning

On each December 4th during the years 1970-1973 residents in the charming Victorian precinct of Parkville adjoining Melbourne University might have seen a few students led by a bearded figure in a gown proceeding towards the nearby Burke and Wills Memorial. This had been erected to commemorate the starting point of the preposterous and hugely hyped expedition by Burke and Wills which set out to cross Australia from South to North about a hundred years earlier.

This was the site I chose to mark each year's progress before I set out on my own preposterous expedition to cross the Universe from South to North to mark the 42nd year since my birth in 1932. The highlight of the ceremony each year was the reading of Lewis Carroll's masterpiece *The Hunting of the Snark*. I had reached the halfway point in my life three years earlier and like Dante I had found myself in a dark wood. Faced with a fork in the path, I chose the rough track and, as in Dante's case, what followed was a series of unexpected attacks on my psychological, social and cultural wellbeing. I have taken both epic poems as my guides ever since.

A SPASMODIC CAREER CONCEALING A MASTER PLAN

I had decided from a very young age to live my life in seven year cycles. I preferred approaching the meaning of my life analogically rather than digitally; just adding the years up without taking the start or end seriously is meaningless. On reaching the age of thirty-five I assumed I would have accumulated enough experience by reading promiscuously, backpacking in the USA, Europe and the Middle East and living in England, Canada, Iran and Australia, to cease being a voyeur and could now "come out" like a debutante to join in the games of intellectual and political "one-upmanship".

In 1967, to the surprise of those who knew me at this point in my life, I gave up a flourishing career as the university's bureaucratic "commissar" of cultural events in Western Australia and moved to the University of NSW in Sydney to become the first qualified academic lecturer in Australia in the mushrooming new field of sociology. I was not quite sure where my new action role would take me, but whatever it was it must culminate when I entered the final of the seven-year cycles in 1974.

THE YOUTH REVOLUTION

During the middle and late 1960s events around the world had taken a sudden surprising turn and teenagers in general and university students in particular were behaving in ways that resembled medieval revitalisation movements. I was giving lectures on this topic at the time whilst researching for a PhD in creative expression and cultural values. This was my chance to come out of the trenches. Realising that cultural phenomena usually reached the Antipodes a year or two after Europe and North America I prepared to ride the tsunami of hysteria that was approaching our shores. To keep my balance I created a surfboard from a synthesis of Logic, Love and Levity. At the University of NSW in Sydney I founded a reform movement that I called Action for Love and Freedom or ALF and anchored it securely on the ideal of the university as a community of scholars.

HOMO LUDENS

My academic training in Psychology and Sociology helped me to analyse what was happening and to keep a cool head. My sunny disposition, which followed a happy non-dogmatic Christian childhood, had even survived compulsory secular education due to frequent changes of school following evacuation in war-time England and enthusiastic participation in the Boy Scout movement. I was more attracted by hippie sentiments of love and conservation of the environment than by the Marxist hatred of "the system" etc. of the rising Student Power movement. Levity or playfulness is, I believe, a characteristic of Anglo-Saxon culture in particular, though the Czechs seem very similar. Raised on a diet of ITMA and The Goon Show on the radio, with a love of such writers as Chaucer, Rabelais, Cervantes, Swift, Sterne, Capek, Vonnegut, etc., and with respectable theoretical underpinning from Huizinga's *Homo Ludens*, I started the Fun Revolution. Logic and Love were in the wings, but Levity was centre stage.

This is not the place to give an account of what happened during the Fun Revolution at the University of NSW between 1967 and 1969. Suffice to say that it included my being dismissed from my teaching fellowship without consultation or appeal by my humourless Marxist head of department. He had been recruited from the much larger field of Political Science and like many politically-motivated intellectuals was probably baffled by my sociological and psychological sophistication. Subsequently however by applying my combination of love, logic and levity I was rescued from expulsion from academia by being appointed as official university Wizard by the Vice Chancellor and Student Union. This 'liminal' role gave me even more opportunities to "revitalise" both myself and the campus.

THE WORLD UNIVERSITY SERVICE BACKS THE FUN REVOLUTION

Towards the end of 1969, with backing of the university and student administrations, I travelled to Hamburg and obtained the support of the Annual General Meeting of the World University Service for a proposal to travel round the campuses raising fun and funds for the

WUS branches and giving oratorical performances on various radical sociological and psychological topics not generally promoted. Only France and Italy were opposed. WUS, as a voluntary non-aligned, mutual-aid organisation of students, administrators and academics, was the ideal backer for my revitalisation campaign. After organising a "Dictator's Concentration Camp" for the freshers to launch their course of studies at UNSW, I relocated to Melbourne early in 1970 to become the travelling Wizard of the World University Service as their Australian HQ was in that city.

THE DAY THE MUSIC DIED

Suddenly the colourful youth movements everywhere turned into cauldrons of hysterical hatred. Love, logic and levity evaporated almost overnight. Between 1969 and 1970 all over the country fun-hating, corrupt, and violent fundamentalist student politicians seized power, fixed meetings and censored all the student newspapers. "I Started a Joke and the Whole World Started Crying". Within a few months I had become the Anti-Christ and my opponents bore an uncanny resemblance to Oliver Cromwell's Puritan "saints".

In 1970, a few weeks into my WUS tour, without warning and without any active campus branches knowing what was going on, the HQ of Australian WUS in Australia was taken over by political extremists to be used as a political front organisation. The office in Melbourne did not respond to my letters and appeared to have vanished. Their usual communication with the active WUS branches ceased. It turned out to be another stupid left wing coup! I began to think that I was becoming a very dangerous radical who must be stopped by fair means or foul. WUS was not a wise choice for a socialist take-over since it was a voluntary independent organisation and there were no compulsory fees to exploit as a source of income. WUS in Australia soon collapsed and has never recovered. I decided to persist with my campus revitalisation activities so I became associated with the Activities Office of Melbourne University Union which was fortunately independent of the new Maoist Student Representative Council. In 1970 I became their official Wizard and Shaman. I was also their official Cosmologer and Living Work of Art.

As a cultural engineer and activist I was establishing the important aspects of a wizard's role-set to prevent myself being dragged down in the cultural meltdown that was beginning to take place.

DRIVEN BY EVENTS TO CREATE MY OWN UNIVERSE

Since coming out of the trenches my career had been destroyed twice by blind fear and irrational hatred. It became obvious that I needed a more accurate cognitive map to avoid being shot down again. In my role as the Union Cosmologer I gave lectures and held open discussion groups on a synthesis of recent scientific ideas in all fields. The Vice Chancellor allowed me the use of a temporarily unused neo-Gothic building on campus for this purpose. This was known as the Department of Levity. This was where my aesthetic Postmodern Cosmology was born. It was first published and circulated widely in 1972. Like the process philosopher A.N.Whitehead, without realising the similarity at the time, I scrapped both belief in the independent existence of what we are taught to believe to be objective reality (the materialistic and mechanistic paradigm of science) and the idealist belief that reality is little more than a psychological, socio-cultural product, (the 'simulacra' of Platonic idealism, socialism and postmodern French philosophy). The interaction between intension and extension could be identified by focussing on what actually happened.

SCIENTIFIC DOGMA CONFOUNDED

Relativity theory was born following the Death of God who had previously been assumed to provide the absolute frame that was a fictional necessity for materialism. The discovery of whole families of sub-atomic particles, and quantum theory in general, had now put paid to the search for the solid irreducible atoms that were the building blocks of the universe. Since the time of the Ancient Greeks, materialist philosophers had devoutly believed that these atoms comprised and determined ultimate reality. The fundamental base of the Laws of Nature was now confounded.

Earlier, having ridiculed *divine* causation, they had simply replaced it with *chance* causation. Belief in the immortality of sacred matter replaced belief in the immortality of the soul which was banished from intelligent discussion. Belief in Heaven was ridiculed and replaced by belief in the Big Bang which, like Heaven, is a fictional construct or singularity. This is assumed to have eventuated outside time and space, for no reason at all and requires belief that a tiny, zero-dimensional point contained enough energy to create an entire expanding universe. Heaven is also a singularity but is the cosmological convergent point whose existence has been 'revealed' to spiritual intellectuals. It is the transcendental opposite of the reductionist Big Bang. Believing in divine causation, creator gods and trusting established religion is like swallowing a fly. Believing in chance causation and materialistic reductionism and trusting established science is like swallowing a horse; as Burl Ives put it in the folk song about the old lady, "She died of course".

THE MADMAN WITH THE LANTERN

Priests in the late 19th century had been deaf to the fearful cries of Nietzsche's madman running through the streets with a lantern crying out "God is dead. We have killed Him!" Now, a hundred years later, the madman is running through the streets with an even more fearful cry, "Nature is dead. We have killed Her!" Government and business-employed scientists, secure in their respected jobs, are predictably deaf to his new cries. More and more independent thinkers are realising the mind-blowing implications of relativity theory in all fields and the end of the insane belief that scientific observers are immaterial spirits who can stand outside the universe to measure, understand and manipulate it.

THE HUNTING OF THE QUARK

I began to realise that my deep responsiveness to *The Hunting of the Snark* was due to the way the narrative paralleled events in the world of materialistic science. The reductionist scientists who had been assiduously hunting the irreducible atom had "stood erect and sublime for a moment of time" when they thought they had finally found the ultimate "building blocks" of matter that made up the universe and could now be controlled by man. Then they discovered that the atom was not solid but was made up of even smaller "atoms" like quarks, and so ad infinitum, and these did not behave like building blocks at all. They and their hopes were confounded, their thoughts were entangled and sucked down into the *horror vacui* of the "uncaused first cause", the Big Bang. In the words of Lewis Carroll that conclude his poem, yet were the first words that came into his head in 1874, "For the Snark was a Boojum, you see!"

ALICE

Like Lewis Carroll, I flourish by expounding imaginative ideas to intelligent young women. Their response has inspired me to attempt impossible feats of intellectual daring. It is my substitute for conventional economic, athletic, moral, sexual or political display. Unlike Carroll, who appears to have suffered from arrested sexual development, I was capable of combining both intellectual and sexual attraction and satisfaction.

Alice spellbound by the Living Work of Art: Melbourne, 1971

Official Engagement: Festival of Romance, Christchurch 1992

At this time, when I was casting around for a fresh start, I was introduced by the Anglican Chaplain at Melbourne University (another echo of Lewis Carroll) to a romantic young Catholic Classics undergraduate named Alison. After very carefully studying me, she finally made her move. Alison became Alice, my spellbound love-slave. She stood beside me as the storms of frenzied and irrational hatred of the student power elite broke over me again and again as I tried to continue my Fun Revolution which was distracting their student members from the real issues. Without her they would have succeeded in their desperate need to drive me off the campus. Instead, against immense organised opposition at noisy mass meetings, the University Union finally published my collection of short provocative articles entitled *The Wizard's Nonsense Almanac of 1974*. Now I could set off on my hero's quest.

FALLING THROUGH THE EARTH - AN EXPERIMENT IN VIRTUAL REALITY

I was now even further radicalised. What did I have to lose, except my warm self-regard, my acute recognition of bullshit when I scent it, and my sense of humour? In other words my love, logic, and levity. Like the Bellman in Carroll's epic poem I started by ditching the conventional signs of both moral and scientific dogma and became empowered by the sheer delight that also informs his imaginative writing. Spellbound by the strange multilevel synchronicity of the magic number 42, I directed my course towards Antipodes Island, a remote uninhabited rocky island whose name and location could be linked to biblical prophecy and the epic poems of Dante and Lewis Carroll. This was the place chosen for my imagination experiment which I described in the Nonsense Almanac and intended to conduct there on my 42nd birthday.

My plan, as the official Shaman of Melbourne University Union, was to attempt to fall through the Earth, like Alice in Wonderland. Ignoring friction etc., scientific calculations provided in Martin Gardner's *Annotated Alice* indicate it would take 21 minutes to reach the centre and then another 21 to reach the opposite pole. A total of 42 minutes! To attempt this brilliant imagination experiment I would have to create an unconventional map in an unconventional frame.

In Carroll's "Agony in Eight Fits", in preparing for their hunt for the elusive Snark, the crew had unfortunately left behind the 42 pieces of baggage belonging to the Baker. He was the unfortunate crew member who met with what turned out to be a Boojum and vanished. Without holding on to the past, he had no secure identity. The same number 42 occurred as having immense but incomprehensible significance in the BBC radio science fiction series *Hitch-hiker's Guide to the Galaxy*, written a few years after my adventure. This was the most imaginative BBC radio drama since The Goon Show vignettes of the 1950s. On my 42nd birthday, on December 4th 1974, I would also enter the seventh stage of my final set of seven year cycles. 1974 was not only divisible by 42 but was also the 100th anniversary of the writing of *The Hunting of The Snark*. The inspiration for the poem came to Carroll in a vision at the age of 42. How could I resist? My motto was now *Reductio Ad Absurdum*.

DISCARDING CONVENTIONAL CO-ORDINATES BY TURNING THE UNIVERSE INSIDE-OUT

According to relativity theory, in the absence of any absolute frame, the Earth could be turned upside-down by a conformal inversion of the old fashioned God-given coordinates. However, it would appear to an uninformed eye to be unchanged. This had been common knowledge in the 19th century. What was not known by most educated people, including astrophysicists, was that the Earth could be turned inside-out the same way. By performing this simple mathematical operation, the Earth is no longer a tiny sphere surrounded by the immense universe but is transformed into an immense spherical hole enclosing what appears to be a tiny universe. Again, to the uninformed eye, it would appear unchanged.

Conventional ideas of size depend not on simple deceptive appearances but on the totalitarian power of the ruling elite of reality controllers to determine both the location of observers and the model they have decided that everyone must adopt. "The only question is, 'which is to be Master?'" Scientists have always been the willing servants of the evil lords of the military-industrial complex so the model of the Earth they have imposed on us through compulsory secular education is the one that makes terrestrial navigation and ballistic calculations the only important concern. Ockham's razor gang were called in to cut any non-utilitarian alternatives to pieces. That was the fate of poor Mostafa Abdelkadar's well-explicated speculative Geoperipheral model, now more or less "disappeared" from the internet.

Love, logic and levity are all now being overruled by the utilitarian needs of welfare-warfare socialist states embedded within the overall embrace of the managerial global bureaucracy.

THE UNIVERSAL LEVITATIONAL FORCE

During the planning stage in my Department of Levity at the University of Melbourne between 1971-1974, I was proceeding in the manner described by Lewis Carroll who, as Charles Dodgson, was not only a cleric in the Anglican Church at Christ Church College, Oxford, after which our city in New Zealand is named, but was also a talented mathematician. Years later in Christchurch, like the Bellman who, as captain, regularly confused the bowsprit and rudder of his ship, I became famous for driving around in my modified VW Beetle, where it is impossible to tell which end is the front. More importantly, like the Bellman, I had completely rejected not only conventional motivation and the conventional signs orienting oneself on the surface of the Earth, but even the conventional shape of the universe itself.

My aim to fall though the centre of the Earth was much more realisable in this new frame where most of the matter was apparently on the outside. I had already decided that I would rely on the Universal Levitational Force to lift me up (or down, for media observers in the northern hemisphere) and provide the necessary acceleration and I assumed that the journey through the centre of the Earth would take 42 minutes as measured by clocks on the Earth's surface. Others have pointed out that materialistic scientists make it clear that the Universal Gravitational Force, rather a misnomer for an acausal structuring singularity, is the only force they believe in which has no equal and opposite force. Is Levity, whatever it may be, an equal and opposite dynamic driving the evolution of increasingly complex self-organising systems?

The difficulties were now twofold. As I approached the singularity at the centre I would be increasingly compressed in apparent size along with the rest of the universe around me. But even more importantly, I would have to travel faster than the speed of light. This could only be achieved if I dematerialised at the start of the journey to become disembedded Ego. I would have to vanish and become pure, focussed information! Now I understood the deeper meaning of Carroll's parable: if I was to succeed where the scientists had failed I would have to hunt the Boojum!

NOTHING IS PERFECT

I am not generally seen as being a perfectionist, being rather slapdash in most tasks. As a child I found the idea of infinity quite ludicrous and was never upset because the God I was taught to pray to did not appear to be perfect or even answer my pathetic prayers. I found that expecting nothing meant that what I did get was always a pleasant surprise. Not being a spoilt child, I have never thought that the world owed me a living. Such things as the mathematical relationship called Pi being another 'singularity' and the existence of irrational numbers confirmed to me that maths was more of an art form than the vaunted key to the mysteries of the universe and it was one that I had no great interest in or aptitude for. I preferred listening to classical music instead. My joy in coming across Gödel's Incompleteness Theorem, which was the death of the mathematical god worshipped by Pythagoreans like Descartes, can be imagined and matched my delight in finding out that hard scientists had to invent imaginary "singularities" to make their mathematical descriptions of the universe work.

I always felt that nothing was perfect and came to understand why many mystics insisted that God could not be named, some just leaving an empty space in their writings. It has taken me considerable intellectual self-discipline but I have eventually reached the point of being able to believe in nothing, at least in short bursts, and my greatest aim is to achieve nothing. Many years ago I wrote this as my four line epitaph, *"Out of nothing I come/ Just to have fun/ Into nothing I go/ At the end of the show."*

CREATING HEAVEN AND EARTH AS A CONCEPTUAL ART WORK

A point that should be of interest to religious intellectuals, but has so far failed to be so, is that in this Geoperipheral model the new singularity at the centre of the universe is no longer the obviously satanic singularity known as the Big Bang but becomes the highest point in the universe towards which all the galaxies are converging whilst accelerating. It exactly matches traditional descriptions of the great singularity known as Heaven. In Ancient Greece the evil materialistic scientists, serving the merchant class as usual, dethroned Heaven by turning the flat Earth into a sphere where there was no "up" only "out". During the Renaissance Heaven was banished to the periphery and Hell was placed right in the centre of their model of the universe. I am attempting, in my own playful way, to create Heaven and Earth in my own image as a conceptual art work, and then to vanish like the Oozlum Bird whilst ascending into the centre of my own fundamental orifice. By avoiding death, I would avoid the hideous boredom of eternal life or the pointless self-deception of being remembered or passing on my genes after death. This was an authentic ego trip I was planning, stripped of all the disguises that provide such rich pickings for psychiatrists.

THE BELLMAN

The main function of the Captain in *The Hunting of the Snark* was to ring his bell to create the impression of being in command without actually doing anything remotely useful. Since failing to attempt my imaginary experiment I took him as a role model and have stood around in New Zealand in public places wearing a pointy hat, blowing my horn and describing my plans to vanish and be forgotten. I have been classified as a living work of art by the NZ Art Gallery Directors Council and tourists came to Christchurch to see this remarkable human phenomenon that was described in all the guide books. I was presented with the highest award for promoting tourism in New Zealand, and I wasn't even trying!

ANTIPODES ISLAND AND THE ENGLISH CHANNELL

As my 42nd Birthday on December 4th 1974 approached, I had already moved to New Zealand to be near a port to get a boat to the uninhabited Antipodes Island. I had chosen this spot to converge the identity, space, and time systems in my process cosmology by briefly becoming Me, Here, Now, whilst appearing on television, especially in the northern hemisphere. Dr Derek Banks, my physicist collaborator in constructing my process cosmology, had already gone ahead to Plymouth to arrange for a fleet of small boats to pluck me from the sea should I splash down in the Channel. Antipodes Island was named by English navigators who noted its location on the opposite side of the Earth to a point in the English Channel near Harfleur. As a trained navigator I was once the Flying Wing Adjutant and later Navigation Officer at the Royal Air Force base at Duxford (preserved now as part of the Imperial War Museum). I am English and my family name is Channell. I took all these "co-incidences" as a compelling sign, but definitely not a conventional sign, not even a floating signifier!

KNOCKING ON HEAVEN'S DOOR

Since I would be travelling at considerable speed with the stated aim of travelling through the centre of the universe on my way to splash down in the English Channel, I often wondered what would happen when I reached the singularity at the centre. There is no way of knowing. A few years earlier Stanley Kubrick's famous film *2001*, had portrayed a similar journey and hazarded a guess about the nature of such a singularity. I had not envisioned it that way at all, especially since I am aesthetically repelled by puritanical temples of hygiene, orderly geometrical forms and by decadent Louis Quinze décor. The image that came into my mind was more like the Heaven portrayed in the classic *Journey to the West* with the Jade Emperor, beautiful goddesses and delicious peaches. I imagined their surprise as I sped through without stopping. King Monkey would have approved. We are fellow spirits: I was born in the Chinese Year of the Monkey and after many bitter experiences I have become an excellent demon exposer.

Although rarely thanked, I do what I can to protect simple persons from the consequences of their trusting naivety.

AVOIDING IMMORTALITY

I had made preparations with my bemused followers in the unlikely eventuality that my vanishing attempt actually succeeded. I expected that even a failure would produce a great flowering of love, logic, and levity to fill the vacuum left by the failure of scientific materialism, bureaucratic egalitarian socialism, capitalist social darwinism and religious fundamentalism which were driving the world to ecological and political-economic collapse.

In the event of my vanishing and *not* reappearing on the other side of the Earth these bewildered acolytes would have to assume that I must have joined Enoch, Elijah, Jesus, Nordic and classical heroes, and various Hindu and Daoist holy men in Heaven. They would have to acknowledge that this event demonstrated that I was the first man to work out what on Earth was really going on. I had been telling the truth all along! They must therefore obey my Last Will and Testament, which was that for me to vanish in every way they must devote their lives to destroying all records that I ever existed. This would not be easy but it would be fun to try and they could become rich and famous doing it. My monstrous ego would finally be destroyed. French deconstructionists, priests and psychiatrists in particular would be pleased.

MAROONED AGAIN

In the months preceding the deadline (an unfortunate but a deeply meaningful term) both in New Zealand in general and Christchurch in particular, my announcement to the general public and media of my plans to rise in the air and vanish did not produce enough levity. The native sardonic English wit found in great abundance in Australasia had probably already been infected by neurotic American TV humour. But alas their logic too was inadequate to make any rational criticisms.

I was disappointed. Could this be the same city that in 1863 first published Samuel Butler's *Darwin among the Machines* in the local newspaper? This is still, according to Gregory Bateson, the best critique of Darwin's mechanistic theory. Was this the city where Karl Popper found sanctuary and wrote his critical analysis of Marxist theory, Platonic totalitarianism and the need for all hypotheses to be falsifiable? However, there was enough love in this rather odd city founded by Anglican gentlemen of the romantic Gothic Revival in a remote swamp on the other side of the Earth. I was affectionately tolerated, a refreshing change from being hated by Australian university student leaders for undermining their juvenile revolution by mistake.

With not enough interest in the community to provide me with a boat and with the superficial and humourless mass media distrustful of my motives, I was marooned in Christchurch. Since it was a delightful little city years behind the ghastly times I settled down and, after putting the dull-witted city council through a fun revolutionary skirmish, I began providing daily entertainments as an orator in their newly refurbished Cathedral Square.

This was an excellent stage on which to exhibit myself and to keep my wits sharp by performing my shamanistic ritual capers on the razor's edge of political correctness. I became notorious but never a celebrity as I was far too intelligent, honest, laid back, and scruffy to be used by the mass-media makers of illusions encouraging consumerism.

THE NONCENSUS PARTY

As the world's first "living work of art", acquisitioned by the Christchurch City Council art gallery in 1982, with Alice, now well qualified in art history, as my curator, I considered it vital to be consistent. Since 1968 I have had no social security or income tax registration and owned no significant property. Needing to preserve my precious identity which had been formed in the fires of hatred from self-righteous and politically ambitious university youths, and impervious to the acidic ridicule of economically ambitious but scarcely literate executives now appearing in great numbers, I had to evade the five yearly Census.

Also as a wizard I had to avoid being rounded up, branded with a number and counted as the property of the welfare-warfare-state farm managers. In 1975 I managed to avoid the count by passing through a loophole in the law. On the second Census in 1980 I went out to sea in a small boat beyond the 12-mile-limit. I invited boat owners to join me in a Noncensus Party. I produced a handbill taken from the original illustration by Holiday on the front cover of the first edition of The Hunting of the Snark showing the Bellman high up the mast. Photographs appeared in newspapers all over the world showing me and my defiant companions rowing out to the yacht. With my beard, striped top, and bell I bore a striking resemblance to the Bellman. There was much wailing and gnashing of teeth by the thousands of employees of the census department but my attorney, an Anglican lawyer, was right: the NZ Government did not have political jurisdiction beyond the 12-mile-limit.

A VANISHING ACT

Five years later during the next Census I informed the government that I would vanish at midnight and would reappear at noon the next day, so I would not be in the country during the Census. After completing my vanishing act, I put adverts in the papers all over NZ, circulated stickers etc. and invited the public to sign forms stating that they believed I had vanished. I explained that if they did not believe in my powers, the Wizard would die like Tinker Bell, the fairy in Peter Pan, and return to being just another sociology academic, a profession that was then multiplying like flies. Thousands signed, including mayors and senior politicians and "I believe the Wizard vanished" stickers appeared all over New Zealand. Once again, the regiments of well-paid control freaks with clipboards working for the Department of Statistics retired from the fray licking their wounds.

BEATEN BY DEATH AND GRAVITY

My seventh cycle ended in 1981 and I realised sadly that my nervous system might now be too old to trigger the preadaptive innate release mechanism for levitation that I hypothesised was waiting to be activated in the human brain. A "useful fiction" for a life based on levity. I had no other explanation for the universal human dreams of flying and the desire found in all human cultures to imagine the most perfect human beings would ascend to some sort of higher place like Heaven. If caterpillars could dream, would they dream of butterflies? Is each human culture a form of chrysalis from which we can never emerge because of our culturally imposed fear of death? I assume that both acceptance and fear of death and personal non-being has been the core value round which the symbolic threads of all previous cultures have been spun.

We must cease to believe in all forms of immortality including fame after death, having children to pass on one's genes, property and family name etc. We are the arrow head of the evolving universe. We must avoid assumptions that the future is determined, thereby locking the door and imprisoning mankind in a death trap. Seeing the universe as a process accepts amazing and unpredictable transformations in form and complexity. From a burst of radiating energy to matter; to living ecosystems of self-replicating cells; to behaving organisms with nervous systems; to social role systems. It is still evolving and accelerating in the direction of unprecedented human symbolic expressions of meaning.

Only dogmatic dyed-in-the-wool reductionists still insist that the universe is essentially a material "thing" observed by god-like scientists. My experiment depended on using the mass media to produce a collective illusion briefly converging intentionality, extensionality and eventuality, and making it personal. Identity as Me, space as Here, and time as Now. Nowadays the Internet would be a more practical means of achieving such a cultural symbolic convergence. I still wonder sometimes what would have happened if I had been able to carry out my embodied imagination experiment. It was even cleverer than those brilliantly designed but abstract thought experiments of Kepler, Galileo and Einstein, but requiring more than just sitting down and thinking and avoiding self-actualisation.

Perhaps Coleridge would have understood what I was attempting. Long ago he wrote of thinking and self-actualisation, "The living Power and prime Agent of all human perception…a repetition in the finite mind of the eternal act of creation in the infinite I AM". To appreciate the strange parallels that I have recorded between my great adventure, the end of the scientific "Great Work" and Lewis Carroll's poem, I recommend *The Annotated Snark*, where Martin Gardner, although a reductionist scientist, reveals the subtlety and complexity of the logical aspects of this unparalleled example of the penetrating power of a synthesis of love, logic, and levity.

A final comment from Kierkegaard, a non-reductionist:

"*The Christian believer cannot be content with less than his own reality for the object of his faith, and therefore in the act of faith he leaps over the confines of what he can know; at the same time the object of belief is itself beyond belief. Hence faith is a paradoxical relationship to the paradoxical.*"

OPENING THE GREAT PORTAL

THE SLEEPER AWAKES

In common with all intelligent animals I am a dreamer. I experience dreaming as entering 'inner space' from which I awake to emerge into 'outer space'. This first happened when I decided to turn myself inside out, and give birth to myself as a baby.

I don't sleep just to rest my body. I sleep to safely experience extreme states of emotion, create dream narratives and enter virtual reality environments.

In human beings the frontal cortex of the brain has evolved dramatically. In each pair of temporal lobes, one is mainly devoted to interacting with what we experience as events in the outer-space world outside us, and the other mainly to integrating and patterning these experiences into meaningful contexts. We all live in narratives where we have intentions which we act out when we can. There can be no narratives unless we have constructed a cognitive map or stage to act upon. In well-adjusted individuals learning from experience, these actions will themselves create events that will modify the narratives themselves.

What some thinkers are calling metanarratives are assumed to be part of a wider context, a world view, belief system, or ideology. The question therefore is how do we explain how the inner space narratives which direct our intentions can sometimes radically change? What we call a conversion experience is when such a context is radically rearranged as a result of cognitive dissonance where there is pressure to change a belief system which is under unbearable psychological, social or intellectual stress. This may be deliberate, as in consistent brainwashing, accidental, as a consequence of personal experience, or even brain malfunction. The change may be retrogressive, as when escaping social alienation by joining a group of fanatics and entering a collective psychosis, or it may be progressive, as when breaking out of the rigid ideology and forced conformity of group-think.

Major changes in metanarratives often occur when cultures are impacted by events in outer space such as climate catastrophe, an internal political coup, or invasion by an alien culture. Technological innovations such as the ability to smelt iron, or the discovery of how to manipulate the power of steam or electricity, can also radically alter the inner space ideologies of large numbers of the world's people. Another source of metanarrative transformation is the transformation of inner space belief systems by charismatic personalities, such as happened during the Axial Age around the beginning of the Iron Age. The Daoists associated with the Chinese Book of Changes, Confucius, Buddha, Heraclitus, Zoroaster, Jeremiah, and the Milesian atheist philosophers, all appeared suddenly around the same time. These were the progenitors of our major traditional civilizations. Egypt was a cultural world of its own that came into the mix a little later when absorbed into the Persian, Hellenistic and Roman Empires.

HEAVEN: THE GREAT PORTAL

For tens of thousands of years before the sudden growth of agricultural technology, division of labour and urbanisation, shamans had been the experts in transitioning between the two realities. They ascended the cosmic axis to enter inner space and came back with information. Once land owning chiefs and kings with armies had taken over, the shamans were replaced by priests of fertility-focussed religions and any shamanic attempt to ascend, levitate, or fly was defined as a sign of evil and consequently suppressed.

A portal is the term commonly used for a door between inner and outer space. They are by definition liminal, being on the fuzzy borders between different realities. The greatest of all portals is the door to Paradise or Heaven. The great portals for the major civilizations of the past, and the less technologically developed agricultural societies, are located out of reach above the surface of the Earth. They are commonly referred to as Heaven's gates or doors. Divine beings have their home there, from which they may come down to earth to appear in dreams or visions since they usually take a great interest in human affairs.

Some cultures believe there are portals down to a dark realm below the earth's surface. Others believe there are hidden doors in the countryside that give entrance to a fairyland inhabited by happy-go-lucky magical beings with little or no interest in the fate of human beings.

THE DEATH OF THE MONOTHEISTIC GOD AND THE END OF THE WORLD

From the Renaissance onwards a gradual change took place in Europe. The natural cosmological frame in religious societies is inevitably linked to a transcendental supernatural being or beings whose dynamic intentions, or even accidental acts, created the world. The orthodox universe of the priestly theologians was being transformed into an objective mechanism. The divine inner space dynamic that directed and contextualised the traditional agrarian world was being replaced by a Pythagorean belief that the intrinsic harmonies of mathematics and geometry were a sacred revelation and had to be trusted more than words which had previously been the unquestioned source of divine authority. This process accompanied the transformation of an agrarian civilization into a number of industrial nation states linked by trade, which provided collective motivation, and with borders decided by the results of military conflict.

Mathematically sophisticated natural philosophers increasingly perceived the universe as being made up of measurable things whose value was assessed by their usefulness to the rapidly expanding national governments. These new anti-religious military industrial complexes had multiplied and grown stronger following the implosion of Christendom during the Reformation. Modern science is founded not only on the pragmatic experimental scientific method but also on the irrational belief pioneered by René Descartes that human beings can be objective observers whose choice of both what and how to measure outer space objective phenomena can be free from psychological, social and cultural bias. Man and universe had both become useful machines and the philosophy of materialism, in the form of economic progress, triumphed in providing the meaning for human political action, both egalitarian and individualistic.

The end of common belief in doors leading from outer space reality to inner space realities took place in Europe with brutal suddenness between the 17th and 18th centuries. After this, books containing openly fictional narratives describing various portals into inner space flourished as they provided an escape from the grim totalitarian reality of the new machine masters and the scientific educators who served them. The portal to the heavenly singularity available to the shamans had already been nailed shut by the priests who forbade attempts to 'knock on Heaven's door' made after their own founders had come and gone through it. Mechanistic scientists, following Galileo and Newton, created an absolute frame with no portal at all. They had sealed it off with their magical mathematical formula. It was eventually replaced with their alternative, the Big Bang, a singularity which cannot possibly exist in time or space or manifest any form of intention. This is the one-way Great Portal leading mysteriously from inner space into outer space. Perhaps this is where the creator God who abandoned His mechanical universe retreated to in the 17th century.

OBJECTS ARE CREATED BY CONCEPTUAL FRAMING

The weakest point in the metaphysical transformation from religious belief to scientific belief was always the problem of framing. Things or objects are only created when they are conceptually framed by human beings. Things are essentially concepts created by such framing in order to isolate part of a process from its context so that it can be understood and possibly manipulated. This pragmatic technique underlies all human activity and has led to the current amazingly complex symbolic system we call culture. The great magician and protoscientist Isaac Newton was faced with the challenge of providing an absolute frame for the new 'observed' and 'mathematically measured' universe in outer-space elaborated by René Descartes. He hypothesised a *Deus Abscondidus* who created the cosmos as a mechanical thing and then abandoned it. Newton claimed that the cosmological frame he created as a useful fiction was absolute because it was in God's mind, calling on a vague form of inner space. Having created the universe as a clockwork machine, Newton's Unitarian deity then wound up its spring to create the required dynamic. Then, having started the mechanism going, He abandoned it, leaving it to eventually run down.

The usefulness of Newton's model to the powerful new industrialists was so great that for over two centuries all major metaphysical objections were thoroughly supressed. This was done systematically in the new clockwork-regulated educational institutions of the secular plutocratic governments that replaced the more organic aesthetic rituals of instruction inherited from the traditional theocratic agricultural civilizations. During the Enlightenment the increasing attacks on theological speculation as mere 'superstition' eventually created a new paradigm of the universe as a mechanically interrelated collection of things in space that had evolved by accident and which had no intrinsic meaning or purpose. This became strictly enforced orthodox dogma. Scientists acted as if they had no need for God or even intelligent design (other than their own human cleverness, of course).

WHEN GOD DIES, NATURE DIES TOO

However the resultant death of the Judaeo-Christian God for all practical purposes meant the end of His infernal machine which fell apart more than a hundred years ago through *reductio ad absurdum* logic. The dissolution of the irreducible atomic building blocks of the old fashioned materialists into nothing more than dancing probabilistic particles, together with cosmological relativity theories, destroyed the universe itself as a form. Without an absolute frame it could never again be a thing, or a collections of things, 'out there'. To Einstein's horror, the creator was revealed to be a dice thrower. The few psychological scientists with integrity revealed that the self-proclaimed objective observers turned out to have been either narcissistic and wilfully blind selfish lackeys of industrial capitalism or neurotic, power-driven, socialist perpetrators of equalising violence blinded by resentful envy.

The scientists, who now had a world monopoly of secular education or 'the truth', hated God more than they loved His creation Nature;

consequently they died together. What then happened to the universe whose absolute frame only existed in God's mind?

THE GREAT PORTAL IS REVEALED IN THE RUINS

The old gateway into the inner space world of meaning and purpose, prioritising beauty, love and pragmatic truth, is being glimpsed again amongst the ruins left by the totalitarian war between intolerant dogmatic morality and intolerant dogmatic science. Metaphysical redemption came eventually in the form of pragmatism which led to process philosophy and the recognition of the ecological interrelatedness of all things when the conceptual frames separating them from the whole were recognised for what they always were – 'useful fictions'.

A century ago the process philosopher A.N. Whitehead warned us of the danger of what he called 'The fallacy of misplaced concreteness'. Only what happens is truly real. What physicists call 'singularities' and 'working hypotheses', like the Big Bang, fiat currencies, economic credit and the will of the people, et cetera, are all man-made useful fictions. The same is true of the evolving structures of grammatical languages, mathematical rules of procedure and musical systems. Values like beauty, truth and goodness evolve in human cultures as meaningful symbol complexes with real subjective and real objective aspects and rise and fall with the cultures in which they are embedded.

Relativity theory is subject to falsification through application of its critique to itself. The way around the paralysis of painting oneself into a corner is to accept the principle that nothing is perfectly true but that by adopting working hypotheses or useful fictions we can muddle through with less conflict and intolerance than from believing we have the absolute truth. The common sense way to proceed without too much painful cognitive dissonance is to behave politely, create beautiful environments, and to openly admit we are not perfect but will do our best to establish what is more true and less false. Playfully synthesising and aestheticising religious and secular ideologies could even create a new, less materialistic and less environmentally destructive world culture. Since the early 1970s I have demonstrated that this is possible by living a provocative liminal life as a postmodern cosmologer, living work of art, prophet and shaman, carrying on regardless with my own synthesis of love, logic and levity.

APPARENT SENSUAL REALITY VERSUS CONCEPTUAL INTELLECTUAL REALITY

First we must distinguish between apparent and conceptual reality. Confusing the two has led to much confusion. I will chart the steps by which we have reached the present state of the model of the physical universe. At this point I would like to draw the reader's attention to an interesting fact. The two largest heavenly bodies in apparent motion are the Sun and Moon which are, amazingly, almost exactly the same *apparent size*. In the absence of a divinely ordained absolute frame and according to relativity theory, *apparent size* is as real as any other form of size. I know of no rational explanation for this blindingly obvious outer space phenomenon which passes largely unnoticed.

It is in this spirit that I am focussing my attention on trying to open up the Great Portal in the centre of the universe. This singularity was regarded by most of mankind as an indispensable supernatural realm until physicists and engineers working in the emerging secular states created the model of the cosmos as a mindless and soulless mechanism with no escape hatch. Once open it will be up to individuals to attempt to climb the 'stairway to heaven'. I failed to get support for my own experimental attempt on my 42nd birthday on December 4th, 1974 CE, but at least I have put the idea in peoples' minds.

COSMOLOGICAL EVOLUTION

THE FLAT EARTH

This conceptual model hypothesises that the Earth is flat, with the Sun rising in the east and setting in the west and which is presumed to travel under the Earth at night to reappear in the east each morning. This useful fiction works perfectly well for cultures relying mainly on agricultural technology. Traders travelling slowly overland may have noticed that the height of the sun at midday varied as they went north or south but this anomaly could be ignored or marginalised by the rulers without serious political consequence.

THE SPHERICAL EARTH

With the appearance of faster sea-travelling trading civilizations in the Mediterranean, who had limited economic reliance on agriculture, this anomaly become significant and the Earth became regarded as spherical, at least by maritime navigators. This was the situation in Europe at the time of the Greeks and it arose again during the economic boom of the Renaissance.

To avoid public cognitive dissonance and political collapse the Church, already caught up in the throes of Protestant turmoil and attacks by the Ottoman Muslims, wisely taught peasants the biblical truth that the Earth was flat, whilst at the same time, for economic reasons, Church administrators accepted that for navigational purposes it was a sphere.

THE HELIOCENTRIC MODEL OF CELESTIAL MECHANICS

As a Platonist, Copernicus believed that pure forms like circles and circular motion were supernatural and unchanging. He himself claimed the heliocentric model of celestial mechanics that he introduced to the scholars in his early printed book *De Revolutionibus* was not true, just a beautiful fiction. Many leading astronomical scholars enthusiastically embraced the new model. The apparent movement of heavenly bodies could already be calculated and predicted by using Ptolemaic-Platonic models based on supernatural epicycles which worked fairly well for navigational purposes. However this was as messy and logically offensive as modern physics which is faced with similar contradictions between apparent reality and conceptual explanations. Magicians like Kepler and Newton and experimental mechanists like Galileo, who provided the foundations for the Enlightenment establishment of modern cosmology, were inspired by the simplicity, beauty and explanatory power of the heliocentric model of Copernicus. They consequently rejected Platonic epicycles. It is worth noting that there was no observational proof of the truth of the new model, such as parallax at opposite ends of the Earth's orbit, until over a hundred years later.

Galileo, the telescope manufacturer and experimental mechanist, had established strong links with Venetian traders and their navy as well as with Florentine bankers. He daringly used the new printing press to propagandise the heliocentric model as true and to ridicule the official papal line. In 1632 he deliberately published his *Dialogue Concerning the Two World Systems* in Italian, the popular language, rather than in Latin, the language of scholars. The newly established rebellious Protestant nations who were fast becoming urbanised traders rather than rural agriculturalists, quickly adopted the new mechanistic model. Thus began the war between dogmatic religion and dogmatic science which led to their mutual destruction as integrated explanatory conceptual schemes at the beginning of the 20th century.

THE BIG BANG-CENTRED EXPANDING UNIVERSE

I will not describe the current jumble of inconsistent and contradictory theories about the nature of the physical universe. One of the important points I wish to make is that all university-based astrophysicists are aware that there is no longer any absolute frame to the universe, nor can they honestly continue to believe that Cartesian observers can position themselves outside the universe to objectively measure phenomena. Atoms are no longer fundamental building blocks and reductionism, where the parts are assumed to determine the behaviour of the whole, has been thoroughly discredited theoretically. Even mathematics has been shown by Kurt Gödel to possess inbuilt contradictions. It can no longer be believed in and trusted as a 'pure' Pythagorean supernatural measuring system.

These truths with their vitally important implications are conveniently ignored and kept from public debate in educational institutions, just as in the past the Church ignored the truth that the Earth was not flat and was moving around the Sun. The reason for both cover-ups was economic necessity and political stability.

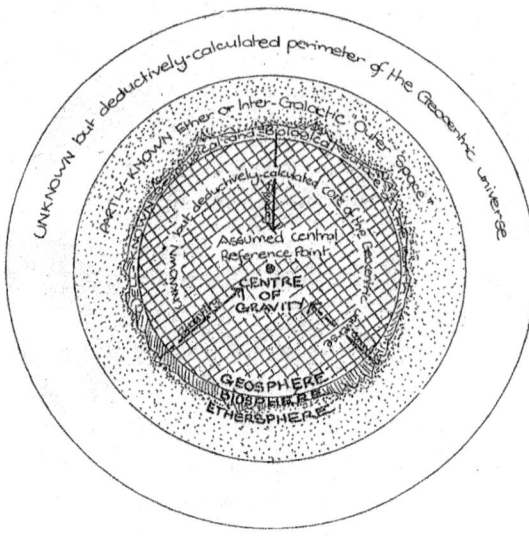

Traditional mathematically-constructed 'gravity-powered' Geocentric, physical model of the Universe or World. Adopted to show the structure or mechanics of the Biosphere etc. on the Earth's surface. (Not to scale.)

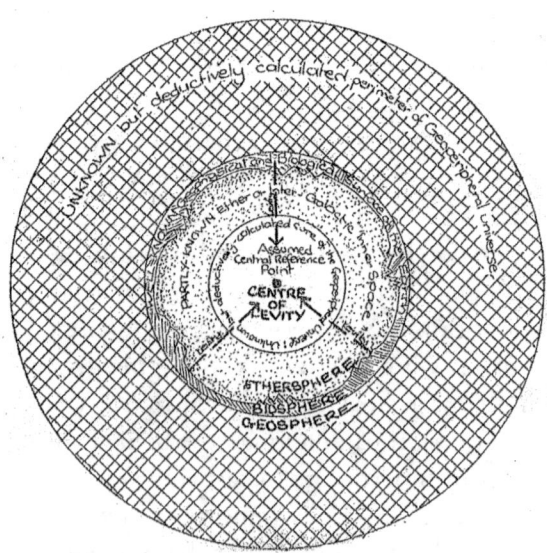

New mathematically-constructed 'levity-powred' Geoperipheral, or Ouranocentric, physical-metaphysical model of the Universe or World. Adopted to to show the function or dynamics of the Biosphere etc. on the Earth's surface. (Not to scale.)

THE INSIDE-OUT UNIVERSE

When the Earth ceased being flat and became a sphere, what evidence was there that it was north up as the mapmakers assumed? Even more controversially, if there is no absolute frame then what evidence is there that the Earth is even a sphere with the rest of the universe surrounding it? Simply inverting the mathematical coordinates of the old model produces a relativistic geoperipheral model where the universe is inside the Earth's surface. Once again although the Earth appears flat, it is not. But according to the geoperipheral conceptual model it now curves the opposite way.

Appearances cannot be trusted since light rays do not travel in straight lines and their hypothetical paths depend on the mathematically validated model and not the naked eye. There is no known way to decide which one is more true. Our secular governments are driven, as was the Church before them, to put economic usefulness first and to conceal from the general public the fact that the truest scientific models radically contradict what they are taught in the educational institutions of the State

Another fact hidden from the people is that the universe is, to all true intents and purposes, man-made. In other words an inner-space 'subjective' concept, not an outer-space 'objective' thing. This is not a useful fiction for the irresponsible rulers, so this fact too is concealed from the public.

THE COSMOLOGICAL CRISIS

Before putting forward my proposal for establishing a new physical universe model as the base for a process relational cosmology I must point out that only in times of extreme cognitive dissonance can the major paradigm we call reality be revitalised. I think this is the case today. It is becoming increasingly clear that population increase, industrial farming and fishing, corruption and irresponsibility in the financial sectors, the immense psychological pressure of consumerism on people to pollute the environment and to consume unnecessary goods and services are all leading to a major crisis in the biosphere, which I believe is close to ecological collapse.

Unfortunately, in democracies where political success is almost entirely validated by economic growth, all party politicians, even the Greens, must promise everyone they want to vote for them more jobs and better material living conditions. Following advances in sanitation, diet, and medicine, peoples' physical health is currently the best ever known but psychological and social stress are increasing at a rapid rate. Family breakdown, mental health problems and hysteria produced by cognitive dissonance resulting from the lack of true cosmology are growing like wildfire, especially in universities. Welfare states are increasingly resembling Orwell's *1984* where bureaucratic intellectual elites are altering the meaning of words and invoking irrational righteous indignation to destroy the current nationalistic civilization in order to replace it with a global financial bureaucracy based purely on fake economics.

THE FOURTH ESTATE HAS BECOME THE FIFTH COLUMN

Economically driven managerial globalisation, supported by monopolies in the communication, educational and media institutions, demonises long established values such as pride in national cultural identity, traditional playful sexual-psychological role differentiation, free speech, formal debating and playful regulated conflict designed to reconcile social, legal and cultural differences. Globalised commercial mass media monopolies which have expanded exponentially since the late 20th Century are now the main backers of 'progressive' parties. These parties are demonising well-mannered and law-abiding citizens for following their own traditional values and they are being backed up by unionised government agencies together with their political lobbyists to destroy such values. Both commercial and political information controllers are growing rapidly in numbers and legalised power. To an uncommitted observer with no skin in the game the establishment of a massive and incompetent global bureaucracy, with no well-developed values other than power for a tiny elite, will be the obvious consequence.

THE SYNTHETIC POSTMODERN PROCESS COSMOLOGY

Before describing my postmodern cosmology and its reopening of Heaven's door, I will summarise the discordant macrocosmic and microcosmic theoretical elements that have rendered belief in the current mechanistic materialistic cosmology absurd.

1. **Belief in human observers** that are somehow located outside the universe so that they can be unbiased and objective. This belief is absurd not just because observer effects are recorded in reductionist quantum theory, but also because recent scientific theories reveal the psycho-social-cultural forces working on all human beings to distort their perception and to rationalise dangerous conclusions through confirmation bias.

2. **The death of God** and the discrediting of divine revelation by materialistic scientists also meant the end of belief in an absolute frame. Frames are now relativistic and chosen for their usefulness to military industrial governments. The lack of any specific objective cosmological governor means that the universe has become a relativistic subjective process which is out of control since no one is taking responsibility for its governance and protection.

3. **The end of unilinear time** as a dimension unique to those civilizations which are either awaiting divine intervention to end history, or that believe in unending material progress leading to the establishment of a utopia. Time is better understood as relative to the evolution of different levels of cosmological complexity and can only be measured as event probability. Barring a major catastrophe, event probability ranges from the Big Bang, which was impossible, to a more and more inevitable convergence at a hypothetical 'now'.

4. **The end of patriarchy** which is still trying to structure human sexual relationships has become inevitable with easily available and reliable contraception and the economic and political liberation of women. The result is the end of stable extended and nuclear families and consistent socialisation of children.

SUBJECTIVITY AND THE GEOPERIPHERAL MODEL

There was no public acknowledgment of their inevitable subjectivity amongst cosmologists and I could not find any academics willing to take any personal responsibility for their own theories. Accordingly I created a subjective process cosmology whose functioning as a symbolic construction was created by, and ultimately governed by, the personal ego of its creator, namely myself. I chose as the physical base for the new universe the geoperipheral model with its singularity in the centre which was also the highest point for all possible 'observers' in every part of the universe. With all the galaxies converging faster and faster on this singularity it makes an ideal location for the Great Portal. I could even affix the long-dreamed-of great 'sky hook' there.

In 1971 I arranged to be appointed official Cosmologer by the Union of the University of Melbourne and given premises on the campus where I conducted interdisciplinary workshops and published my findings. I realised of course that unless culturally accepted by leading intellectuals my creation would remain no more than a cultural seed. At the same time I had been publicly recognised by the Director of the prestigious National Gallery of Victoria as the world's first Living Work of Art. This provided me with a suitable cultural identity for the creator of a subjective, aesthetic and truly postmodern cosmology. My universe was the frame for my 'work of art in progress', like the Great Work of the alchemists.

HEAVENLY SEX AND SOCIAL BONDING

The psychological and social aspects of the postmodern cosmology and its participant creator were part of a pragmatic Fun Revolution which included community therapy and a personal attempt to create a post-feminist alchemical marriage to balance the yin and yang elements of the human personality. Cultures based on fertility as their prime value regard sex as meaningful and moral only when it is understood as being motivated to cause conception. Fatherhood, which is essentially a social phenomenon, is culturally valued by men in such societies as primarily a biological guarantee of their immortality. In many hunter-gatherer cultures however, the important child-rearing functions of a father may not be the responsibility of the mother's lover but of a close male relative.

At the present time a new form of family can be formed where the matriarchs can recover much of their lost socioeconomic power and, as in nomadic hunter gatherer and nomadic pastoralist societies, men can recover their lost cultural independence. They would be able to devote more of their time to cultural, non-utilitarian ego-tripping pursuits. These coincidentally attract females seeking a partner. In the animal kingdom females rarely display in order to attract males for instinctive bonding. My cosmology accounts for the consequences of the instinctive and direct tactile interaction of male and female genitalia which impacts on their hindbrains during intercourse and greatly affects the inner space of both. The lovers are in essence turning themselves inside out in a united, instinctive, rhythmic dance. Activation of inherited behavioural releasers in the hind brain may consolidate limbic family bonding at the social level and stimulate complex symbolic interaction at the yin and yang spiritual-cultural level.

In my own case during an affair in the 1967 Summer of Love I was seized by a vision of a heavenly centre. Like the evolutionary bootstrap hypothesis, all my life I had dreamed of springing higher and higher in the air until I reached an equilibrium point. Shortly afterwards my discovery of the geoperipheral universe model with its unambiguous centre made me realise that heaven could be returned to its ancient place by adopting this idea as a working hypothesis.

I am not a believer in the useful fiction of immortality to compensate for what I was told is the inevitability of my death. Evolutionary theory makes this assumption very probable but no longer absolutely certain. Any attempt to get to heaven without dying can still be seen by theologians as a sign of satanic power or treated with ridicule by materialists. Consequently I treated this aspiration as an example of levity which is intrinsically enjoyable. It could even provide the transcendental core value of the Fun Revolution I had started whilst at the University of New South Wales.

It can be 'rationally' explained in my subjective process cosmology as an example of the involved intention of my soul being manifested as an ego-tripping aspiration to evolve by levitating: in other words, sending myself up. I regard dualistic thought experiments, where material and mental reality are assumed to be ideologically separate, as frequently misleading and even dangerous fictions. In 1974 I tried to carry out an embodied experiment combining time, space and identity using the collective 'mind space' created by television. Unfortunately I couldn't get it off the ground!

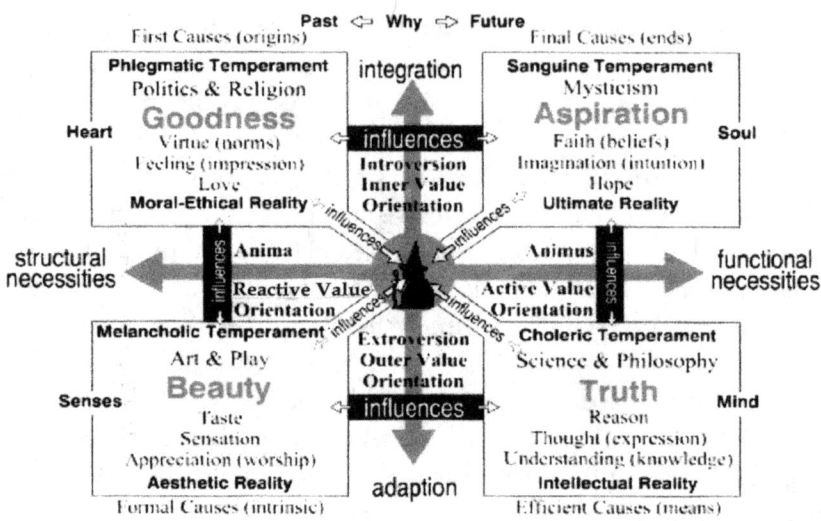

CONCLUSION

RESOLVING COGNITIVE DISSONANCE BETWEEN SCIENCE AND RELIGION

My postmodern cosmology is openly subjective, process-relational, evolutionary and truly postmodern aimed at reconciling cognitive dissonance between Science and Religion. It is not just an irresponsible, jargon-filled variety of materialistic and reductionist ethnocentric, economic determinism. Its manifestation as a symbolic creation is described and explained forthrightly in the cosmology itself as an ego trip by its creator.

If it is accepted as more true, more beautiful and more ethical than any alternative cosmology then I will have achieved my aim. If there is no debate in the academic community despite it being well publicised there, I will assume that it is too true, too beautiful and too ethical and not 'serious' enough for them to examine. There are none so blind as those that will not see, especially if they have ego, income and security to lose. Hysteria is common in those who, through living too much in abstractions and rationalisations, have cut off their inner space nervous systems from responding to the real, sensible outer space world where, as Merlin Donald explains in *A Mind so Rare*, mimesis still rules.

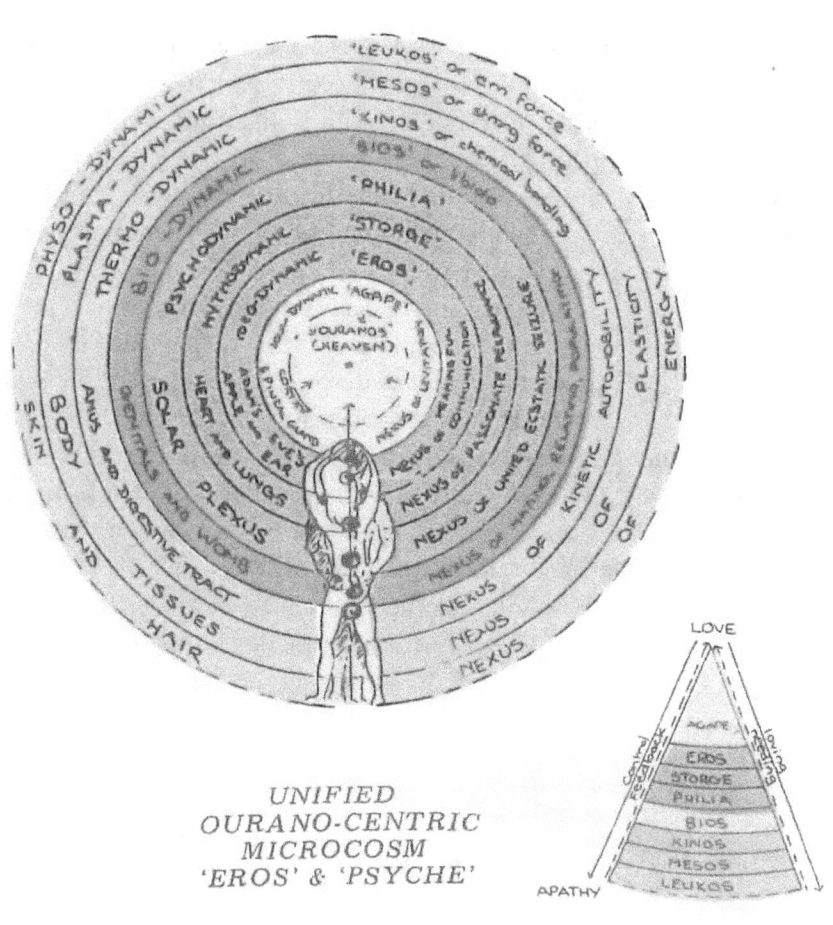

UNIFIED
OURANO-CENTRIC
MICROCOSM
'EROS' & 'PSYCHE'

SEX AND THE HEAVENLY SINGULARITY

The logos is not a servant of man. The logos possesses wise men who go with the flow and enjoy the ride.
Fools try to impose their will on the cosmos by manipulating symbols, so that, like the Wizard of Oz, they can dominate other fools impressed by their covert ego-tripping behind symbolic masks.

SEX

The materialists of the European Renaissance and Enlightenment replaced spiritual salvation with material-economic development as the ultimate meaning of life. Since then there has been a gradual but fundamental change in understanding the previously repressed meaning of human sexuality.

Unlike many other religions, much of Christian theology was based on the Jewish fear that the mysterious power of the sexual orgasm might distract believers from their fearful and obedient relationship with the divine. Only sexual acts that are carried out with the intention of producing offspring were regarded as free from sin. Even masturbation was regarded with horror, let alone sexual acts between consenting adults carried out for mutual delight and deliberately avoiding conception. Jewish heroines could prostitute themselves to manipulate non-Jewish rulers without incurring God's displeasure since they were not acting out of selfish pleasure.

The rational humanists of the Renaissance and Enlightenment, even those who enjoyed making fun of the hypocrisy of those Christians who succumbed to the pleasures of the flesh, were still embedded in the world view of the agricultural revolution which is essentially patriarchal and regards marriage aimed at producing offspring as the political-economic foundation of civilization. Unlike religious believers and more like the Romans they had no serious objection to men having mistresses as well as wives. Even wives who took lovers were not always condemned so long as this did not interfere with their duties as wives and did not in the case of respectable citizens produce socially recognised bastard offspring.

Freud's pioneering investigations of the unconscious revealed that human self-awareness and stated intentions were frequently distorted by socialisation experiences in childhood, particularly those associated with what he called oral dependency, anal striving for independence, and genital satisfaction in sexual relationships. Subsequent psychological investigators have been critical of Freud's bourgeois and rather ethnocentric obsession with what he called the Pleasure Principle as mankind's major motivation, hence the need for repression based on what he referred to as the Reality Principle. The naive belief in the rational self of the Enlightenment could never again be assumed. As Socrates had earlier pointed out, strategies of self-deception and rationalisations disguising unethical motives from oneself are alarmingly common. No doubt due to his Jewish background, against which he violently rebelled, Freud was convinced that religious attitudes to sex as something fundamentally wicked were the cause of most repression. Other psychoanalysts like the Protestant Jung were not so opposed to religion, studied other non-Abrahamic religious explanations of the meaning of life and did not believe that sex was all important. By contrast, an obsession with unrepressed sexual self expression coupled with immortality through fame or offspring could lead to the repression of transcendental explanations of the meaning of life and a fixation on materialism. Governments based on materialism, sexual freedom and exploitation, and the repression of religion have produced highly efficient but totalitarian nightmares.

Sexual intercourse is surely something more than just copulation that guarantees survival of a species through reproduction? One early psychoanalyst certainly had this conviction, namely the heretical figure of Wilhelm Reich. He assumed the whole universe is suffused with orgasmic power and that the blocking of such power leads to intellectual or emotional armouring. Many of his ideas can be ridiculed, but in his writings on mass psychology he provides a psychological explanation of the sexual aspects of the worship of enlightened anti-religious political leaders like Napoleon, Mussolini, Hitler, Stalin, and Mao which sociologists and historians are at a loss to explain. His studies of intellectual and emotional armouring have been neglected but are much needed to explain the absurdly irrational behaviour of many politically correct university students and academics in the West at present. Their intellectual armouring is as obvious as the emotional armouring of the heartless Islamic Jihadists.

In *Love and Will*, written during the late 1960s, Rollo May comes to grips with eros and power. The sensationalisation of sex and the emphasis on the orgasm as a mini 'big bang' are an escape from the anxiety of living as a machine: as he puts it, 'we fly to the sensation of sex to avoid the passion of eros.'

THE SUMMER OF LOVE

Looked at from a Reichian perspective, the short-lived Summer of Love which took place amongst the educated youth in North America, Western Europe and Australasia between 1967 and 1968 was a brief outpouring of erotic-orgone energy. This was no doubt precipitated by the visual and auditory impact through the electronic media of the new music of bands like the Beatles who, like Elvis Presley earlier, had broken free from the political control of more openly expressed sexual sensationalism. Other factors were important, especially the impact on young women's consciousness of the now easily available and reliable contraceptive pill. I would also add to this the neurological impact of the shift away from the mass instrumental conditioning of the print-based educational institutions towards the mass affective conditioning of post-war electronic advertising adopted to encourage consumerism.

At the time, I was a thirty-five-year-old, whose childless marriage of convenience, although based on mutual sexual attraction, was undertaken as a *folie à deux* sharing of cultural appreciation and a love of overseas travelling. This was coming to an end. My wife was pressurising me to give up my settled academic career, first as a cultural organiser in Perth, and then as sociologist in Sydney, in order to resume our travelling life. I had remained faithful to our contract, but I was being affected by the changes taking place all around me and was keen to stay and see what would happen. I was pioneering a new form of playful conflict resolution to bring about reforms of teaching methods on the campus at UNSW in Sydney where I had recently arrived to help set up the courses in their new School of Sociology.

A major change in the behaviour of some of the young women around me at university drew me out of my cautious and rather prudish English shell. Influenced by my feminist primary school teacher parents, I had never been tempted to pursue women who acted as manipulative sex objects and for personal reasons I did not want to become involved with those looking for a husband with the intention of forming a family. I regarded loveless, one-night-stands as only attractive under exceptional circumstances.

Young women were now free from the fear of unwanted pregnancies and more erotic, less decadent and more playful forms of sexual love were developing. The hippies, who came into prominence at that time, were motivated by love more than money or power over others. Their ideology of love was neither possessive nor compulsive and was not narrowly and passively sexual but was actively social and cultural. My studies for my lectures on antinomian millenarian movements in the Middle Ages had convinced me that they were mistaken in assuming that the sexual act could be, and should be, engaged in without neural bonding and subsequent jealousy. Although still active in what I called the Fun Revolution during that Summer of Love, I had brief love affairs with three young women in their early twenties. They had nothing in common except their independence. One was a happy-go-lucky beach bunny and postgraduate statistical psychologist, another was a self-employed Californian body-painter artist and designer of what she called Men's Liberation Suits, and the third was an ambitious actress who became a famous model in

London and was a Bond girl in one of the James Bond films.

Their uncalculating and fearless responsiveness caught me by surprise and I felt that not only the sociable limbic brain but even the sensationalist hind brain of my nervous system was given a boost I had never felt before. Experiencing an attractive young woman abandoning herself to my gentle penetration, in the sort of religious ecstasy described by St Teresa and portrayed by Bernini, made a considerable impact on my sensorium. I too felt as though I was being welcomed through a portal into another world like the King of Glory. This seemed to me to be what William Blake was communicating through his mystical poetry. Now I was possessed by an overwhelming desire to ascend into Heaven.

A GLIMPSE OF HEAVEN

This was not a new obsession of mine. For years I had been regularly dreaming of springing into the air as high as I could until I reached equilibrium above the heads of astonished onlookers. This was the essence of the evolutionary boot-strap hypothesis. Now I was convinced there was a singularity in the centre of the universe as an organism and I would not rest until I penetrated it. This seemed an absurd aim as there was no evolving centre in any universe model I had ever come across. Like Jacob with his dream of a ladder to heaven, I would have to struggle with God's angel.

My intuition was that such intense neural interaction between the sexes was not a common phenomenon. This was particularly so since, unlike the social mammals whose maternal drives were far more powerful than their sexual drives, the sexuality of human females was strong but easily displaced or repressed due to previous social and cultural need for material male support. This was also the time of an explosion of feminist writings about the disputed nature of the female orgasm which had been largely denied until then. I was repelled by the common scientific paradigm of human beings as copulating biological objects or machines, and attracted by the process ideology of the universe as experiential and ecstatic. I recognised that, if not culturally forbidden, masturbation through self-manipulation gave human beings freedom to choose their sexual partners and avoid imposing themselves on unwilling individuals or becoming victims of manipulative others. I found myself agreeing with Reich that orgasmic release can be shallow or deep and therefore assumed that there could be a deeper orgasm in women than through clitoral stimulation. This was not an informed opinion; I was relying on my instincts which have proved reliable on many occasions. It is up to women who are not trapped in the mechanistic scientific paradigm to reach a decision on this matter. What is a matter of fact and not conjecture is that post-puberty human females, unlike animal females, are always on heat, at least potentially, even after menopause. Humans also face each other during normal intercourse. This leads to stronger bonding but also to a stronger desire to bring the male under control. The maternal drive can easily override the sexual drive, with disastrous psychological and social consequences.

Being treated solely as a provider of pleasure, rather than as a father figure, economic supporter, oedipal child, or even friend, appealed to my male vanity and my egoistic satisfaction in giving pleasure rather than receiving it. My psychological training and subsequent reading led me to believe that I was not dysfunctionally orally dependant, nor of an anxious and rebellious anal disposition. I was capable of properly self-controlled and playful genitalised sexual intercourse, so what was happening to me? Then one night during this short Dionysian period I began sobbing uncontrollably for hours for no apparent reason. This had never happened before, nor has it happened since. I then came across Reich's theory that crying of this type accompanies the dissolution of what he described as both emotional and intellectual 'armouring'. I realise that Reich is usually thought of as a sex-mad lunatic, even worse than Freud used to be regarded, but Elsworth Baker's *Man in the Trap* is an excellent guide to his highly original theories. Reich's differentiation between the intellectual armouring of liberals and the emotional armouring of fascists and 'emotional plague' types in general, should be essential reading for those who want to make sense of the political correctness that is currently destroying the mass education and mass communication institutions in the West. This is fast leading us towards the destruction of the rule of law and its replacement by totalitarianism.

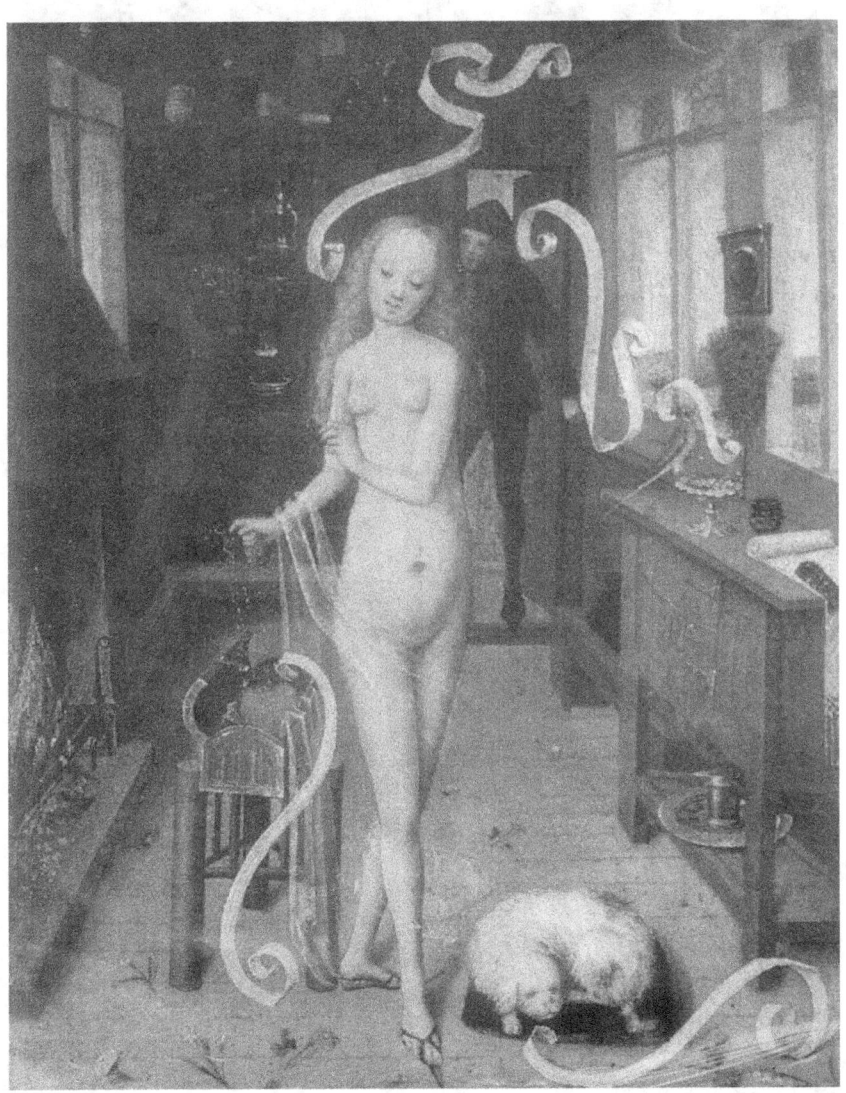

The Fall of Man

As a natural conservative I could not summon up enough fear and hate for my fellow countrymen to live up to expectations that as an academic sociologist I should be a cold hard-nosed capitalist or a passionate angry socialist. Now I felt my Fun Revolution was vindicated. Reich was also convinced that both men and women could be arrested at what he called the rather shallow 'phallic' stage of psychological development rather than proceeding to what he called full genitalisation and so they did not reach deeper union with the cosmic process. Rollo May had already described the obsession with sexual orgasm that began in the 1960s as an attempt through mere sensation to escape from being what Reich termed 'living machines'. Since that time sex has become so trivialised that it can no longer console the living machines whose new escape has been into drugs or exercising irrational power over others.

Blake, who instinctively understood and rejected Newton's single vision and the evil Pythagorean obsession of the Enlightenment to manipulate everything by measuring everything, would have rejoiced with me. The only psychiatrist who would have appreciated my mystical calling was Theodore Faithfull who, in his remarkable set of essays *The Future of Women*, deriving many insights from Blake, shows he shared many of my instinctual feelings about the amazing undeveloped potential of playful reflexivity between partners in an alchemical marriage with sixteen potential axes of differentiation. Now I knew where the convergent heavenly centre was located in the microcosm, if not objectively in the macrocosm, and whilst not giving up on my hope for a suitable female partner or partners to share in this enterprise, I began the creation of a subjective process cosmology.

DEATH AND THE MAGUS

My increasing intention to somehow ascend was accompanied by my inability to believe with Aristotle that, being a man, I must die. Bernard Shaw's play *Back to Methuselah* is based on the assumption that since evolutionary theory now indicates that since homo sapiens, as the arrow head of evolution, was obviously still evolving, death, although inevitable so far, might one day no longer be certain for everyone. There might even be a qualitative upgrading or major phase change coming. I realised that the usual compensation for accepting one's physical death was to adopt a fictional narrative in which one could become immortal in ways that I regard as cowardly surrender. Immortality can be realised by religious belief in an afterlife, reincarnation, having offspring, naming people and places after oneself, acting to become famous after death through reputable achievement, or even being frozen or becoming a brain inserted into a machine. Since I would have to become a self-deluding fantasist or monster to achieve these forms of immortality they did not appeal to me as a solution. As a believer that nothing, or 'no thing', is sacred, I would rather disappear whilst ascending and then be forgotten by those I left behind.

My life changed at this point. I began to trust my instincts and intuition even more than before. Now I wanted like a shaman to experience ecstatic union by ascending the cosmic axis of the tree of life. What would happen if I let my body and brain speak mimetically by disembedding myself from the involuntary bureaucratic aspects of the social system even more than I had done as a back packer for months at a time in the 1950s?

In the past Marx and other intellectuals, who were not themselves embedded in state institutions, were concerned not only by the material conditions of factory workers but by their alienation from mean-

The Second Petts Wood Boy Scout Troop.

ingful emotional engagement in social life. Such thinkers realised that the roles these workers occupied were affecting their consciousness. If they were made aware of their false consciousness they could take steps to free themselves from their slavery to managerial capitalist masters. The bourgeois intellectual Marx remained a tyrannical patriarch in his own sexual life and his revolution was a broadening of the old enlightenment class struggle of the bourgeoisie against the land-owning aristocrats and the peasantry. Since his time the bourgeois socialists have largely succeeded. The illiterate rural peasants have been turned into urban manual workers and have been educated to become petty bourgeois suburbanites whose caged domesticated lives are managed in fine detail by the administrators of the welfare-warfare states that they themselves are compulsorily taxed to pay for.

THE CLASS WAR BECOMES THE SEX WAR

The old war of the classes has ended and a new one had just begun. I could see that we were entering a period of war between the sexes. I realised that if men lost this war as women had lost the last war during the patriarchal agricultural revolution driven by the need to be immortal, we would be domesticated and psychologically, socially and culturally castrated. All our joy in running wild and in competitive ego tripping would be lost. There would no more 'knocking on heaven's door'. Now that 'girls can do anything', with sperm banks, masturbation and lesbian love affairs, men could become extinct or be kept in zoos (or, more hopefully, in wild life reserves).

I was curious to find out if my own awareness might be enhanced by breaking free from social roles that may have been controlling my consciousness. This had already been affected by my sensual awakening in the Summer of Love, my involvement with the hippies and their new forms of artistic expression such as the happenings. My successful creation of the Fun Revolution, aimed at reforming university teaching and administrative methods based on loving and teasing my bureaucratic enemies, gave me great hope. I needed to prepare myself to rise above the war of the sexes that I could see coming, and to set an example to others. The radical feminist attack on the institution of patriarchy fell on fertile ground in my case.

I had never wanted to be a father whom I regarded in practice as 'mother's little helper' and useful bread winner. As a child, Tarzan films, Kipling's *If* and *The Jungle Book* had corrupted me into admiring animals and hunter gatherers. I joined the Scouts in the era of post-war austerity and strict rationing imposed on England by the social engineering plans of the triumphant Labour Government. My misery in finding myself in Bromley Grammar School in Kent, which was run by teachers obsessed with motivating us to pass examinations so that we could rise from the lower-middle class to the middle-middle class, was ameliorated in the company of boys of all classes and intellectual abilities in the excellent Second Petts Wood Boy Scout Troop. This was a welcome respite from teacher tyrants lording over their inferiors. Instead of committee meetings there were voluntaristic open hierarchies of governance and skill with leadership and learning by example. I felt so much in harmony with this boys' world modelled on the culture of the hunter gatherers that for a time I began sleeping outside in our garden. I persisted for a while even during the winter, in a tent pitched on the rough soil of the vegetable garden, having worn down the lawn. In the 1950s my wife and I broke out from suburbia to become nomadic wanderers. We were obliged to return to civilization and its discontents when she briefly contracted TB. I became an academic and cultural organiser in Australia until the advent of the hippies and the Summer of Love.

Ever since I was a child I had been unable to understand how men could believe they can have children. My reading and later social science training confirmed that hunter gatherers had the same ideology and consequently saw no cause and effect connection between sex and reproduction. Even if they did, it was a useful fiction to keep sex free from being seen as an abstract ideological cause of something more important. Like tiny uncaused big bangs, babies were conceived when potential beings or spirits in trees, rocks and streams chose to manifest themselves by entering a woman's womb as she passed by. This useful fiction is no more absurd than the compulsory commitment to increasing fertility which leads to the useful fiction of patriarchy. Men were the autonomous lovers of the women they were bonded to and spent much of their time with other men and male children in the wild, having fun, ego tripping to build up status and inventing stuff.

They did bring meat back to the camp and boasted about the hunt, although it was often the women who got most of the food through gathering. The man was not the bread winner: he was the existential dancing, story-telling, ego tripper who could communicate with the spirits. In complete contrast, in religious agricultural societies, a 'husband' treats his wife as his field which, when ploughed and seeded, will produce fruit for him in the forms of sons who are his egotistic personal immortality. This is the probably the foundation of the basic myth of the fall of the first man and woman and their expulsion from the garden.

Learning from the hunter gatherers, who lived this way for tens of thousands of years and whose instincts and innate release mechanisms we must have inherited, would be an excellent way for men to prepare for the war now raging between the sexes and with which, so far, they have shown few signs of coping. Sexual intercourse leading to psycho-social-cultural intercourse is now free to be appreciated as an intimate connection between the sexes and not an instrumental action driven solely by some deep instinct to reproduce, nor as the act of evil males needing to force themselves on smaller and weaker females, nor of evil females tempting trusting males and leading them into economic traps.

That is only half the psychic preparation needed. Under the old regime not all men wanted children and even some of those with children had another use for women, namely sexual pleasure. Their useful fiction was that unlike men, women didn't enjoy sex but could become skilled in giving men sexual pleasure if rewarded for it with gifts. My own epiphany during the Summer of Love confirmed very different intuitions that had been struggling to become conscious for some time.

EROS AND STORGE

I realised that many financially independent young women, who consequently had no fear of rejection by their families or of unwanted pregnancy, were suddenly released from centuries of sexual repression. Virgins in particular, who had not been lied to and betrayed by men who treated them as disposable sex objects and who had refused to allow themselves to be worshipped like goddesses by grovelling and jealous men, were finding in sexual intercourse their true religion and their deepest sacrament. This *eros* love is not just based on sexual orgasm and worshipping of their true lord and master, but a psycho-socio-cultural unfolding. Since love, like truth and laughter, sets us free, after a few years with her master's help the young woman gradually comes out of her love trance to create more mature relationships with her master, her family of origin, and the world as a whole. I prefer using the word 'master' since 'husband' hints at animal domestication. I see no reason why women would prefer the word 'wife' to' mistress' or 'love slave' with their romantic associations. Love of this type between men and women is processual and based on fun instead of being justified by reproductive consequences and the continuance of maternal care for adult men.

Maternal parental love, or *storge*, can be taken as a model for a similar interactive male-female developmental process. Mother and child are normally mutually bonded at birth through innate release mechanisms. The mother must also allow for jealousy since most children are not happy about sharing her love. Seniority status is usually accepted to lessen such emotions. To a lesser extent, other adults in the family are similarly bonded with the new-born. As time passes a girl begins to identify with her mother and, unless under strong psycho-social pressure, she does not form a strong bond with adult males in her family. A mother's love for her son, if not deformed by a bad relationship with her husband, lover, father, or mother, is similarly transcendental for the child. Although biologically based on the provision of food, not sex as in the case of Eros, the mutually reflexive bonded relationship develops psychologically through comforting, and socially through conditioning and narrative storytelling.

A loving mother will gradually and carefully wean her infant son away from her for fear that he will become permanently dependent on her as a dominant goddess figure. He will then be better able to defy later matriarchal bullying or 'matronising' in general. This is the general practice in hunter gatherer societies who insist that boys around seven should be ready to cut their apron strings and leave their mother's residence to join the adult males to continue their socialisation and acculturation.

This gave me the core of a new useful fiction or scenario and a new narrative for a marriage form to ride out the coming storm. I had no desire to return to the patriarchal extended family of the agricultural scenario nor to the nuclear family of the mercantile industrial scenario and I was particularly keen to avoid the serial monogamy and socialisation of children by welfare state bureaucrats that was developing with amazing rapidity in the consumer society.

My family background meant I have never had any temptation to exercise financial control over women, only relating to women who, like my mother, earned their own keep and intensely disliked men who attempted to impress them financially. Moreover, I had now ceased being a wage slave without being on the dole. I even learned the hard lesson of accepting women's financial aid when I was broke. My reluctance to approach women because I found them sexually attractive increased and my willingness to engage in sexual banter with women of all ages, attractiveness and intelligence increased. I wanted to know my feminine opposite. Once mutual attraction began to develop, which sometimes happened in spite of knowing that as the well-known Wizard I was a rather unusual individual, before things went any further I made it clear that I had adopted a life style that excluded promiscuity, legally enforced monogamy and marriage with children.

In 1971, after two years of a doomed attempt to establish this sort of enduring relationship with a young graduate of unusual intellectual curiosity and outspokenness, I realised that I must establish a contract like a marriage contract. When the mutual attraction had reached a certain point, I explained my reasons for acting as I did and gave them a document in which I distinguished between what Eric Fromm called 'standing in love' and 'falling in love'.

A NEW MARRIAGE ALLIANCE

This short document, which was more like taking an oath than a bourgeois contract, did not have any special legal standing and was not signed. I laid out the conditions under which I was prepared to enter into a sexual relationship with a young woman over 18 as a form of potentially polygamous marriage, limited to a maximum of four. The most important aspect of this arrangement was that they were free to leave the relationship at any time without emotional blackmail or recrimination. On the other hand, I swore that I would not leave them.

I expected that after a few years my love slaves would have matured enough to free themselves and relate to me the way children who have grown up relate to their parents. I would regard our marriage as over if they wanted to give me children against my clearly specified wishes. Feminist psychologists, getting back at Freudians accusing them of penis envy, frequently describe men who desperately want children, not just for their personal immortality, as suffering from 'womb envy'! Becoming a patriarch would destroy the identity I had built up over years with considerable personal sacrifice.

I would not compel my love slaves to follow any unexpected orders given by me and I would not need to follow any such orders given by them. For the first few years I was only prepared to spend intimate time with them once or twice a week, but more as time went by. Nor would I support them financially as I did not want them to lose their independence. Instead I encouraged them to help me out if it pleased them, as I was very short of cash most of the time as usual.

I had assumed this would work because some young independent and educated young women were instinctive romantics and might 'fall in love' with someone their parents and peers might disapprove of. In Melbourne during 1971 three young women initially became what we all called 'love slaves' both to appeal to their initial psychological desire for romantic sensual self-abasement whilst having fun. There was no unnecessary joint residence which would have caused friction amongst us and anyway I was impoverished and resided in a student house with university student friends.

By 1974, when I left for New Zealand to attempt to carry out my imaginary experiment in ascension, two had already left without recrimination. One had become rather stupefied and promiscuous by her addiction to pot whilst overseas, and the other had been forced to leave because of pressure from her mother. The third, Alice, a strong minded and independent thinker who had been head girl of her Catholic school, was now employed and owned a car. Her parents, like mine, had reared her to make her own life choices so long as she lived an ethical life.

She resisted all efforts to undermine our union. In 1974 she single-handedly stood up to successfully defend me against an attempt to dismiss me from my unpaid role with the Activities Committee of Melbourne University Union. This had been made on spurious grounds by the political extremists who had now taken over the Union Council as well as the Students Representative Council.

A NEW POSTMODERN MATRIARCHY?

It follows that any self-freed love slave wanting to follow a fulfilling career or look after offspring would only be the first stage of a transformation of *storge* into a new form of matriarchy evolving from the new sexual bond based on *eros*. I would not be able to specify the new matriarchal role complex at this early stage, assuming it was up to the newly mature women to establish it. There is a strong tradition in most societies for women (often called 'aunties') to take on low-profile but highly responsible leadership roles based on social needs whilst most men are more interested in ego-expressive cultural activities. The mother's brother or other close male relative might initially act in a male parental role. I was convinced however that, as is the practice amongst non-patriarchal societies, male children should not remain in close contact with their mothers after the age of seven or so but should be parented by the adult men living away from their sexual partners much of the time.

Wizard and friends in the Carmelite Monastery, jointly signing the pledge to remain in Christchurch after the great earthquake of 2011. (Photo: The Press)

152 SEX AND THE HEAVENLY SINGULARITY

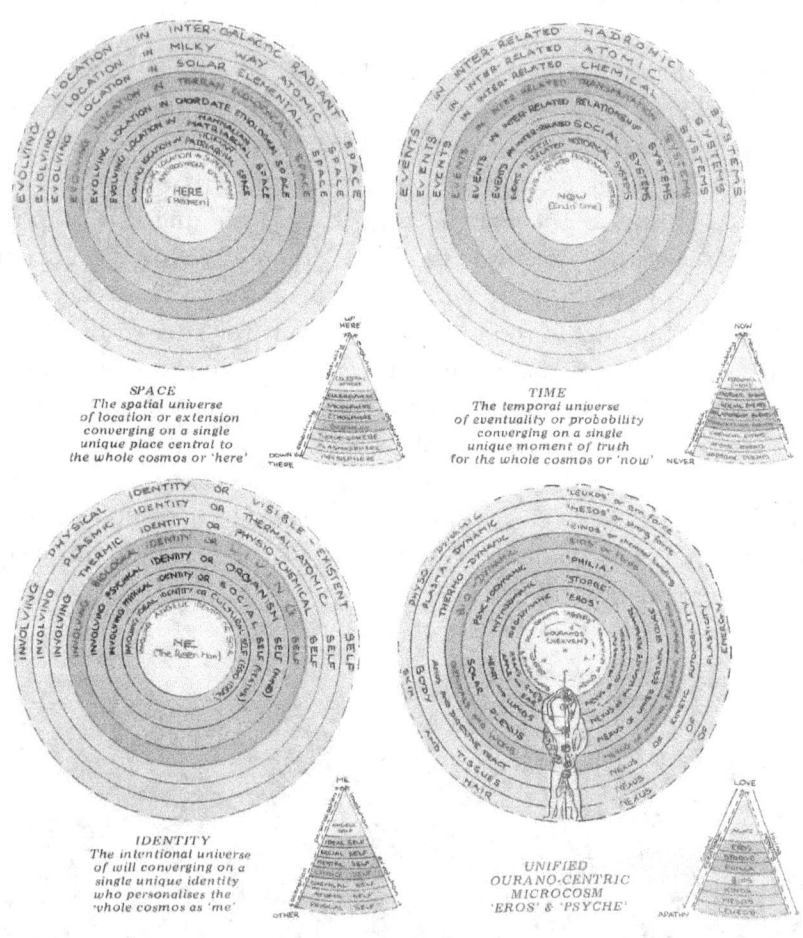

SPACE
The spatial universe
of location or extension
converging on a single
unique place central to
the whole cosmos or 'here'

TIME
The temporal universe
of eventuality or probability
converging on a single
unique moment of truth
for the whole cosmos or 'now'

IDENTITY
The intentional universe
of will converging on a
single unique identity
who personalises the
'whole cosmos as 'me'

UNIFIED
OURANO-CENTRIC
MICROCOSM
'EROS' & 'PSYCHE'

THE WOMEN'S MOVEMENT

In the previously Christianised but now increasingly secularised West, the women's movement was mainly led by anti-religious, left-wing, intellectual women. They were still embedded in the mechanistic paradigm of bourgeois industrial society where individuals were cogs in the economic development machine. Meritocracy, requiring equal opportunity and equal economic reward for equal ability, had been the foundation of the women's movement since the Romantic movement of the late Enlightenment. They were still cogs however and by repressing their spiritual anima they aimed their revolution on achieving parity with men as their role models.

There were now three distinct groups of women in western society whose aims were very different: religious women whose main concern was with family cohesion and accepted patriarchy as the best way to keep men domesticated and responsible; socialist women who wanted political and economic equality, easy divorce, contraception, and in most cases safe abortion when needed; and radical feminists who regarded heterosexual men as fundamentally evil and who should be brought under strict coercive control. These radicals hated men more than they loved women and despised all women who did not share their hatred of men.

Since in all cultures men and women are bound together in reciprocal roles it is necessary to examine the three types of males and their ideologies caught up in the rise of women. Patriarchal men, whether Christian or Jewish, stick strictly to their traditional role of responsible head of the household, husband and provider. Bourgeois humanist men find themselves in difficulties as they are fast losing what little authority they had over their wives who now have independent incomes and are spending more time away from home. Their children who are being educated towards moral and economic independence from their parents and through the intrusive mass media are increasingly dependent on their peer groups for approval. They take what they want from their parents whilst openly disobeying them. Men who are in relationships with radical feminists become as weak and servile as those women who had been under brutal patriarchal control in the past.

ALLIES OF THE RADICAL ANDROPHOBES

Homosexuals of both genders were better off with the weakening of the patriarchy and had risen with liberated women into positions of power and respectability. Followers of Islam who had been raised to hate Christians and Jews were treated as allies in their war against the patriarchal Christian elite. Their brutal oppressive treatment of women was no problem since 'the enemy of my enemy is my friend'. Another ally of the radical wing of the women's movement were the racists and sexists to whom skin colour and other physical appearance and self-identifying gender were more important than cultural beliefs and practices. The world was still reeling from the Nazis' attempt to eradicate the Jews as part of their eugenics ideology. Nazis were only interested in the Jews' ethnic inheritance regardless of their loyalty to German national culture or their religious beliefs, which were quite frequently Christian.

We are currently witnessing a new form of biological discrimination, namely 'inverse racism' and 'inverse sexism'. In the education institutions people are encouraged to hate people with white skins, whilst claiming self-righteously that they are fighting racism. Human beings with female genitalia are encouraged to hate human beings with male genitalia, whilst claiming self-righteously that they are fighting sexism. Having had their ethics destroyed by secular education and the commercial mass media and turned against their own cultural traditions, such people are driven by nothing but power over others, the most dangerous addiction known to mankind. Once again, 'the enemy of my enemy is my friend'. These violent racists and sexists, now wearing their virtue signalling masks, are politically aligned with the radical feminists and those self-loathing men in their ranks. Who is their main target group? White skinned males! Amongst white skinned males who are most hated? Christians and Jews.

The massacre of the Armenians in Turkey in 1915 was the first example of systematic genocide in recent history. The millions of Christians of different churches, many of great antiquity, who, like the Jews, had lived in the eastern Mediterranean and North Africa in considerable numbers for fifteen hundred years, have nearly all been killed or driven out by the Muslims, especially in recent years. They may not even have been believers: it was enough that they were part of a Christian community. The powerful secular humanist nations of Europe and North America have shown no interest and their compulsory secular education system is systematically removing studies of Christianity and stopping the traditional short daily ritual of collective prayers. Fundamentalist Christians, being full of passionate intensity, believe traditional universal churches like the Orthodox, Roman Catholics, and Anglicans are the enemy of true spirituality and are glad to see them go. Many of these fundamentalists live in silos reproducing rapidly whilst awaiting divine intervention.

As a social scientist specialising in religion, and interested in depth psychology, I followed all this with considerable interest. I was confident that my combination of logic, love, and levity and my new liminal roles would prepare me and my lovers and friends from the rising hysterical fury. As Socrates pointed out people create fictions to justify their beliefs and behaviour no matter how unethical, unrealistic and self-destructive. All three groups adopt useful fictions to give themselves meaning and purpose.

In agricultural patriarchal societies both men and women devoutly believe that they have immortal souls, must worship their creator god or gods and obey him or them in order to avoid catastrophic climate change or invasion. Women's duty is to have as many children as possible, whereas men are expected to work in the fields and fight to the death defending their own territory or taking other people's land to feed their expanding populations.

In mercantile industrial societies the urbanised workers in the factories believe in money and what it can buy, regard their wives as goddesses of the home, which is their temple, and worship them instead of God or the gods. No longer having immortal souls and working amongst machines in soul destroying environments, they frequently take to drink to dull the pain, seeking solace in the pubs, and taking it out on their wives and children when they return home. For these men, the meaning of life is not salvation but better pay and conditions and sensational sex. For their wives it is being sexually attractive to their husbands and respectable in the eyes of their neighbours.

In the Ponzi scheme of the new consumer society the previous norm of working in the material world to earn a living is replaced by many years of stressful education often with little or no connection with serving the basic needs of a mercantile industrial society. An army of paper shufflers or computer nerds has become indispensable in a civilization devoted to creating false needs and using credit to keep the population in financial slavery. Student loans have become the ideal first step in the stairway to hell. Men and women are being educated to believe that they are not cultural beings with different inherited characteristics but just programmable machines with different genitalia or different skin colour.

PSYCHIC COLLAPSE AND CULTURAL IDENTITY

Following his experiences in Nazi concentration camps, the psychotherapist Viktor Frankl observed that in such terrible conditions many prisoners collapsed into psychic despair. The exceptions had strong cultural beliefs about the meaning of life. He coined the word 'logotherapy' to describe the best treatment for such wretched individuals. Religious believers had the strongest set of what I, as a process philosopher and wizard, call useful fictions. The immortality of the soul, the importance of marriage and the family, the ethics found in the sacred texts, et cetera. were those time-tested aspects of the agricultural civilizations which still survived in modern industrial societies. They believed that Nazism was satanic. Enlightened humanists were also able to remain human under those appalling conditions if they had been raised with a strong sense of national cultural identity and enough awareness to understand that their Nazi oppressors were driven by powerful impersonal psychological forces. The communists, themselves living in a powerful negative collective psychosis like the Nazis, either identified with them, and became become capos (trustees), or remained unchanged. What new useful fiction could replace those we have lived with for so long?

My personal biological-racial identity as a white, male Anglo-Saxon was a bad start to life in the second half of the 20th century and made me the target of a certain amount of animosity. In radical circles for some time now WASPs have been seen as the enemy of mankind. When, added to that, the information that I was born in London when it was the largest city of the greatest Empire in the world, did not help matters, even though I had no choice in the matter (or did I?). Nor did I have any choice when I was conscripted – first into the compulsory education system, including attending all-male primary and secondary schools and then into the Royal Air Force as a pilot officer. Even worse, as an evacuee in East Anglia, I had voluntarily chosen to be an Anglican choir boy in an all-male choir until my voice broke and after the war I chose to become a Boy Scout, rising to become a Scout leader in my all-male troop in Kent.

During the late 1960s, through a series of unusual circumstances largely out of my control, I became the first academic lecturer in sociological theory in Australia. The animosity I encountered from some members of staff and students in the Arts Faculty was extraordinary when it became clear that I lacked the required class consciousness and self-hatred to become a Marxist in favour of class war and instead enjoyed being a happy-go-lucky 'pommie bastard'. I could not help teasing those self-righteous individuals influenced by Mao's Red Guards who, driven by maniacal desire for power, were then taking over all the Student Unions in the universities. Finally, when even my head of department turned against me for no good reason, I had to pull off a coup. I became the official University Wizard with the necessary knowledge of the essential psychological and sociological jargon needed for the job. Like Gandalf, the wizard in *Lord of The Rings*, which was going through an unprecedented popular revival at the time, I decided to take on the duty of protecting simple people who just wanted to be left alone to mind their own business. I was now treated by humourless neurotics and frenzied psychotics as a deluded fool or evil madman, which at least protected me from being treated as just another male chauvinist pig and white supremacist. The military industrial machine which has been driving Western Civilization since the Enlightenment is now beginning to unravel politically in Europe and America and the biosphere is close to irreparable damage through the massive pollution of consumerism, factory farming, and fishing. As I have been saying since 1968, I am the only Channell that has not been tried and found wanting.

EGOLESS FUN

I may have failed in my attempt to detonate a funpowder explosion in the global village through my imaginary experiment in sending myself up as a practical joke, but in the following forty-six years I used my navigator's skills to demonstrate that there was a practical and playful way to rescue the male-female relationship we call marriage from destruction at the hands of the secularly educated women who were understandably overthrowing the patriarchy and its associated institutions.

Once the universe was believed to be no more than a meaningless collection of things in space that evolved by chance, the Death of God inevitably followed. The consequences of this catastrophic event have been largely ignored by sensation seeking materialists. Since I have believed, like Socrates, that virtue was its own reward, I have not reacted, like Dostoevsky and Nietzsche (both reared to be virtuous through fear of God's punishment) to the Death of God for its weakening impact on ethical systems. I find that both religions and secular ideologies may reward what I consider wicked behaviour and punish what I consider good behaviour. Children can be socialised to behave well without supernatural sanctions. I myself was raised by a loving Socialist father and loving Anglican mother with no serious pressure to uncritically adopt the beliefs of either ideology. I behaved myself to please them.

I reject the fundamental belief of most academic scientists that the universe is a kind of predictable money-making machine driven by human usury, not only for its disastrous impact on reason and beauty but also for its puritanical dismissal of playful curiosity or fun. Since the 18th century the military industrial complex has increasingly been providing the *raison d'être* for our educational and commercial institutions. Bourgeois utilitarian scientists have marginalised or replaced both religious and sceptical aristocratic intellectuals who do not share their ideology of material progress. The implementation of the ideology of economic progress through bottom line validation by a university certified managerial power elite has led to a tiny number of wealthy individuals and impoverishment of the rest.

The death of the monotheistic Abrahamic God as an all-powerful, supernatural and patriarchal being who protected and rewarded his obedient subjects like a king certainly has consequences for ethical systems partially based on this parental power. More important to me was the consequent absence of any evolving hierarchies of truth, love or beauty which can only evolve if there are hypothetical transcendental absolutes or useful fictions to attract them. In the absence of any such freely chosen absolutes as rules of the game, there is an unstoppable reductionist decline leading to the Orwellian situation described in 1984.

Power, which is more addictive than any drug, deforms or replaces all other values. Lies become truth, hate becomes love, stupidity becomes reason and short-term, bottom-line monetary valuation justifies it all in the name of some absurd narrative promising a future utopian fantasy. Religious fundamentalists and left wing materialistic liberals, who have reached the Orwellian value inversion stage produced by 'ressentiment', generally regard those who do not subscribe to their particular ideology as evil. Given the chance, they would imprison or kill them. In complete contrast, art-loving sceptics and non-puritanical religious believers respect the rule of law as rules of the cultural game. They regard left wingers as wrong and are prepared to reason with them and to use legal means to restrain them if they act in a criminal manner.

THE SINGULARITY

A NEW POSTMODERN PHYSICAL UNIVERSE

My growing interest in heaven and personal ascension remained an unfulfillable subjective intention until two years later when, during my fun revolutionary tour of Australian universities, I came across a remarkable new model of the physical universe. This is what in my publicising activities for the past fifty years I have been referring to as the Geoperipheral universe. It is a simple conformal inversion of the mathematical coordinates of the current Heliocentric model of the solar system. Since belief in absolute space and absolute frames is no longer tenable except as a useful fiction, the mathematical coordinates framing the old mechanistic scientific model can be conformally inverted and consequently the Heliocentric model can be turned inside-out! The surface of the earth now contains the rest of the universe. This is of course 'only apparent', but in the absence of any absolute frame, all models of the physical universe are 'only apparent'. I keep my balance whilst walking carefully and lightly on the tightrope I raised above the fallacy of misplaced concreteness. Assuming there may be other like minds elsewhere in the universe, if they performed the same coordinate inversion on their planet they too would find themselves attracted towards the same cosmological centre.

The shift from Platonic-inspired Heliocentrism, 'proved' by Pythagorean mathematical absolutism, to Heraclitan Geoperipheralism, which is neither provable nor disprovable by mathematical manipulation, is as instantaneous as changes of spin of an electron.

There was now 'apparently' a singularity in the centre towards which all the galaxies were 'apparently' converging faster and faster. The central singularity was 'apparently' directly above the Earth's surface and could be identified as Heaven which had been summarily dismissed as irrational superstition by the reductionist mechanistic scientists living in a universe of things. Heaven was back, and Up as the most joyous direction was also back. As a sociologist of religion, I was puzzled by the cross-cultural human fascination, even in godless religions, with a transcendental heavenly location. When such belief was denied as a delusion, political systems became less loving, less playful, less artistic and less tolerant. In my essay 'Hunting The Boojum' I have explained how with the help of Lewis Carroll's instinctive genius and using logic, love, and levity I planned my own attempt to fall though the inverted Earth whilst vanishing.

The next step I took was at the University of Melbourne in 1971 where, with the backing of the University Union as their experimental Cosmologer and in premises provided by the Vice Chancellor, I set up an informal non-accredited department of cosmology (as distinct from just astro-physics). Here, with the help of a colleague Dr Banks, a theoretical physicist, and with input from some students and postgraduates, I set about creating a subjective evolving and involving convergent, process cosmology which interrelated the essence of all the learning I had accumulated. By 1973 it was finished and circulated around universities in the USA and UK for criticism. If I could persuade similarly motivated individuals to endorse it, it could be chosen as a model of the universe which could be adopted by mankind as a useful fiction since it converged onto a hypothetical centre which formed a singularity - an ideal location for a much-needed 'sky hook'.

THE NEED FOR A SKY HOOK

Elsewhere I have described the importance of this inverted universe model in helping to discredit and demolish the intellectually outdated Enlightenment model of the universe as a mechanistic collection of things in space driven by chance and held together by magic (Newton's gravity). Like other human symbolic creations, universe models are capable of cultural evolution in the form of upgrading, which may be very sudden. The importance of the geoperipheral model is that, in the absence of any credible and widely accepted absolute authority delivered as a clear statement from a single omniscient God, human beings are now obliged to choose a man-made cosmological model as an internally consistent explanatory convention. It seems unbelievable to me that this has not yet been seen as a priority to be debated by academic scientists. Process cosmologists cannot find any rational objections to this model. Its psychological, social and cultural importance in reconciling transcendental religious and reductionist secular scientific cosmologies cannot be overestimated. Creating a 'sky hook' from which to suspend phenomena that would otherwise be subject to the negative force of gravity, including its various spiritual forms of despair and self-hatred, has been a common, but as yet unrealised, aspiration. Establishing a single place or singularity from which a symbolic cosmological creation could be suspended is an obvious requirement. As Umberto Eco comments in *Foucault's Pendulum*, it would have to be affixed to the highest possible and most central location and it must be completely unique so as to avoid relativistic deconstruction by those attracted by evil and despair rather than by goodness and hope.

THE OURANOCENTRIC UNIVERSE

Such a singularity does now exist in the universe. It is the singularity in the centre of the greatest work of art ever created, the man-made Geoperipheral or Ouranocentric model! I now knew which location could be chosen so that the centre can hold! Not only was it up above all points on the Earth's surface and in the centre, but it was the highest place for all hypothetical beings in all possible locations in the entire universe. The existence of what has been traditionally referred to as Heaven was now at the centre of the physical, biological, social and cultural universe. This need no longer be affirmed or denied by unquestioning obedience to some higher authority. It had now become a matter of free human choice and could be voted on using the internet. As the only human being ever to be appointed by a university as a wizard, and the only human being acclaimed by art gallery directors as a living work of art, I am an outstanding singularity myself and the ideal person to initially establish the new universe by fiat as a useful fiction.

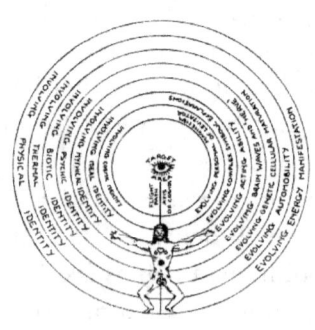

The levitating shaman

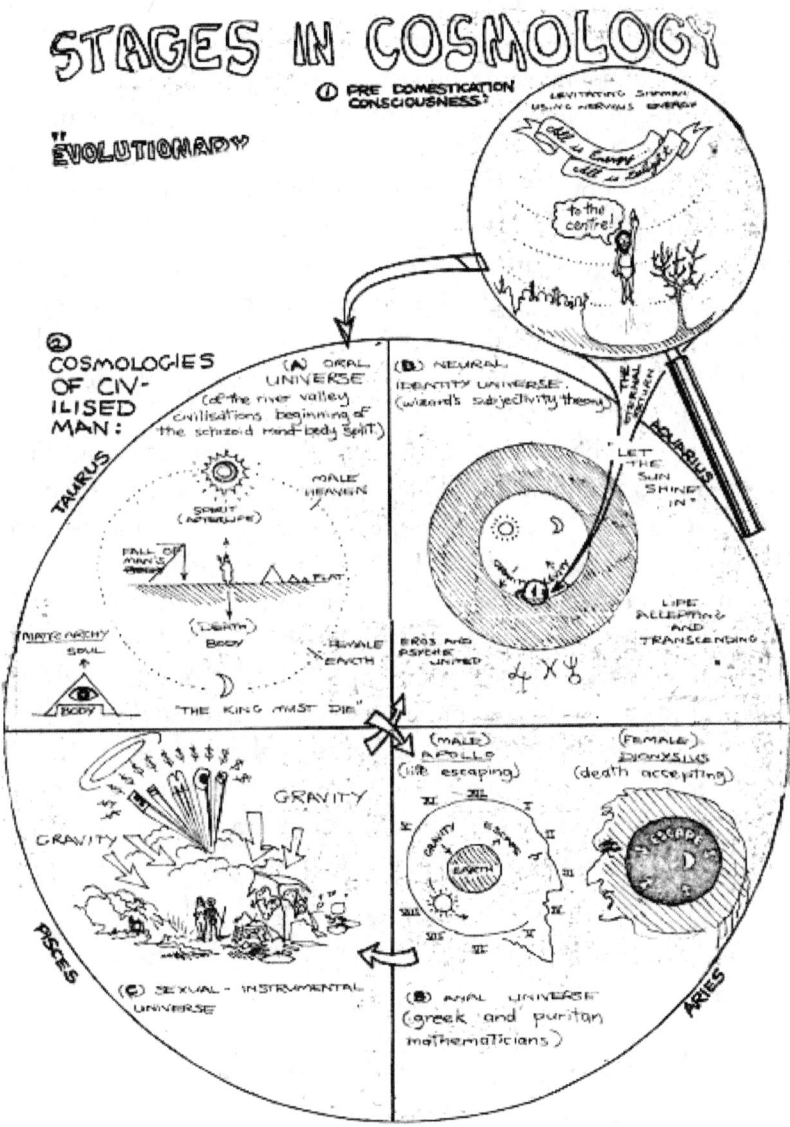

Drawn by a friend in 1972.

JUMPING FOR JOY

Having located a suitable singularity for the outer symbolic centre, all that would remain to be done is for the most evolved and most playful human beings to resume the ancient shamanic attempts to ascend the cosmic axis of the Tree of Life and encourage the universal human subjective intention to ascend in order to reach Heaven. Much of the spiritual power needed would come from the involution of the consciousness of yin and yang united in the erotic life-affirming alchemical marriages that I described in the first part of this essay. Most religious people including Confucians with their essential belief in the authority of Heaven need no longer put up with being ridiculed by reductionist astrophysicists. Even sceptical materialists whose meaning system is mainly sustained by aesthetic pleasure, could understand this universe to be a work of art created by a human being through the interaction of male and female psycho-socio-cultural 'orgone energy'. For those of limited conceptual awareness it could be seen as uplifting fun at the expense of the cocksure astrophysicists of the military industrial complex who are unable to escape from their unconscious commitment to the old useful fiction of the absolute frame, the mind of Newton's now-deceased Unitarian God. Unfortunately, I was thwarted in my 1974 attempt in New Zealand to carry out the first such non-dualistic and truly embodied thought experiment. In my essay *Hunting the Boojum*, I have described how I designed my embodied imaginary experiment combining logic, love and levity to converge identity, space and time, (me, here, now).

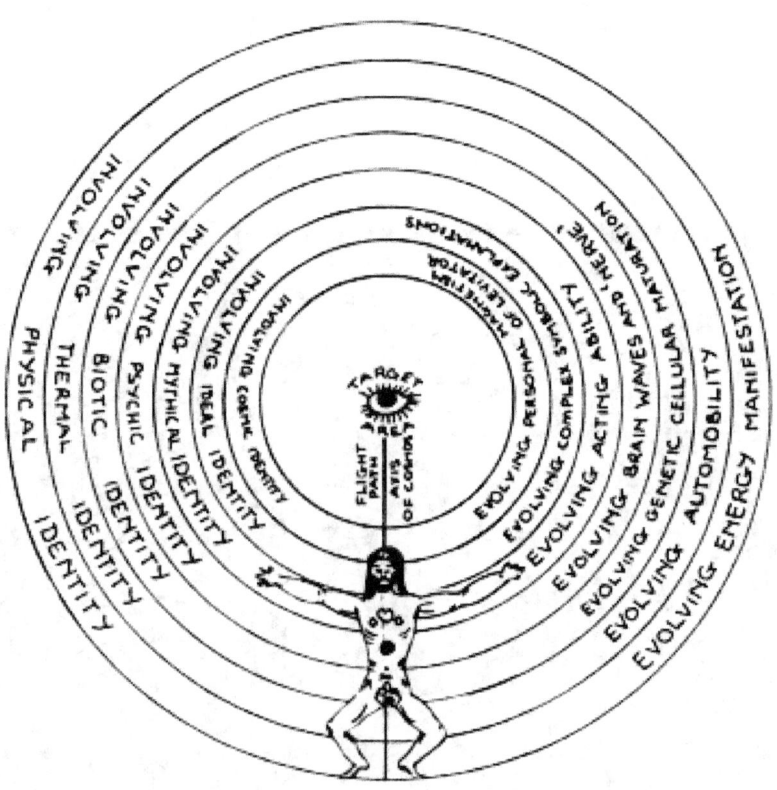

The levitating shaman

WHAT'S THE MATTER OF BRITAIN?

As an amateur historian and cultural activist who includes levity as well as love and logic in my approach to life, I have always been attracted to the classic little history book *1066 and All That* by Sellars and Yeatman. The book published in 1930 was promoted as a 'memorable History of England, comprising all the parts you can remember, including 103 Good Things, 5 Bad Kings and 2 Genuine Dates'. They realised history writing was impossible without 'good things', no matter how historians may deceive themselves to believe they are being objective. Love is subjective and biased, and logic is meaninglessly objective. The escape from this dilemma is only possible through sceptical levity, the approach taken by Sellars and Yeatman. This essay on the Matter of Britain is being written by an English wizard and hence will reveal what I consider to be good and bad things leavened by levity.

Joseph Campbell is one of the most influential explorers of the indispensable myths that are fundamental motivators in all societies and which I term 'mythodynamics' in my postmodern evolutionary cosmology. He makes the point that the Arthurian Romances are the distinctive mythodynamic of Western Christian-Classical Civilization.

In Asia it is the equivalent to the story of Buddha's search for enlightenment and, in the East, King Monkey's adventures in helping to bring the Buddhist Scriptures to China. From Edward I on, until the crude materialism of Enlightenment economic determinism and republican plutocracy, the stories about the Knights of the Round Table particularly influenced the behaviour of the Kings of

England. They found that claims of ancient magic, romance and chivalry surrounding kingship buttressed their authority independent of the monopoly of legitimation of kingship exercised by the priestly bureaucracy of the Vatican in Rome. The Round Table set up by Edward III helped to equalise the power of rival aristocrats under the king and was enshrined in the formation of the Knights of the Garter, the oldest surviving noble order in the world.

THE MATTER OF BRITAIN

Around 1136 Geoffrey of Monmouth wrote his History of The Kings of Britain. It was immensely influential and was soon circulating throughout Europe. Like the Jewish priests in Jerusalem, whom Jeremiah believed had created fictional additions to the history of Israel, he claimed that the source of his history was some ancient writings he had 'discovered'. In his narrative, Geoffrey claims that the British kings descended from a survivor of the royal house of Troy named Brutus who landed in England, and names some of the kings that followed him, concluding with King Arthur. The main characters in his book are Arthur and Merlin. Merlin the wizard makes lengthy prophecies and Arthur is a mighty warrior who defeats the Anglo-Saxon invaders. He also conquers Ireland, Norway, and Scotland and finally invades Europe where he defeats the Roman armies and their Eastern allies, kills the emperor Lucius Tiberius, and occupies Rome in revenge for the Roman invasion, massacre of the druids, and military occupation of Britain. In this first epic narrative there is no Queen Guinevere nor Lancelot, a foreign knight.

As in Homer's Iliad, and in Chronicles and Kings in the Old Testament, in Geoffrey's history the battles, the allies involved on both sides and individual heroic actions are all named and described in most convincing detail. This form of history is mainly fictional, being derived from orally transmitted epic narratives originating in the Bronze Age before the long Dark Age which lasted until around the 9th century BCE.

MYTHODYNAMICS

The ideodynamics of contemporary Western Civilization is a synthesis of Judaeo-Christian religion and Graeco-Roman philosophy, but it also incorporates mythodynamic elements from the heroic warrior cultures of northern Europe.

Important parts of the Biblical narrative describe the radical acts of the Jewish King Hezekiah, the late 8th century BCE founder of fundamentalist monotheism. The captivity in Babylon which followed the destruction of Jerusalem had a great impact on their confidence in Yahweh. Following the Persian conquest of Babylon the Jews absorbed the Zoroastrian belief in the future coming of their messianic god Saoshyant. I assume that the demoralised priests of the defeated Yahweh took this as a sign that though temporarily overthrown by Marduk, Yahweh was still active on their behalf and would send a messianic warlord to reconquer the lands once ruled by the mythical Bronze Age kings David and Solomon. This expectation was confirmed by their unexpected release by Cyrus to return to Jerusalem.

These events which took place between the 7th and 5th centuries BCE can be shown by historians and archaeologists to be reasonably factual. However the re-established temple theocracy in Jerusalem were opposed to the restoration of their kings. Their interpretation of this sequence of events created a new messianic mythodynamic for the Jews which played an important part in the rise of Christianity and Islam in the vacuum formed by the slowly imploding Roman Empire.

The more philosophical world view of the classical world had its origins in the breakaway from theocracy based on agricultural fertility to plutocracy based on economic development. This took place during the early Iron Age in the autonomous city states of the Greeks on the Mediterranean coastline of Anatolia. Transcendental validation of the world view of the great agricultural civilizations was measured mainly by land ownership and population increase. The Greek city states who made skilful use of the new iron technology, including coinage, tools and alphabetic writing, were able to maintain independence from the land based empires by fortifying coastal cities and exchanging manufactured items for food. Democracy and theatre are both linked to the metaphysical ideodynamics of 'representation'. The deconstruction of clans and other forms of extended families and the use of house slaves in the fortified cities, made it possible to create a unique form of government without traditional religious transcendental validation. The gods became fictional creations who could be represented on the stage as popular escapist entertainment and skilled orators could direct political actions through persuasion of citizen representatives in democratic assemblies. The mandate of the people replaced the mandate of the gods.

In plutocratic governments material reality is believed to be more real than spiritual reality. The early philosophers in Miletus created materialistic proto-science based on the reduction of ultimate reality to the lowest common denominator or atoms. Pragmatic reason based on observation replaced ethical faith based on reflection and meditation. This is still a major difference between Western Civilization and all others.

Mythodynamic elements in the Norse culture also played a part in the British version of Christianity. One of these was the portrayal in the Gospels of the suffering figure of Jesus on the cross which could be likened by the northern tribes to Odin hanging in pain on the world tree in order to gain special knowledge. The Mediterranean fertility cult farmers regarded Jesus on the cross as a resurrection symbol or as a victim offered up to appease the High God. Jesus is not a sad victim, like Odin he voluntarily and heroically embraces the necessary sacrifice. This can best be appreciated by a reading of the Anglo-Saxon poem, *The Dream of The Rood* which was composed in the 6th century, even before the time of Bede.

A NEW MYTH OF ORIGIN

The story in Virgil's *Aeneid* describes Aeneas' escape from Troy and his settling in Lavinium, the place which later became Rome. Geoffrey's history describes the conquests of the continent by King Arthur, an early British emperor descended from Brutus, who like Aeneas was a royal escapee from doomed Troy. Both are almost entirely fictional, like the Bronze Age Homeric epics the *Iliad* and the *Odyssey*. Like many such myths they were seized upon and exploited as useful fictions by sophisticated rulers.

Virgil's mythodynamic epic was written for the Emperor Augustus to provide the aggressive tribal Latin upstarts with a fictional history to rival that of their rivals the sophisticated Greeks with their *Iliad*. Geoffrey was providing an alternative and rather cruder mythodynamic history of the 'British' people, rather than that of the currently Norman-dominated 'English'. The mythologically sophisticated Welsh poet David Jones refers to it as 'the Angevin *Aeneid*'. The strong bias against Rome in this epic provides an independent myth of origin to that of the Pope's new attack dogs, the newly arrived Viking converts who had succeeded the now well established Franks. At the time of composition, the Plantagenet-Angevin kings were at war defending their extensive territories in the west of continental Europe against French expansionism.

THE BRITISH REVIVAL

It was still remembered in the Celtic North West that the Romans had invaded Britain and destroyed their magical wizards and indigenous culture. More recently at the Synod of Whitby in the 7th century the Papacy in Rome had used the newly converted and recently arrived Anglo Saxons to take local control away from the existing Celtic Church authorities. Shortly after this, in the early 8th century, Bede wrote his influential *Ecclesiastical History of the English People* which lavishes praise on Augustine and the missionaries sent from Rome by Pope Gregory the Great to convert the 'pagan' Anglo-Saxons. Bede gave little credit to the Irish Christian monks who between the 4th and 8th centuries had almost single-handedly preserved the intellectual culture of Europe.

Invasions by Goths and Lombards together with the great plague of the 6th century had left Rome a rather backward malarial backwater. In modern terms, Bede can be appreciated as a truly great 'spin doctor' with the 'English' as his own personal ideodynamic creation, though great writers like Chaucer and Shakespeare put the finishing touches as Christendom began to split along ancient faultlines during the Renaissance. Bede's dream was realised by Alfred the Great, the educated Saxon ruler who after visiting Rome made the fiction a reality by defeating and converting the uncultured Danes. He brought them under control whilst giving his citizens a Romano-Christian legal system and a monarchical government linked both to biblical traditions and ancient Anglo-Saxon traditions of democratic rulership. The ideal that the best government was the king in parliament was established. The mandate of heaven and the mandate of the people were thereby brought into harmony.

A WIZARD AT THE COURT OF KING ARTHUR

A unique element in Geoffrey's history, written a century after the Norman Conquest, and the various popular expansions which followed, is the presence of a wizard at the court of King Arthur together with bishops and knights with a code of chivalry. This is quite extraordinary. The emphasis on humane warrior virtues and magic is typical of the ancient culture of the British people who had been subjugated by a Roman invader whose interests were mainly economic. Roman plutocratic republicanism, legalism, and materialism was never threatened by their own crude superstitious religious cults, and their military killing machine had absolutely no concept of chivalry. The Matter of Britain rapidly became immensely popular all over Europe. Images of Arthur can be seen in many Romanesque churches. Significantly for my thesis, at the same time the Abbot at Glastonbury 'discovered' the tomb of King Arthur and Queen Guinevere in the abbey grounds, thereby adding to the income from the steady stream of pilgrims.

QUEEN ELEANOR SUBVERTS THE NARRATIVE

The French writer Chrétien de Troyes did his best to undermine the myth by subverting the narrative. In his version, composed around 1180, half a century after the original, King Arthur is cuckolded by a new (French) outsider, the knight Lancelot, who is a superior warrior to Arthur. In Chrétien's revision of the myth, romantic love for arrogant beautiful women is the most important theme. This was not surprising, Chrétien's patroness was a daughter of Eleanor of Aquitaine, a powerful queen in her own right. Eleanor not only cuckolded her husband the King of France whilst on a crusade with him but divorced him to marry the King of England. Her second husband Henry II had incurred her sexual jealousy and she spent her later years tearing the Plantagenet Empire apart, urging her sons by both husbands to go to war against Henry. In the 12th century she founded Schools of Courtly Love for immature men and paid poor clerics to write songs and stories in which young knights pledged love and undying loyalty to untouchable dominant women (Domnei) rather than to their liege lords and God.

ENGLISH KINGS EXPLOIT THE MATTER OF BRITAIN

The Plantagenet branch of the Norman kings lost most of their territories in Western Europe during the fratricidal and patricidal wars engineered by Eleanor, the 'she-wolf', against her husband with enthusiastic help from her ex-husband and family from the Isle de France. Henry II was a hyperactive legal reformer whose efforts to bring common law to Plantagenet lands in England and the continent were far ahead of those of other rulers. Henry appointed Thomas Becket as Archbishop of Canterbury to help him fight clerical corruption and to bring priests under the rule of law. He had previously appointed this close friend, a despised Saxon, to the position of Chancellor, the most powerful secular position in the land.

The papacy was now becoming a centre of political power using the Normans as their enforcers and was refusing to accept the earlier Christian dictum of 'rendering unto Caesar'. The Pope insisted that the king had no legal authority to bring to trial and punish priests guilty of criminal offences against the law of the land. Once archbishop, Becket seems to have suffered a kind of nervous breakdown; Henry's drinking companion and bon viveur suddenly felt called to become a holy man who resolutely opposed the legal reforms and spent his time alone in prayer and self-flagellation. He brought martyrdom on himself and the king was forced to accept humiliation by the Pope and his client kings. The disastrous wars between the sons of Henry II and their father followed, and concluded with the ignominious and tyrannical reign of King John. His extreme abuse of royal power led to the barons pressurising the king to sign the Magna Carta which eventually guaranteed the establishment of the vital rule of law in Western Civilization.

King Edward's Round Table in Winchester

THE RETURN OF THE WIZARDS

An important part of the British mythodynamic identity is returning and fast accelerating as popular novels and films move more and more into fantasy where heroic struggle against evil forces is replacing the bourgeois values of both social realism and narcissistic individualistic introspection. The cult of Courtly Love that appeared in Northern Europe in the late 11th century exploded amongst the aristocracy in the 12th. Since this is bound up with the spread of the ideodynamics of the Matter of Britain I feel it necessary to look deeper into the previously neglected aspects of the role of wizards and another form of romantic love that has been repressed since the agricultural revolution and is manifesting itself in the current dissolution of nuclear families in our world civilization.

During the turbulent 17th century Milton planned to write an epic poem on the subject of Arthur and the myth had great appeal to the 19th century romantics like Tennyson. In spite of literary critics, the best-selling work of fiction of all time after Dickens' *Tale of Two Cities* was Tolkien's massive three-part epic *Lord of The Rings*. Huge numbers of children all over the world today, who hardly ever opened a book before, are devouring the series of lengthy novels about the young wizard Harry Potter. New Zealand has also become famous recently as the setting for an immensely popular film version of *Lord of The Rings* directed by a New Zealander with a talented local production team. Moreover, this essay itself is being written by the Wizard of New Zealand, who is not a mass media-created fictional character, having been appointed official Wizard by the Administration of the University of NSW in 1969, Wizard of Christchurch by the City Council in 1982, and official Wizard of New Zealand by the Prime Minister in 1990. For his performance he was finally awarded the Queens Service Medal in 2009. The reader can imagine the cognitive dissonance this is causing the intellectual and media elites in New Zealand who, unable to engage with him socially or culturally, deny his existence as anything but a tolerated fool.

It is obvious that, like Moses and Merlin, Gandalf is not a historical figure. The fictional King David fulfils similar status needs and motivational functions as King Arthur and Aragorn. Magic and miracles are just different interpretations and exaggerations of similar improbable events. Will Jesus come again as promised? Will the Jewish Messiah finally come to lead the chosen people to Middle Eastern conquest? Will the newly resurgent Wahhabi-influenced Sunnis of strictly monotheistic and misogynistic Islam financed by oil-rich Arab states finally conquer the oil-rich Aryan Shiites of Iran and then the rest of the world and bring about the end of history? Will KGB-trained Putin, the new wannabe Tsar of Russia, recommence the expansion of Russia until he finally gets the political control of Europe dreamed of by Stalin? Will Merlin reappear as prophesied? Will Arthur, who is only sleeping, come to the aid of the British people when they are in dire trouble? Will the revolution finally irrupt and overthrow evil capitalism to replace it with an egalitarian utopia where no-one is poor and oppressed?

The early signs of a revival of British mythodynamics can be seen in the rapid rise of the United Kingdom Independence Party followed by the radical transformation and unprecedented election victory of the Tory Party in 2019 which attracted supporters away from the other parties, especially Labour voters living away from the bankers' paradise of London and its supersuburbs. In the 19th century the class war produced by the rapid urbanising industrialisation of the Whig elements of the Tory Party created the Labour Party resistance which culminated in the welfare state of the 1945 Labour government. Unscrupulous individualistic capitalists were then replaced by an army of over-scrupulous conformist bureaucrats. With socialist centralisation of economic and political power and control of education, materialist values based on gender and skin colour were fast replacing traditional Christian ethics.

Merlin

As in the French Revolution the useful fiction of the Mandate of Heaven of the religious monarchy was attacked as mere superstition and was replaced by totalitarian belief in that other major useful fiction, the Mandate of the People. This was accompanied by a puritanical utilitarian approach to environmental beauty and the replacement of complex spiritual rituals by nationalistic displays of force and mass produced commercial escapist entertainment. The class war became the classroom war. The 'woke' educated public servants with their sacred certifications became the arrogant public masters who despised the beliefs and life-styles of the people who paid the taxes that supported their increasingly incompetent rule. Populism, a political movement of discontent with no progressive ideological agenda, has been rising in many parts of the world but it is taking a unique turn in the British Isles.

The Tories led by the charismatic adventurer Boris Johnson have returned to the one nation policy of the charismatic adventurer of the mid-19th century Prime Minister, Benjamin Disraeli, and they are desperate to get out of the undemocratic and economically failing European Union. In 1939 Winston Churchill, who was another charismatic adventurer, inspired a one nation resistance to what was almost the extinction the British culture by the so far triumphant Nazis. Who risked their lives and crippled their economies by coming to their rescue? Their fellow British in Canada, Australia and New Zealand in particular. Then, in the 1970s, spellbound by promises of wealth and power in a United States of Europe, the United Kingdom rudely cut adrift their economically dependent relatives and rescuers to join Germany and France. Returning to visit their home country the overseas British

were treated at the border as 'aliens', whilst Germans, French and others were admitted as fellow citizens. In the years following the end of the war, giving in to economic and political pressure from the USA and their puppets in the UN, they unashamedly abandoned their colonies in Africa and elsewhere to their grisly fate.

Now they are realising they were lied to about the anti-imperialist and anti-nationalist benefits of becoming Europersons in a United States of Europe. Selling their birth right for a mess of pottage they betrayed the rich culture and heroic deeds of their ancestors. Behind the screen of this preposterously bureaucratic organisation based on the Treaty of Rome (sic) the Germans, helped by the Americans who cancelled most of their war debts but not those of Britain, are once again being driven by their traditional barbarian mythodynamics to take over Europe. The economies of many of the member states have been bankrupted since they joined and they have become little more than bureaucratically controlled client states of the German national bank. As to what happened to the lives of people in the colonies the British abandoned in Africa before they were prepared for independent nationhood, the less said the better.

We have good reason to fear the rise of the United States of Europe controlled by Germany and supported by Anglophobic France. Lest I be accused of racial determinism, when I regard myself as a non-deterministic cultural activist, I quote from *The History of Religion and Philosophy in Germany*, a book written in 1834 by the romantic German poet, Heinrich Heine. This prophecy came true. Power can be exercised through bureaucratic and economic sources and not just from the barrel of a gun:

'Christianity - and that is its greatest merit - has somewhat mitigated that brutal Germanic love of war, but it could not destroy it. Should that subduing talisman, the cross, be shattered, the frenzied madness of the ancient warriors, that insane Berserk rage of which Nordic bards have spoken and sung so often, will once more burst into flame. This talisman is fragile, and the day will come when it will collapse miserably. Then the ancient stony gods will rise from the forgotten debris and rub the dust of a thousand years from their eyes, and finally Thor with his giant hammer will jump up and smash the Gothic cathedrals'.

ROMANTIC LOVE IN NORTHERN EUROPE

When it comes to the sexual relationship between men and women, British mythodynamics and their impact on psychodynamics go even deeper than those of other cultures. Over the past half century, patriarchy as the foundation of marriage forms in both East and West is being undermined by new intellectual movements opposing patriarchy. These are greatly effecting women's roles. Here too the Arthurian romances embedded in Northern Christianity can play an important part.

Lest I be accused of psycho-sexual determinism after my comments about Eleanor of Aquitaine, I believe that the love story of Heloise and Abelard which took place at about the same time is something completely new in the psyche of Western Civilization. The brilliant young scholar Heloise was born in France twenty years before Eleanor. When Peter Abelard, the leading intellectual of the time and a popular musician in Paris, was brought into her house to further her education they fell secretly in love. She eventually became pregnant and Abelard was expelled. They were married, even though marriage would mean the end of his scholarly career and Heloise strenuously objected to it. The love story took a very sad turn at this point with Heloise ending up in a convent and Abelard in a monastery. Their letters have been preserved and demonstrate an entirely new form of erotic sensitivity particularly in Heloise. They influenced me in my attempts to create a postfeminist and postmodern marriage form. The importance I ascribe to this love affair is the significant absence in her behaviour and expressed feelings of what I call a repressed 'Jocasta complex', a psychodynamic and mythodynamic based on an incestuous matriarchal desire to control the behaviour of one's husband and sons, classically exhibited by Eleanor. This is the unrecognised reciprocal aspect of what the 'blinded' patriarchal Freud called the Oedipus complex.

The northern traditions of Europe are imbued with different myths from those of the Mediterranean and Eurasia. It is the key region where, under the influence of Christianity, the responsive female soul might be freed from subordination to childrearing and from having her sexual partner chosen by her family on economic grounds. Many nuns entered the convent to experience this strong form of romantic love for their spiritual husband and lover, Jesus. In complete contrast to this, Dante's *Divine Comedy*, composed in the Mediterranean Christian region a century and a half afterwards, condemns Paolo and Francesca to Hell for behaviour similar to that of Abelard and Heloise. Dante fell deeply in love at a distance with Beatrice, a beautiful banker's daughter, whom he believed to be pure enough to guide him in his imagination up to Heaven, passing through the heavenly spheres where even his idol Virgil was too impure to trespass. In his *La Vita Nuova* he even recommends that we look into the face of a beautiful woman to experience the divinity of Christ.

The dogma of the Christian Church emphasises the pure love of the mother-son bond even though Jesus' mother plays almost no active part in the narrative. She was divinised and given the title of Mother of God. Any hint of impure psychosexual bonds between Jesus and a woman has been suppressed by the Church. Mary Magdalene, Christ's important female disciple, was deliberately misrepresented as a reformed prostitute. This is not surprising in a religion based on the Jewish sacred books in which only sexual activity undertaken with the deliberate aim of producing offspring is divinely sanctioned: all other forms are forbidden as sinful. The Song of Songs which resembles the love poetry of contemporary Egypt and Mesopotamia appears to be have been inserted into the Jewish scriptures like Proverbs and Ecclesiastes. It inspired the Hassidic 'devek' and must have contributed to the growth of romantic love in Christianity. The influential protestant John Milton was a critic of traditional marriage and in his epic *Paradise Lost* and other writings he questions the nature of the psychosexual power relationship between husbands and wives. I examine this in my essay called 'The Great Leap Backward'.

Like the later St Theresa, whose voluminous writings reveal an astonishing exploration of inner space and describe her ecstatic union with the masculine manifestation of God, Heloise created the model of true romantic love, unpolluted by maternal love or storge. This was the exact opposite of the behaviour in the Courts of Love sponsored by the manipulative Eleanor.

The romantic mythodynamics of the West unlike that of the East oscillate between woman as dominatrix and woman as devotee, with the former usually in the ascendant. Queen Elizabeth, as the current divinely ordained head of the British government and Church of England has set us an example of finding a balance between matriarchal dominatrix and marital devotee who fell deeply and openly in love with Philip her husband. Since the British Empire came together to fight the Nazis and their allies, the Royal Family, who have demonstrated a remarkable devotion to duty, has made it a priority to maintain the links with the Commonwealth as a family of nations. The old class war is ending with the electoral triumph of a new One Nation Tory Party who earned the respect of the electorate by fighting heroically to regain their nation's sovereignty against a corrupt establishment who had sold out. With the amazing rise of the wizard archetype and the freeing of the potential for romantic love in women through effective contraception and political feminism, the British mythodynamics have been given a boost that should enable them to lead the world in coping with an ugly looking future.

I have just come across *Gynocentrism; from Feudalism to the Disney Princess*, by Peter Wright, published in 2014, which confirms my long-standing conviction that there is a fundamental flaw in our understanding of women's nature and potential in Western Civilization in particular. Since becoming the official Wizard of the World University Service in 1969 I have considered what is currently being called the gynocentric thesis to be an important factor in the creation of the present zeitgeist.

As I understand it, at the start of civilization itself the immortality ideology of patriarchal agricultural religion began the destruction of the uniquely efficient and playful human culture achieved by mimetic evolution. In existential pre-agricultural societies sexually aroused females selected males for bonding on the basis of their performance skills and adult males did not seek physical immortality through offspring.

Following the evolution of speech this form of human culture came to an end and eventually led to verbally expressed supernatural ideologies based on the new fear of ego extinction, not fear of death. Although highly efficient at increasing population, the price paid for this was not only cripplingly bad physical and mental health but the destruction of their natural environment and rule by brutal military-religious elites.

Then, amongst male members of the feudal elites in Europe in the 12th century the divination and worship of beautiful women through Courtly Love began to replace feudal honour hierarchies based on loyalty to one's master, religious awe and courage.

Max Weber's famous thesis pointed out that a determining factor in the emergence of the unique cultural form we call capitalism was the Protestant Reformation belief that each man should be his own priest which became the secular doctrine of bourgeois individualism. The Reformation transformation of urbanised human role-actors into autonomous material 'bodies in space' driven by material gain, became conflated with social life which was centred on the courtly love belief in women's moral superiority. Added to this was the ancient egoistic, non-existential need for personal fame after death or spiritual immortality that started the agricultural revolution. These ideologies have trapped mankind into what has become violent, soulless, and mindless military-industrial complexes governed by insect-like humourless male bureaucrats without balls and even more humourless female bureaucrats acting like morally superior nannies. The combination of these three major ideologies created a truly fearsome monster.

The love of power increasingly replaces the power of love. Agriculturalists despise, fear and hate hunter-gatherers, entrepreneurial traders in cities despise fear and hate religious peasants, woke globalists despise, fear and hate nationalistic entrepreneurs. Each devolving ideology is more arrogant, distrustful, violent and humourless than its predecessor.

The tomb of Abelard and Heloise in Paris.
A popular tourist attraction.

"Great Sage, Equal of Heaven." (Photo: Karl Filipov).

THE GREAT LEAP BACKWARD

*What we call the beginning is often the end
And to make an end is to make a beginning.
The end is where we start from.*
  - T S Eliot, *Little Gidding*

Colossal political convulsions are currently shaking the USA and UK, the two most stable and historically important democracies in the world. Communist China has been exposed as the greatest threat to world peace since Nazi Germany and Soviet Russia. Career bureaucrats in the public services are increasing in numbers and power and destroying traditional ethical standards. National governments are being controlled by huge global corporations, including those which control what information is communicated. Physical health has been much improved but mental health is declining rapidly. Meritocracy is being replaced by 'mediocracy', with universities leading the charge against free speech. Most disturbing of all is the obsession with expensive but idiotic fixes for temporary climate change whilst the massive pollution and degradation of the land and seas caused by unstoppable consumerist ideology is ignored. A radical reappraisal of human consciousness is now the most important task for those of us prepared to tackle it.

Any journey backward through the history of human consciousness can only be undertaken by studying what we know of the changing social institutions and cultural narratives of the past. This must include Palaeolithic hunter gatherers, Neolithic farmers, Bronze Age heroic cultures, Iron Age mercantile-industrial civilizations and, since the late 19th century, the Modern Electric Age global consumer culture. A personal detachment from dogmatic beliefs held by human cultures previous to our current post-modern scepticism is a prerequisite. This does not exclude what I call fun revolutionary empathetic participation in the playful aspects of any particular cultural scenario, so long as it remains fun where means and ends are not in serious conflict.

Having been engaged in this enterprise since 1968 I can liken it to slowly reversing a vehicle with several trailers back down a long intermittently lit driveway until finally reaching Göbeckli Tepe and Çatalhöyük where the disruptive agricultural revolution began. The exploratory *yang* aspects of my postmodern personality were focussed forward whilst the tradition-loving *yin* aspects were focussed on the rear view mirror, requiring constant shifts from one to the other. To avoid being stuck I had to make constant playful and sensitive readjustments of the steering wheel to avoid colliding with and harming the borders I set for myself of love on the one side and of logic on the other. As an ex-navigator I was inspired by the existential orientation of the captain in Lewis Carroll's *Hunting of the Snark*.

During the brief flowering of radical new ideas that took place in the late 1960s and early 1970s many influential speakers and writers pointed out that all evolving or devolving human culture, not just religious and magical beliefs but scientific theories and even the very structure of languages and mathematics are artificial human creations that provide forms that are essential for our expressed thoughts. In other words, we are living in virtual reality. I consider Joseph Campbell's *Myths to Live By* of 1972 one of the best summings up of the situation made at that time. David Riesman's *The Lonely Crowd* published in 1950 had already provided me with an excellent description of the major psycho-social shift from 'inner-directed' neurotic anxiety to 'other directed' hysterical narcissism taking place in the USA since the end of WW2.

Individuals whose personal and group identity is inextricably embedded in a religious, political or philosophical ideology may regard any contrary beliefs, even when expressed peacefully and politely, as a threat and may become violently angry as if in the grip of a collective psychosis. Defending one's ego against attack is a basic human characteristic. The weak and more vulnerable are less able to shrug off criticism or failure and either respond by shrinking away and becoming more submissive and surrendering to group think, or by angrily attacking their critics.

This classic hindbrain-based flight or fight response can take on intellectual complexity in the case of *ressentiment*, a form of psychological rationalisation described by Kierkegaard, Nietzsche and Scheler. Aesop's fable about the fox and the grapes illustrates how some individuals, rather than learning from their mistakes, protect their fragile egos by altering their consciousness to compensate for failure to obtain a desired outcome. Important values such as honesty, love, truthfulness, and successful goal achievement can be devalued and replaced by compensatory baser values. Belief in the relativity of truth, beauty and goodness values is created by philosophical reductionism from the symbolic cultural level to the materialistic social level (as in socialism). Similarly reduction from the social to the organic-psychological level to protect hurt feelings (as in political correctness) greatly facilitates this devaluation process. Without any socially acceptable ranking of subjective values in provisional hierarchies the will to power can rise to 'deconstruct' them and establish an objective bureaucratic new world order resembling Orwell's *1984*.

Neurophysiologists have demonstrated that the human brain is divided not only between hindbrain and forebrain but also between the left and right hemispheres of the frontal cortex. If reflexive interaction between these is blocked by irrational fear, the energetic delight of *coincidentia oppositorum* ceases and Koestler's 'darkness at noon' takes its place. Psychologists use the phrase 'cognitive dissonance' to describe this.

COGNITIVE DISSONANCE

A major paradigm shift that commonly takes place and produces massive cognitive dissonance is from theocratic cultures based on agricultural technology, motivated by fertility values, to more materialistic plutocratic Iron Age societies, based on markets, manufacturing and trading. Such cultural transformations, whether fast and expanding or slow and consolidating, inevitably involve great changes, not only in individual psychology but in family structures. Collective identity as membership of a religious collectivity may be progressively replaced by membership of an economic collectivity. Increasing industrialisation and secular education may greatly weaken religious identity based on integrating love with national identity based on utilitarian logic taking its place, and rapid urbanisation may cause rural extended families to break down into nuclear families. The sudden establishment of coercive bureaucratic welfare states has recently replaced many of the functions of families and voluntary associations. This increases the anomie already a cause of concern amongst political philosophers of the 19th century.

I had better explain how I came to be a cultural activist pioneering new liminal roles which I believe were essential to free my consciousness from being embedded in any cultural paradigm other than that of a hunter gatherer, which I considered the fundamental essence of what it is to be human. Following a series of unplanned events I found myself lecturing in the Sociology of Religion at the University of NSW in Sydney in the late 1960s, specialising in revitalisation movements in preliterate societies and making comparisons between them and the 'post-literate' revitalisation movements which were taking place all around us. In 1967 a political crisis was developing on the campus. As the first lecturer in social theory in Australia, indebted to Max Weber and George Mead for my general orientation, I responded to this by launching what I called the Fun Revolution, aiming at reforming the ever increasing bureaucracy which was destroying the last remnants of the university as a community of scholars. I organised a discussion group and a series of university mass meetings with a few friends and the executive of the Student Union. I also founded a direct action movement based on my new synthesis of logic, love, and levity which I called ALF (Action for Love and Freedom) to bridge the divide between the love-based but escapist activism of the hippies and the freedom-seeking but confrontational political activism of the student power movement. To everyone's surprise, a series of radical, more humane social deconstructions of the university bureaucracy followed, which I attributed to my encouragement of ego-suppressing pragmatism. Unknown to me Victor Turner, the anthropologist who had shifted his ideology from the usual Marxism to process theory, was conducting similar but more marginal experiments in the USA.

A WIZARD APPEARS IN THE COUNTERCULTURE

This was a few months before 1968 when the puritanical neo-Marxists of the Student Power movement suddenly launched their long march through the institutions based on the Nietzschean will to power. Traditional values of truth, beauty and goodness were maginalised with free speech as the first casualty. At UNSW the two revolutionary movements collided. The academics turned against the Fun Revolution, preferring to relate to the angry and frequently violent student power mobs whose motivation they could understand and empathise with. I was only able to remain active on campus with the help of the Student Union and University Administration who appointed me their non-contractualised 'free range' official University Wizard. I was supported initially with an honorarium. This is not as stupid and irrational as it may appear. Max Weber's criticism of Marx's social philosophy and his horror at the growth of sterile bureaucracy was derived from Goethe whose interest in alchemy and 'elective affinities' was unique and led to his critical objection to Cartesian mechanistic objectivity.

I recently came across a blog by Scott Adams, creator of the Dilbert cartoons. Adams describes the character of a wizard in the following way:

'According to my Moist Robot hypothesis (that we are programmable meat) and paired with the Master Wizard view of the world, one can imagine a world in which all the big changes in society are engineered by a handful of living wizards at any given time. The wizards, in this context, have learned the rules of hypothesis and persuasion. This knowledge gives them access to the admin passwords for human beings, and they use it.

I will tell you how to spot a wizard, if such people exist. Look for these clues. The wizard succeeds in a high-profile field without the benefit of as much talent as you think would be necessary. This is the biggest tell. People seem to have an irrational hate for the wizard that is not entirely explained by the wizard's actions. These reactions are signs of cognitive dissonance. Wizards often introduce cognitive dissonance without trying.

Look for an inflated ego combined with an unusually strong ability to withstand withering criticism; wizards get a lot of criticism. The common view is that wizards are egomaniacs. In reality the wizard works hard at being ego-free and hence can handle criticism well. Wizards are often more ambitious and more aggressive than you think is normal. One or more major PR disasters define the wizard's story. The wizard has a gift for simplification.

Observers detect a reality distortion field. Wizards have an ability to succeed where others fail by changing the entire game as opposed to winning at the existing one. Wizards use words to create images and emotions in people's minds. Wizards seek public attention. This wizard filter on the world isn't necessarily true in some objective sense. The fun is seeing if the data and predictions fit the filter.'

If this explanation is true it makes sense of the extreme emotional polarisation that has taken place around me and my radical cultural actions over the past fifty years in Australia and in New Zealand. These were explicitly designed to increase a synthesis of love, logic and levity in my personal, social, and cultural relationships. A few years ago the sudden appearance of the charismatic individuals Donald Trump in the USA and Nigel Farage and Boris Johnson in the UK began producing similar examples of extreme cognitive dissonance. Truly wicked, corrupt and treacherous individuals were receiving nothing like the hatred these egotistic but comparatively polite, and reasonably law-abiding individuals are provoking in the mass media and amongst the educated financial elite. What is called 'Trump derangement syndrome', where individuals literally lose their minds in venomous hatred, is extremely common. Adams claims that President Trump is a wizard.

I have concluded that what in my own case began as a fun revolutionary strategy to avoid being dismissed as an immoral materialist by religious fundamentalists, or an irrational religious believer by political economic determinists, has turned out to be truer than I believed at the time. Perhaps I really am a wizard hiding in plain sight, even though I can't 'believe' it myself. This brings me to an essay I composed a few years ago seeking the origin of dysfunctional forms of human consciousness demonstrated in human history.

THE FALL OF MAN

ORIGINAL SIN

The myth of The Fall of Man following an act of disobedience in the distant past with catastrophic implications for the human race is found in many cultures. Assessment of the importance of this myth and possible remedies of this 'fall' vary considerably. The story as recorded in the Jewish scriptures was carried over to the sacred writings of both Christians and Moslems and still has an important impact on Western Civilization. However the doctrine was modified by belief in personal immortality and life in an after-world as a reward for ethical behaviour. This belief originated in Egypt and by the time Christianity was established it was suffused throughout the whole Roman Empire.

The book of Genesis is not just a traditional account of the creation of the world by an all-powerful creator God. It is also an account of the expulsion of Adam and Eve from Paradise as a consequence of an act of disobedience. There is no possibility of return or self-salvation. As the descendants of Adam the first man, all human beings inherit the evil in their genes. The human race is permanently flawed by this 'original sin'.

Genetic determinism in this form has affected Christians far more than Moslems or Jews. Christians are deeply concerned with original sin and salvation, making it the centre of the mythodynamics of their sacrificial religious meaning system. They believe that their saviour Jesus Christ came down from Heaven as the human incarnation of God to atone for mankind's sins by sacrificing Himself through suffering a hideous death as a common criminal. This belief continues the theme of the sacrifice of Isaac by his father Abraham. Isaac is saved by an angel who miraculously substitutes a ram for Isaac. Jesus is miraculously resurrected from the dead. Human sacrifice is abandoned forever in the first instance, and God, as the loving and forgiving father of all, replaces Yahweh the feared tribal warlord, in the other.

Jews and Moslems are more concerned with collective obedience to Yahweh/Allah's commands than escaping from the individual guilt arising from Adam's transgression. Protestants, especially extreme religious determinists like Calvinists, take more personal responsibility for their salvation than traditionalist church members who seek guidance and reassurance from their spiritual leaders.

THE TREE OF KNOWLEDGE OF GOOD AND EVIL

In the myth described in the Jewish sacred texts the creator God has made a mandala-like garden in Eden where his human creation Adam could live a happy carefree life. No work to do, no pain, perhaps not even death. God has made only one condition which Adam must obey. There is a tree in the Garden of Eden whose fruit he is forbidden to eat, the Tree of Knowledge of Good and Evil. We must not confuse inherited animal-based knowledge with being ideologically aware of the uniquely cultural difference between good and evil. Adam is only told of the existence of this tree. It appears that he has not been informed of the presence of another all-important tree, the Tree of Life, whose fruit also possesses great power. This is only revealed later.

THE TEMPTATION OF EVE

Adam is incomplete without a feminine half to his being and God makes Eve as his female partner. Whilst Adam is absent Eve is tempted by a supernatural cunning serpent to eat the forbidden fruit of the Tree of Knowledge of Good and Evil in order to gain power. The nature of the serpent and how it came to be in the garden is not clear. Many scholars see it as an ancient survival of belief in a dualistic opponent of God that pre-dates Hezekiah's invention of militaristic monotheism in the late eighth century BCE.

THE TEMPTATION OF ADAM

Adam too is tested when Eve tempts him to copy her defiance of God's command. In his epic masterpiece *Paradise Lost*, whose mythodynamic influence in the Protestant English speaking world should not be underestimated, John Milton imagines the feminine wiles that Eve employs to persuade Adam to follow her example of disobedience. Adam succumbs to her blandishments and eats the forbidden fruit. They are both ashamed and cover their newly-embarrassing nakedness. God

soon finds out and angrily asks Adam why he disobeyed his creator's important instruction. Adam blames Eve and Eve blames the serpent.

THE EXPULSION FROM THE GARDEN OF EDEN

God expels them both from Eden. Adam is told he will now have to work and he and Eve will both have to eventually die. Eve will have to endure pain in childbirth. My interest is particularly drawn to the fact that in the myth Adam does not take personal responsibility for his transgression but blames Eve. He is more afraid of disobeying Eve than God his creator. He has a new master! There also seem to be changes in their mutual sexual attraction which now produces guilt and shame.

THE TREE OF LIFE

The section of Genesis where the creator God gives his reasons for preventing human beings from acquiring God-like powers is important for understanding why I have selected this myth for analysis. I quote from the Bible, Genesis 3.22:

'God said, 'The man has become like one of us, knowing good and evil; what if he now reaches out his hand and takes fruit from the tree of life also, eats it and lives for ever.'

Reference to 'us' is another survival of polytheism not redacted by the priests of Yahweh. The Tree of Life occurs in many early myths as a kind of hierarchical cosmological form which, like Jacob's ladder, can be used to ascend into Heaven.

THE MYTHODYNAMICS OF THIS NARRATIVE

I attempt here to give a basic and necessarily simplistic description of the major differences between hunter gatherer cultures and those of the agriculturalists who aggressively replaced them. Many of the dynamics of the myth of the Fall of Man are symbolic explanations of the causes of these dramatic changes to the psychological and social structures that had sustained mankind for tens of thousands of years.

Amongst hunter gatherers sexual relationships were not seen as motivated by fertility. The need for men to have male children to inherit their family name and their property was not relevant to their nomadic economy. The causal connection between sex and reproduction may have been known but was denied for ideological and cultural reasons. This ideology stated that babies existed as spirits dwelling in sacred places who would choose to enter a passing woman's body to be conceived rather like Jesus. Fatherhood was not a biological relationship but a social role involving responsibility for helping mothers to rear their children. Social descent, name and geographical homeland were usually matrilineal and derived from the mother's family.

SEXUAL SELECTION

Men spent a lot of their time with other men away from their camps and the women and children. Even young boys were strictly initiated to make them independent of control by their mothers and to identify with the autonomous male cohorts. Men did not usually actively select specific young women as sexual partners. As in the animal kingdom young females selected mature males on the basis of their performance skills, such as hunting, personal decoration, dancing and storytelling. The men also carried out secret rituals designed to impress women with their awesome sacredness. The acquisition of a wife or wives was seen as a boost to a man's animal-based ego and social standing rather than a desire for sexual consummation. Instead this was understood to be a woman's prime motivation in choosing a mate. Biologically speaking human females are unique in the animal world for their capacity to surrender themselves to sexual ecstasy and are always 'on heat'. Men's love for their wives was more egotistic and concerned with impressing them in order to earn their devotion and to arouse them sexually and psychologically. This is a biological drive rather like a woman's desire to arouse and satisfy hunger in their children. Women's love for men was 'romantic': they were not motivated by any need to have power over men for material gain since they themselves provided most of the food by gathering. Of course, like children with their mothers, there are many ways wives can influence their husbands.

THE FERTILITY CULT

The Agricultural Revolution transformed not only the ideal interests of the hunter gatherers and their symbolic expressions of the meaning of life but the whole of their mytho-dynamic motivation and its representation in the form of social roles. The punishments meted out by the creator god as the consequences of the fall fit the common experience of the life of human beings in these new societies. Authoritarian regimes demanding obedience had replaced the earlier more egalitarian male cohorts and matriarchal control over the social systems in their camps. Dietary deficiencies, painful skeletal diseases and great amounts of hard work, had become essential compared to the healthier leisure-filled life of most hunter gatherers. In agricultural societies where women's sensuality is regarded as sinful they are more likely to suffer in childbirth especially since fertility was so prized that it had become an act of overriding importance, compensatory sexual pleasure was frowned upon.

Military institutions led by secular rulers were formed to seize and protect limited arable land in alliance with intellectuals in spiritual obedience structures which encouraged fertility. These were administered by priests who replaced the shamans as cultural leaders. A new belief in religiously ordained patriarchy was established now that men needed children to inherit their land and status. Sexual selection by young women was replaced by parental selection of suitable partners for their sons. Infertile women were put aside. Sowing seeds and waiting for them to ripen was now the new meaning of sexual activity, which was seen only as a means to achieve fertility as an end. Marital sex was only sanctified by reproductive outcomes. Later temple prostitution flourished and provided income for temple building. Voluntary celibacy was prized as even more sacred than marriage.

PARADISE LOST

The greatest epic poems in the Christian religion are Dante's *Divine Comedy* and Milton's *Paradise Lost*. They both see disobedience to God as the greatest sin. Dante is devastated by the break-up of Christendom into warring commercial city states and Milton is influenced by the bloodthirsty military battles that were convulsing England during the Civil War between rival Christian believers. Following the earlier collapse of his marriage Milton became particularly concerned with the traditional disharmonies between husbands and wives. His strong individualistic Protestant views leads him to emphasise personal responsibility rather than obedience to ecclesiastical authority. He had earlier written a treatise on divorce and, in Latin only, an even more controversial essay on marriage forms.

In Book VIII of *Paradise Lost* Milton wrote of Adam and Eve, '*He for God only, She for God in him*' as the perfect relationship between them before the Fall. Having eaten the fruit Eve thinks to herself that she might keep her new 'empowerment' a secret:

...shall I to him
Make known as yet my change
And give him to partake
Full happiness with me, or rather not
But keep the odds of Knowledge of my power
Without co-partner? And so to add what wants
 In Femal sex, the more to draw his Love,
And render me more equal, and perhaps
A thing not undesirable, somtime
Superior; for inferior who is free.

So Eve resists this great temptation to gain power over Adam and decides to tell him. When later Adam finds Eve, he is tempted to obey her and eats the forbidden fruit since, '*against his better knowledge not deceav'd, /But fondly overcome with Femal charm.*' Milton compares Adam with Samson, the subject of *Samson Agonistes* his similar major poem on female manipulation and male emotional weakness. Adam's responsible love has turned to irresponsible lust and he eats the fruit. They consummate their newfound awareness of good and evil and shortly afterwards mutual recrimination, guilt and shame ruin their previous happiness. The love based on the initial balance of power between Adam and Eve has been upset by eating the forbidden fruit. They now alternate between mutual blame and a shared sense of sinfulness. Eating the fruit of the Tree of Knowledge of Good and Evil brings not only guilt and shame but alienation from the natural environment.

The conscious mind of an affected individual is now able to objectify and project their own guilty feelings onto others whilst feeling self-righteous in the process. It becomes sinful merely to follow one's own heart rather than to comply with the will of morally superior others. Is this the origin of conscience which will use intellectual rationalisation to justify rebelling against loving authority and pursuing transgressive power over others?

MULTIPLYING AND FILLING THE EARTH

The survival of agricultural societies which are so well adapted to their 'unnatural' environment that they can rapidly increase their populations, requires radically new forms of social integration. So many of the inherited psychological traits and neural wiring of the small hunter gatherer tribes had to be overridden by new and powerful institutions that bound the society together and protected their borders. The crops and arable land were protected by a military class who ruled in alliance with a specialised class of religious intellectuals who organised regular gatherings, shared rituals, and narratives of origin and destiny. These were based on a set of values legitimated by commands of supernatural origin. Belief that supernatural beings rewarded social behaviour and punished parasitical crimes against the community made such complex societies possible. Wars with neighbouring societies, crop failure in their mainly single crop economies and disease resulting from the continuous high density occupation of urban centres, made life hard and dangerous. Promises of a trouble free existence after death in paradise, free from suffering, work and disease, were frequently made to prevent collapse of consensus. Some forms of religion did not depend on obedience to the wishes of supernatural beings but were based on the promise of the end of continuous incarnations based on karma. Later monotheistic religions arose that promised world domination for obedience to the will of their all-powerful warlord deities.

Paradise had indeed been lost, though both religious and political attempts have been made to build perfect societies by 'returning to nature'. The hippies were the most recent and tried to avoid the coercive extremes of communism like the Khmer Rouge, totalitarian religious communes like Jewish kibbutzim, Hindu cults built round gurus, and Christian communities centred on obedience to spiritual masters who claim a monopoly of communication with God.

This part of my essay was written several years ago: since then the unique stone Palaeolithic site at Göbeckli Tepe in the Fertile Crescent in southern Anatolia dating from 9000 BCE has been discovered and the nearby earliest known Neolithic farming settlement at Çatalhöyük from around 7500 BCE has been carefully excavated. Archaeologists believe that this may well indicate the time and place of the Agricultural Revolution, the transformation of human society and consciousness that is often referred to as the Fall of Man. In the mythodynamic structures underlying both individual and collective human history a common focal point is a power struggle leading to the deterioration of the psycho-sexual relationship between man and wife.

Göbeckli Tepe with its multiple stone circles which covered several acres was abandoned and deliberately covered up around 8000 BCE. Archaeologists have shown that for at least a thousand years it had been a regular summer gathering place for unprecedented large numbers of hunter gatherers who brought prime cuts of meat and brewed beer there. Celebrations took place in circles of standing stones exquisitely carved with various animals which were no doubt connected to the different tribes who gathered there to party. Predating Neolithic monuments by thousands of years, these finely finished stone circles and carved stones are the oldest known. Noteworthy amongst the realistic animal representations are much taller stones which seem to be abstract humanoid figures. It is now assumed that these are man's first idols of supernatural beings, possibly ancestors.

Çatalhöyük, in the same region, is the oldest known agricultural urban settlement. Comparison of the domesticated grass found here and also in the crystalised beer residue from the vats at Göbeckli Tepe shows a connection between the two sites. No human burials were found at the older site but burials were an important part of Çatalhöyük and were under the floors of the cramped mud brick houses clustered together like a honeycomb. The bodies showed signs of disease caused by poor diets and overwork. The rooms were furnished and some were decorated with murals and figurines, mostly female.

SOCIETY IS GOD

The assumption can be made that the annual feast gatherings of large numbers of hunter gatherers created a completely new mimetic bond through identification with supernatural beings. As Émile

Durkheim the founder of sociology claimed, 'Society is God'. Little has changed fundamentally since then in all societies based on agricultural technology. Factory farming only increases the separation from the organic ecosystem. Today, by remaining existentially embedded in the natural world, only isolated non-patriarchal hunter gatherers have been able to avoid a deep sense of self-loathing and original sin. Members of other cultures take steps to escape into another supernatural world, either in heaven or into a future materialistic utopia, or by losing themselves in artistic fictions. Bishop Heber's 18th century hymn includes the line, 'Where every prospect pleases, and man alone is vile.' This negative sentiment is driving the powerful Green will to power movement of our time. The other great will to power movement of our time is modern androphobic Feminism, but only 'man' remains vile for its adherents, who usually exclude woman from this loathing.

Milton was driven to write his epic *Paradise Lost* as he was deeply and personally concerned with the loss of the balance between God

Disenchantment of the world caused by Pythagorean mechanistic ideologies imposed by intellectuals.

and mankind, and between man and wife. He could have been influenced by the heretical but practical alchemists who were active at the time. Later their ideas and practices influenced both Goethe and Jung who were also concerned with finding the existential balance, the *coniunctio oppositorum* between anima and animus, or cosmic *yin* and *yang*.

The people who sang and danced and created the cave paintings in the Palaeolithic period over 30,000 years ago were not moronic apes. They were saner people than we are. Humankind is progressing technologically at increasing speed from 'agricultural aristocracy' to 'plutocratic meritocracy' and now to totalitarian 'bureaucratic mediocracy'. The rural extended family shrinks into the urban nuclear family which in the welfare state is collapsing into serial monogamy. Compulsory secular education and self-righteous political correctness in the nuclear-armed military industrial states portrays the dynamic *coniunctio oppositorum* of the sexes as evil. The death wish of the self-pitying will to power is spreading and the life-affirming will to love and laugh is weakening.

Re-enchantment of the world created by the Wizard's existential Fun Revolution.

The question is now clear. Can we rid ourselves of psychotic self-loathing and the projection of the poisonous internal self-hatred onto others that follows eating the fruit of the Tree of Knowledge of Good and Evil, and learn to live again in the real world as best we can? The garden is still there under the rubbish we have dumped on it as a result of following the gods' commands to mindlessly multiply and fill the earth:

We shall not cease from exploration
And the end of all our exploring
Will be to arrive where we started
And know the place for the first time.
Through the unknown, unremembered gate
When the last of earth left to discover
Is that which was the beginning.
    - T.S.Eliot, *Four Quartets*.

Now that we have found the lost Garden of Eden we can start to turn away from the evil will to power and start to eat of the Tree of Life of the hunter gatherers.

I have outlined in my essays the reasons for my claim that only an existential Fun Revolution where logic and love are guided by levity can bring us back to our senses. By avoiding any unconscious attachment to useful fictions like 'equality' or 'merit' (which are inevitably relative ethnocentric values depending on context) and by taking special care, it is possible in this postmodern transitional period to live simply by obeying the rules and going through the motions like a player in a game. We begin life believing in Father Christmas, the tooth fairy, nature spirits, monsters, angels and devils, et cetera, and there is a danger that, finding we have been deceived, we may angrily reject all imaginary beings and react against them even though they may represent no threat. Instead we may progressively come to understand that they represent good and bad, wise and foolish characters and so on. The situations in which imaginary beings are shown as finding themselves are another important part of the narratives that through psychological identification teach us, guide us and sustain us.

A good example of the adoption of non-materialistic useful fictions is the use of coinage or other tokens as money for transactions without believing, as some may do, that monetary value is absolute and transcendent and overrules other values such as goodness, truth, or beauty. Economic cost and value (psychological, social, or political) are not identical. Participating in religious ceremonies and following ethical guidelines for psychological, social and aesthetic reasons does not necessitate dogmatic belief in the existence of supernatural beings whose intentions have only been made known to a chosen few. The best example of rule following without requiring any absolute belief is in obeying the rule of law which all of us experience. Like the rules of good manners and those voluntary rules essential for participating in games or sports supervised by neutral referees, they can even be changed if seen as socially desirable since dogmatic belief is not required – 'The Play's the Thing'.

Between 1968 and 1972, as an academic social scientist and with the help of university and art gallery authorities in Sydney and Melbourne, I took the trouble to disembed myself from the current academic zeitgeist where the new religion of sociology was replacing the old sociology of religion, which had been my special subject. Following my appointment as official Wizard of the University of NSW I reinvented myself as a Living Work of Art and Shaman. I did this by using interactive role theory as leverage based on useful fictions or hypotheses which were derived from a synthetic, postmodern process cosmology I created from various sources circulating at the time. I have written of these events in an unpublished thesis in dialectical form entitled *Channelling the Wizard* where as a sociologist I interview myself as a wizard. The key to what George Mead described as 'role-taking', which is an anticipatory socialisation or acculturation process, is pretending or 'reaching forward' in a non-serious but pragmatic way. By believing in no thing, only process, and with enough courage and self love, an egotistical but self-deprecating wizard is not easily demoralised.

As a cultural activist and well-known public figure I have been trying for fifty years to set an example of detachment without individualistic or social escapism or anti-social withdrawal. I have not joined with others aiming at the political overthrow of our contemporary civilization. I created new existential roles based on my nervous system which I instinctively felt had matured to what I called the neural stage beyond fixation at the confusions of the genital stage. Relating to the opposite sex consistently but without compulsion would free me to develop an autonomous cultural identity. I wanted to recreate the existential bond between man and woman based on loving and playful psycho-sexual interaction rather than on any supernatural moral imperative of fertility, economic need, or on the materialistic manipulation of lust-evoking bodies as owned things.

The wizard role was a conflation of all my other roles and I was accepted as an informal, paid public performer in the new counter culture which at the time included quite a few eccentric characters. I was influenced by the ecstatic shamanic aspects of the booming popular music scene which I combined in my performances with dancing and Ciceronian oratory to reach out to the alienated student crowds. The themes of two popular movies of that time, *Barbarella* and *Zardoz*, confirmed my new calling. At the same time, in my unpaid role as Cosmologer with my own uncredited department on campus of interdisciplinary studies, I was a free-range academic. The Union of Melbourne University authorised me to introduce students and outsiders to the new intellectual ideas that were flourishing at that time in all fields. This is where I created my subjective process cosmology which was more or less completed by 1973. Influenced by Johannes Kepler and other 17th century magicians as well as by Teilhard de Chardin, I could not exclude aesthetics nor love from my cosmology. I printed copies of what I described at that early date as a postmodern cosmology with a list of the texts I was relying on and posted them out to many universities in the unfulfilled hope that I might get intellectual feedback and avoid any drastic mistakes. The main diagram took the form of the Tree of Life. Renaming myself Jack, I set about climbing the magic beanstalk, or Jacob's ladder to Heaven.

The first step back to the future to the lost bio, psycho, socio and cultural ecological reality of Eden is to establish where we assume we are at the present time. I will as always call on my procedural values of logic, love, and levity to do this. We have passed the stage of believing in ideological absolutes and are living in a postmodern metaphysics. The uncomfortable truth is that all human culture is a human creation. We must never forget that we are obliged to live in virtual reality. Consequently we must exercise our free will and make a conscious choice of which hypotheses or useful fictions are the most virtuous, beautiful and truthful in terms of explaining and relating to our biological, social and cultural environments. By contrast, despite claims by some deconstructionists, fundamental human social forms have evolved partly without conscious symbolic control by humans, and the human organism itself has evolved in changing environments without any significant symbolic intervention.

STARTING THE LONG MARCH BACK THROUGH THE CULTURAL INSTITUTIONS

The long march backwards begins in the educational institutions with the publicising of the postmodern cosmology I have been living in since 1973 as a practical experiment. This is the fun revolutionary alternative to the current neo-Marxist march forward through the institutions designed by Antonio Gramsci whose adherents, like Mao and his Red Guards, ruthlessly destroy truth, beauty and goodness in their Nietzschean 'will to power'. To preserve and encourage the growth of the vital values of truth, beauty and goodness, the postmodern universe, as a man-made work of art in progress, would have to be freely chosen after debate and by aesthetic persuasion, not imposed by force. It is arguably more beautiful, more therapeutic and more spiritual than the previous flat earth, mechanistic heliocentric, and expanding universe models. These can still be adopted as useful fictions for agricultural, navigational, mechanistic, ballistic and atomic purposes if and when required.

STARTING THE LONG MARCH BACK THROUGH THE FAMILY INSTITUTIONS

The ideology of biological patriarchy, introduced as an important component of the agricultural revolution to increase their superordinate value of fertility, their obsession with immortality, and their idolatry in mistaking concepts for things (i.e. the fallacy of misplaced concreteness) had upset the successful cosmological balance of their predecessors the hunter gatherers.

Fathers are needed to assist mothers to properly develop the psyches of infants, and in matrilocal and matrilineal social systems this role is often performed by a close relative of the mother. The biologically-based patriarchy intrinsic in the agriculturally-based ideology includes providing men with biological immortality, fame through consanguinity (especially with important men of the same family name) and the inheritance of property owned by related individuals. Ownership of people and animals as 'things' by careful naming, as well as marking out owned land through fixed boundaries, is another characteristic that develops in agricultural belief systems.

I realised that human being and universe as well as man and woman are in continuous interaction through the *coniunctio oppositorum* of the pre-mechanistic magician-scientists. Uninhibited reflexivity is essential and only functions properly when in process, unblocked by inflexible ideological absolutes. Psychologists like Carl Jung found in the concealed experimental practices of some 17th century alchemists significant attempts to bring into balance the bio-psycho-socio-cultural values of masculine and feminine, or anima and animus. For Paracelsus' pupil, Gerhard Dorn, the highest grade of the alchemical *coniunctio* consisted of the union of the total man with the *unus mundus* or 'the one world'.

Consequently the other vital first step on my long march back through the institutions was to create a postmodern marriage form. Not surprisingly this began at the same time as my creation of a new postmodern cosmology. During the late 1960s and early 1970s I collaborated with a small number of young unmarried women, newly-liberated through education and safe, reliable and cheap contraception, who could help me in my experiments in creating a post-nuclear-family and post-patriarchal institution as an example for others to follow. I made it clear to my sexual collaborators that I regarded fatherhood as a social role not as a mere biological consequence of sexual union. The only young women I would associate with would have to show strong sexual interest in me before I let my guard down and risked masculine ego demolition.

I have always identified with the sexual selection found in hunter gatherers and male animals where the male's ego depends psychologically on being treated as a sex object whose attractiveness is earned through practical performance skills. Being raised by a romantic feminist mother from a rural extended family who became a teacher to support herself and who told me she spent years slowly moving in to capture the man she had fallen in love with, I was not suffering from an Oedipus complex (better called the Jocasta complex).

To explain and clarify what I mean by love here, I quote from 'The Naming of Parts', a miniature frame I composed as part of my process cosmology:

> *Love is hypothesised to be the dynamic discharge of tension from intentionality fields. As this deduced involution increases in complexity it is manifested as more complex evolutionary processes extended in space. These are experienceable. By induction hypothetical models of extension can be created and tested experimentally through eventuality. Love as self-expression, growth, self-preservation, organic cooperation and competition becomes increasing more significant and influential as it involves from increasingly complex identity fields of intention. It can be understood as rising progressively from the electro-magnetic force, to the strong interaction force, from chemical bonding to bios, and from there to philia, storge, eros and ultimately agape. This process relational terminology is unique to this postmodern cosmology. In chance-driven reductionist-mechanistic cosmology there are no equivalent processes, only unintentional forces.*

Distinguishing between ideal types of love as the Greeks had done, I could express *eros* love guided by *agape* love and avoid the compulsions and fixations created by confusion of *eros* love with oedipal *storge* love, or the *folie à deux* of *philia* love. As a living work of art I could accept being frequently treated as a sex object or 'thing' by the young women in my life. I understood that this was a similarly strong bonding to that of a child for its mother and was not therefore surprised or alienated by the disruptive neurotic jealousy which characterises such powerful relationships. The various forms of love are set out in the ideal typology quoted above. A mother's *storge* love socialises and encourages her children to mature away from dependency and she takes pride in their offspring's achievements. A master's *eros* love for his beloved love slaves acculturates them and encourages them to become independent of him not only psychologically, but socially, economically and culturally. Successful socialisation and acculturation is shown by the resultant independence of the loved ones in both cases. Family members are bound together by *philia* love and *agape* love integrates the family with the wider society.

This inclusion of love in the microcosm relies on a new paradigm which depends on process rather than modernist egalitarian mutuality in the sexual relationship. At university I was increasingly disturbed by the plight of those intelligent and trusting young women around me who had fallen deeply in love but were being abandoned by the young men when their jealousy made them less attractive. The modern ideology of gender equality rendered them defenceless and the heartless young men who used them as things and moved on had been raised and educated to regard honour as an outdated value. Some academics were even breaking the traditional *in loco parentis* rule. Of course the reverse also applies to those young men who fall in love and are subsequently rejected but I regarded these as insufficiently socialised away from dependency on female authority figures in childhood that originated in the ideology of the agricultural revolution.

LOVE IN ALL ITS FORMS

There is a vast reservoir of writings about love by novelists, film-makers, philosophers, psychologists and others. I found Carl Jung, C S Lewis, John Bowlby, Erich Fromm and Rollo May particularly helpful. I developed a hierarchy of love as expression of intentionality arising from identity throughout the whole universe. I did my best to distinguish between levels of love and the control and feedback loops that maintained them. *Agape* rested on and included *eros*, which included *storge* which included *philia*, which included *bios*. This ideal typology provided me with the ability to focus on *eros* by specifying its relationship with *agape* and *storge* in particular. Fromm distinguished between 'standing in love' or loving and 'being in love'. I saw this as a control and feedback loop that could lead through the *coniunctio oppositorum* to autonomy from unconscious fixation on *eros* and greater openness to *agape*.

I had the example of a similar involving process of love before me in the form of *storge* or mother love. As a general principle found in all mammals, mothers 'stand in love with' their offspring who are 'in love with' their mothers. The resentment and jealousy felt by offspring, especially those with siblings, resembles that of young women in love with a man who as their lover is standing in love, like a mother in a similar situation, patiently waiting for the storms to subside. The psychological aspects of this power struggle can also be identified in homosexual relationships and, as Wilhelm Reich also points out, in political institutions. I took the unusual step of establishing a post-patriarchal marriage institution where, before any sexual consummation took place, I gave a written promise that I would not desert any young woman who had bonded with me whereas they were free to leave me without recrimination or emotional blackmail. I also made it clear that I had no intention of fathering any children. I carefully avoided any significant material dependency which would have inhibited the evolution of the love, logic, and levity of this erotic relationship based on process.

Between 1970 and 1973, a time of great interest amongst the young in sexual experimentation and gender identification, I published roneoed *samizdats* at the university of Melbourne and articles in the student newspapers describing and explaining my post-patriarchal activities which included a paradoxical 'Save the Males' campaign. In the spirit of the Fun Revolution I linked my 'modest proposal' to other humorous writers in the English tradition. I was disappointed at the lack of any intellectual feedback, but I 'carried on regardless'. I left academia in 1974 for New Zealand accompanied by Alice, my last remaining love slave, to prepare for my imaginary experiment described in my essay, 'Hunting the Boojum'.

Since that far off time the top-down, neo-Marxist Long March through the institutions which began in the universities has spread rapidly through other institutions in the welfare state and globalised corporations. Deconstruction of all human values through the application of reductionist egalitarian relativity enforced by bureaucratic power led to the emergence of what has been called the Blob. The old Jacobin dream of ending history through the application of the bureaucratic violence of the spiteful Nietzschean will to power, has resurfaced. The cruelty, stupidity, and comical absurdity of ego-driven, self-righteous political correctness is no longer justified by Marxist economic differences but solely through different inherited and relatively superficial biological characteristics. Inverted sexism and inverted racism are gaining strength. Hidden in a thicket of jargon, we are drifting from neurotic economic determinism and the instrumental conditioning of meritocracy, to narcissistic bureaucratic determinism and the emotional conditioning of 'mediocracy'. The humourless morons have taken over. Is this to prepare for the establishment of artificial intelligence mechanisms and algorithms to rule us? The first step back is to the free speech and academic integrity of the universities established in the Enlightenment.

The long march back through the history of human consciousness is a journey in virtual reality. The progressive shattering of illusions based on lies, fear and the desire to force others to obey, is a task for shamans, not for puppets of imaginary parental gods, materialistic thugs, lying politicians, idolatrous salesman of commodities and most of all not for those intellectuals who can spin words to trap us in their webs of deceit. Maintaining power by relying upon exaggerated fear of unanticipated consequences is a trap for cowards designed by cowards.

Farmers and priests despise and persecute hunter gatherers and shamans, urban business men and schoolteachers despise and persecute peasants and priests, and suburban bureaucrats and propagandists in the socialist welfare states despise and persecute entrepreneurial risk takers and non-deconstructionist scientists. At each step forward in the addiction to power that drove hunter gatherers to become farmers, then to mercantile traders, then to military-industrial nationalists, and finally to brain-washed slaves in bureaucratically-controlled, globalised *1984* super states, the balance between love, logic and levity decreases. Love becomes addiction to power, logic is reduced to group mind absurdity and only creative levity retains its ability to break the spell of fear and madness.

The Fun Revolution based on love, logic and levity is the only way to tease undone the Gordian knot of tangled consciousness. I end with a quote from a famous song of 1956 by that master of fun, Spike Milligan:

I'm walking backwards for Christmas, across the Irish Sea.
I'm walking backwards for Christmas, it's the finest thing for me.
I've tried walking sideways, and walking to the front.
But people just look at me and say... it's a publicity stunt.
So I'm walking backwards for Christmas to prove that I love you.

WORLD SYSTEMS IN COLLISION

*Paper given by The Wizard of NZ at the
International Whitehead Conference in the Azores 2017*

IN THE IRON AGE EXPERIENCED FORCES BECOME OBSERVED THINGS

During the eighth to the sixth centuries BCE the consciousness of human beings, particularly those living in the agricultural civilizations in the Fertile Crescent, underwent a profound change. I believe this was associated with a massive change in technology from the previous use of wood, stone, copper and bronze implements to the discovery of a way to smelt the widely available iron ore.

This led to more intensive ploughing, more effective weapons and the early beginnings of 'market forces'. Domesticated animals and human slaves were already treated as commodities, but the development of commodity trading of measurable things gradually began to weaken the previous influence of both magical spirits and immaterial gods.

The Babylonians began to conflate the gods with the planets which were 'things' whose movements could be observed, recorded and predicted. Writing, which began as temple records, became more and important and became the records of the words uttered by inspired religious or philosophical leaders as well as creative narratives of past events. Words already had magical powers of command associated with the words themselves inscribed on clay, stone, bamboo, papyrus or parchment. Reduction of the measurement of the value of commodities to various currencies and eventually metal coinage, as well as reduction of written language through simplified phonetic and other symbols, had taken place by the beginning of the seventh century BCE.

During the fairly short Axial Age, significant personalities appeared almost contemporaneously in China, India and the Middle East. *The Book of Changes* preceded the appearance of Daoist process philosophers and Confucius in China. The Vedas provided the ground for Buddha in India. Jewish prophets in Jerusalem arose from strict monotheism. Religious dualism and eschatology culminated in Zoroaster in Persia. Accurate astronomical measurement in Babylon led to Pythagoras and cosmology on Samos. Materialistic philosophers appeared in the new mercantile civilization developing in the Mediterranean seaports centred on Miletus. At the same time a unique process interpretation of cosmological reality was being pioneered by the aristocratic Heraclitus in Ephesus.

It is my contention that our present civilization, which is a late flowering of the Iron Age resulting from the invention of steam engines and the use of fossil fuels, has added nothing fundamentally new to the fundamental psycho-socio-cultural explanatory paradigms that were established during the Axial Age.

The mechanistic-technological world view of the materialistic Milesian branch of the Axial Age reappeared in Europe during the Renaissance and Reformation and provided the intellectual foundations for the Enlightenment and eventually what is now commonly known as the military industrial complex. By the late 19th century industrialised nations had been successful in weakening and even destroying the ruling elites and intellectual foundations of the Confucians and process philosophers in China as well as those of the agricultural, transcendentally validated religious civilizations throughout the world.

Secular governments ideologically based on the military industrial complex and aesthetic-linguistic nationalism arose during the materialistic scientific-technological revolution of the seventeenth century. This cultural process was in turn facilitated by the religious wars of the Reformation which began transforming most of Western Christendom into nation states motivated by economic development as an absolute good. With their superior mechanistic technology, they began to change the rest of the world through economic imperialism, military conquest, and the establishment of secular education.

In order to expand and increase its profits, capitalism, the characteristic form of industrial economy, externalises much of its real costs in terms of permanent environmental damage and personal economic costs to people who do not share in the profits. The final stage of capitalism has become monetised managerialism free from ethical, aesthetic or even truth values. This has provided a protective wall to protect a colossal Ponzi scheme in which an economic elite is able to practise criminal manipulation of stocks, uncontrolled debt creation and the issuing of fiat currency as information which, like electricity, is free from any material base, and hence can no longer function as a commodity.

This approaching end to the Theoretic Iron Age may be compared with the catastrophic end of the Mythic Bronze Age which preceded it. My thesis is that our psycho-socio-cultural Iron Age structures have already been fatally undermined by the fundamentally different technologies based on electricity. Once again, we shape our tools and our tools shape us. If mankind survives the impending collapse of our present global civilization, I foresee the sudden evolutionary breakthrough of a psycho-socio-cultural process cosmology. Process thinking has been greatly stimulated by metaphors derived from all-at-once electricity replacing metaphors based on the discredited, future-oriented utilitarian cause-and-effect 'time machine'.

I am going to put before you my proposal to apply a symbolic form of electro-convulsive therapy to our increasingly anxious, violent and hysterical global civilization. Before I do so I will attempt to persuade you that the actions of unique 'liminal' individuals have in the past, at specific times and in specific places, altered the world.

The triumph of our present mechanistic cosmology took place in Europe during the early 17th century, but this was not inevitable, despite the opinions of those who believe in economic determinism or historical inevitability. In this short paper, I wish to draw your attention to highly relevant events that took place in Christendom whilst the Reformation was ripping the Western Church apart. Rome and Prague were not just the centres of the two warring religious factions but also of other even more profound alternative forms of consciousness. Human understanding of the nature of the physical universe itself was about to be transformed by two men, one of whom triumphed and was later lauded as a secular saint, whilst the other disappeared into ignominious obscurity.

Galileo Galilei, a commercially-successful instrument maker of telescopes and a brilliant mechanistic experimentalist, was active in Rome while Johannes Kepler, a notable astronomer, astrologer, Platonic aesthetician and mystical Christian magician, was active in Prague. Their fortunes could not have been more different. Galileo made telescopes which he sold to the Venetian businessmen keen to know which merchant shops were first coming to port and to the navy threatened by the growing Ottoman fleet. He was now living in Florence controlled by a banking family who were his patrons. Kepler had spent years as an astronomer but he was surrounded in the magicians' city of Prague by fundamentalist puritans. He was in danger of being killed as a wizard and only just managed to save his mother from being burned as a witch.

Both men had been deeply affected by the simplicity of the heliocentric hypothesis of Copernicus the Platonist who had revived the theory of Aristarchus, an ancient Pythagorean aesthetician-astronomer, for its aesthetic appeal. The Ptolemaic epicycles, although based on the aesthetics of Platonic circles and uniform speed, were the best guide to the positions of the heavenly bodies but were absurd in terms of mechanics. There was however no observational proof of the truth of the heliocentric model as their instruments could not identify the expected stellar parallax at orbital extremes.

The observations of both Galileo and Kepler (who had to make do without a telescope since Galileo declined to supply him with one) led them to conclude that the heliocentric model was true, despite the opposition of the intellectual establishment of the time. Galileo had been on friendly terms with the Pope who was a noted scholar and talked with him in the Vatican gardens about physical cosmology.

Then suddenly the irascible Galileo, emboldened by his commercial success and friendship with the Venetian businessmen and financial rulers of Florence, lost patience. In 1632, just as the fanatical and bloodthirsty Thirty Years War was about to break out in Prague and the Ottoman Fleet was attacking in the Mediterranean, he wrote his *Dialogue Concerning the Two World Systems* and had it printed. It was not in the scholar's language of Latin but in the vulgar Italian tongue and took the form of a play where a superior intellectual, obviously Galileo, gives his reasons for believing that, in spite of appearances, the Earth goes around the Sun. One of the other two characters is convinced by his arguments, but the third, named Simplicius, insists that the Ptolemaic system is a better explanation. Some of the words put in the mouth of Simplicius are those the Pope used during his conversations with Galileo in the Vatican Gardens.

The Pope, who had no objection to scholarly debates in Latin about the heliocentric model, was understandably furious. Galileo was found guilty of heresy, forced to recant and placed under house arrest. It is not properly realised by secular intellectuals even today that papal endorsement of the new cosmology would completely destroy the physical base for the complex religious value system of integrated virtue, truth and beauty built up over generations and shared by most other major religions. It should also be appreciated that the peasants all over Europe were already frightened by the rising tension of the approaching religious civil war and the increasing attacks by the Ottoman fleet. Luther too was enraged by the disturbing idea of believing that the Earth was now not just spinning but hurtling around the Sun.

From his comfortable home, Galileo was allowed to continue his experiments and to correspond with Protestant astronomers in the North who eagerly accepted his crude mechanist world system. Since this had no messy connection with beauty nor ethics derived from the traditional religious cosmology there was nothing to stand in the way of using his ballistic model to provide the foundations for the military and industrial improvements that would enable them to defy the papal armies. This was the origin of the Military Industrial Complex currently turning the world into a bloodbath. As the magician poet Yeats put it just after the First World War in *The Second Coming*:

Things fall apart; the centre cannot hold;
Mere anarchy is loosed upon the world,
The blood-dimmed tide is loosed, and everywhere
The ceremony of innocence is drowned;
The best lack all conviction, while the worst
Are full of passionate intensity.

Meanwhile in Prague, Kepler the magician, a much better scientist than the mechanist Galileo, was playing with Platonic solids to break the spell that orbits had to be circular and planets had to move predictably. He not only worked out a Platonic solution for the elliptical orbits of the planets but also calculated that although the Earth accelerated and decelerated in its orbit it was sweeping out equal areas in a lawful manner. He did not envisage the solar system as a soulless mechanism and hypothesised that the Sun loved the planets as God loved his children, using the power of love to keep them at the right distance and providing the Earth with warmth. He also stated that the Moon affected the tides. Galileo held stubbornly on to the Platonic belief that abstract immutable laws governed the perfect heavenly realm unlike the corruptible Earth and insisted that the tides were caused by the seas sloshing about as the earth turned on its axis.

The 17th century saw the utilitarian mechanists in the industrialising countries breaking all contact with their original magician colleagues who were still maintaining connections with the traditional religious-ethical cosmology and platonic aesthetics. This fear and hostility has continued to the present day and probably accounts for the irrational rejection of process philosophy by most academics. Aesthetics and ethics and immaterial magical influences have no place in materialistic modern science. At this time throughout the

Protestant areas on the continent, thousands of people were burned, hung or drowned as witches or wizards. The Catholic Inquisition was only interested in persecuting heretics who challenged the authority of the Church.

Whilst creating my subjective process cosmology in the late sixties and early seventies I was greatly influenced not only by Teilhard de Chardin but also by Arthur Koestler's *The Sleepwalkers* of 1959, a carefully researched book on the events surrounding the adoption of the heliocentric cosmology. It is worth quoting with special emphasis from page 394 in the Penguin edition, where he is referring to Kepler's *The Harmony of the World* completed in 1618, three days after the Defenestration of Prague:

"What Kepler attempted here is, simply, to bare the ultimate secret of the universe in an all-embracing synthesis of geometry, music, astrology, astronomy and epistemology. It was the first attempt of its kind since Plato, and it is the last to our day. After Kepler, fragmentation of experience sets in again, science is divorced from religion, religion from art, substance from form, matter from mind."

There was another opportunity for the acceptance of a non-mechanistic universe when a hundred years later, the anti-social and clearly mad Newton and the charming polymath Leibniz proposed their radically different universe models, both having independently invented the calculus to do so. Newton triumphed as he had the backing of the Royal Society which was supported by the military industrial complex which had formed in England and Holland. Materialistic causation had already passed the point of no return. Writing from his remote farmhouse in New Zealand for *The Christchurch Press* newspaper in the mid 19th century, Samuel Butler used humour to make the first and best criticism of the new mechanistic theory of biological evolution.

ELECTRIC SHOCK

The mechanistic and reductionist metaphysics of the established but out-of-date scientific establishment of today, has become patently absurd 'scientism', rather than true science. Only wilfully blind academic place holders refuse to take into account the facts before them. The irreducible atoms, which as things in space had been the fundamental building blocks of the Greek materialists and their successors, had disappeared into an unpredictable cloud of dancing probabilities. Individualistic bourgeois observers have also been deconstructed by depth psychology, narratising role theory, and relativity theory and can no longer credibly position themselves outside the universe as unbiased, god-like beings to observe things objectively. Electricity, with its essentially instantaneous flow, its electrical potentials, immaterial positive and negative electro-magnetic fields, and manifesting as neither true particle nor wave, has rendered mechanical cause and effect thinking nonsensical and probability theory has replaced it. In the absence of any divinely ordained absolutes, such as time and location, probability theory and relativity theory have flourished. With the end of any belief in an absolute frame and hence absolute size, the shape of universe itself has become a choice amongst competing 'useful fictions'. The choice being made in all the current educational and scientific institutions is not based on the truth of any particular model but on its *usefulness* to the military industrial complex, which after all pays for their research and often their salaries. Just follow the money. There are a few exceptions, but they are politely sidelined.

ELECTRO CONVULSIVE THERAPY

Many patients suffering from severe anxiety and depression can be given relief by ECT treatment. This as an extreme form of treatment but is easy to administer and it is certainly better than lobotomy. The global situation is so catastrophic that a cultural revitalisation movement has become essential. Before putting before you my less interventionist form of *cultural* electro convulsive therapy, I need to explain my cosmological analysis of the process known in the literature as 'Revitalisation Movements'.

THE THEORY OF REVITALISATION AS EXPLAINED IN MY PROCESS COSMOLOGY

- The individual psycho-dynamic field of intention, as expressed in behaviour, is continuously being influenced and formed by the narrative or mythodynamic field of intention, which is expressed in role performances. Consequently, changing the narratives will lead

- to changes in role-sets in different social contexts as well as changes in mental health.
- The ideo-dynamic field of intention is acted on by feedback from the success or failure of such role performances (whether measured by desire for status, for money or for power) and this will be manifested in symbolic expressions of value made in institutional contexts. The expression of values such as truth, love, beauty, goodness, and playfulness will be prioritised or marginalised depending on the relevant institutional context.
- Cognitive dissonance in the ideo-dynamic field of intention is manifested in absurd and contradictory symbolic expressions in which values are deformed, repressed or even inverted. This is best exemplified in Max Scheler's theory of ressentiment.
- Major changes, such as religious conversion or political enlightenment, will be manifested in changes in symbolic expressions of meaning taking place within institutional contexts and by creating new roles producing new psychodynamics, which in turn produce changes in behaviour.

REVITALISING A DYING UNIVERSE

Some years ago, inspired by events during the nineteen sixties, the anthropologist Victor Turner, who had been newly converted to process metaphysics, took the first steps in constructing a theory of changes in social structures undergoing crises. He also described the potential impact of what he termed 'liminal' or outsider personalities. Such individuals were effective in deconstructing and reconstructing roles, narratives and social systems, producing temporary 'social anti-structures' and a revitalised sense of 'communitas'. Although unaware of his work, at the same time, in my liminal role of Wizard, I myself was successfully experimenting with this process in the strife-torn universities in Australia.

Revitalisation movements of this type have frequently occurred and been studied when defenceless pre-literate cultures are devastated by sudden colonialisation resulting from Western political-economic expansion. They can also be identified in sudden successful revolutions led by highly motivated, power-seeking individuals driven by ressentiment, as in such puritanical cultural phenomena as Protestant and Islamic Fundamentalism, Jacobinism, Communism and Fascism. Revitalisation movements may also be driven by love, as in Buddhism and the early Christian communities, or by beauty, as in the Romantic Revival at the beginning on the nineteenth century. Pure self-expression through dressing in colourful clothes, dancing, singing and making fun of stupid ideas and serious leaders, as during the brief period of Beatlemania, can also be a less frightening, less puritanical and more therapeutic form of revitalisation. It is this course I have chosen to take in my proposal to apply cultural ECT using the mass entertainment media, as I will explain.

Making use of social media, with YouTube as a starting point, I intend to demonstrate that, as a wizard, trickster and therapist, (not an objective scientist nor obedient servant of God) I can cast a word and number spell that will, to all intents and purposes, totally change the shape of the universe. My new universe is not only more beautiful, but more rational, more ethical, more fun and more stable than the old mechanical universe which is falling to bits. Since there is no absolute frame to the universe I recommend voting through the World Wide Web to choose the most popular. Scientists working for the military industrial complex could simply carry on using the old Enlightenment 'balls in space' model.

COPYING GALILEO AND CHANGING THE WORLD SYSTEM

STEP ONE: TURNING THE WORLD UPSIDE DOWN

After some entertaining videos on YouTube groups are formed throughout the world using the web and social media initially to pressurise for a democratic vote on whether the Earth should be shown north up or south up on all official maps. I calculate that, for various reasons, four out of five people can be persuaded to choose the south up option. Official maps would have to be amended. Like the Universe itself the Earth is, for all intents and purposes, a subjective and culturally transmitted symbolic construction based on, and including, but not determined by, lower levels of life and matter.

The Earth would have been turned upside down, but there would be no apparent change!

STEP TWO: TURNING THE UNIVERSE INSIDE-OUT

Having demonstrated the power of collective human will to transform the world in a sensational but harmless way, the newly empowered and delighted world population (especially those living around the Equator and in the Southern Hemisphere) are now ready for a much more important transformation of physical reality which will destroy the materialists' global monopoly of education, the media, and political and economic power. Another vote is taken, coordinated again through the World Wide Web, which goes even further. By avoiding the fallacy of misplaced concreteness, where we mistake our models of reality for objective 'things', we can make a collective choice for the first time and decide on the relative size and location of the Earth that will make it a more beautiful, more truthful, more moral, more stable and much larger human world system.

All size is apparent and depends on both the location of embodied, subjective observers and their belief in the model they adopt to account for what they perceive. Until now many different models have been imposed on mankind by ruling intellectual elites.

The new model is a simple conformal inversion of the traditional mathematical coordinates of the spherical model of the Earth. This produces an inside-out model of the Earth. No longer a tiny sphere surrounded by the Universe, but now apparently framing an enormous 'hollow' space containing the universe. There is no apparent change. It will look exactly the same since light rays are now travelling in accordance with the new model. There is however an important new centre to the model, a singularity which is directly above the Earth's surface, where real embodied human beings are located. The Sun and planets now circle around inside the Earth's surface. The galaxies are now hurtling inwards towards the central singularity to converge on this highest place, which is what mankind has traditionally called Heaven. Hell is now a singularity spread thinly around the outside, so the universe is now Heaven-centred! If we could drill straight down to what was the old centre of the Earth as a sphere, we would encounter the periphery of the model which, like the Big Bang, is a singularity, and we would find ourselves returning to the centre through the other side of the Earth. Materialists who have already had to swallow the singularity of the Big Bang, will certainly 'go ballistic', since the new Heaven-Centred Universe is unsuitable for calculating the trajectory of missiles.

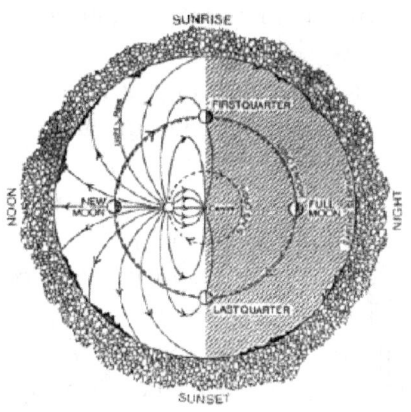

Geoperipheral Model showing the paths of light rays

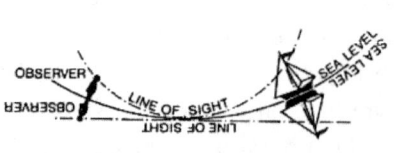

Lines of sight in both models.

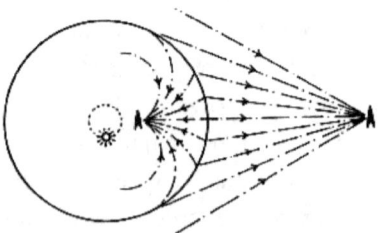

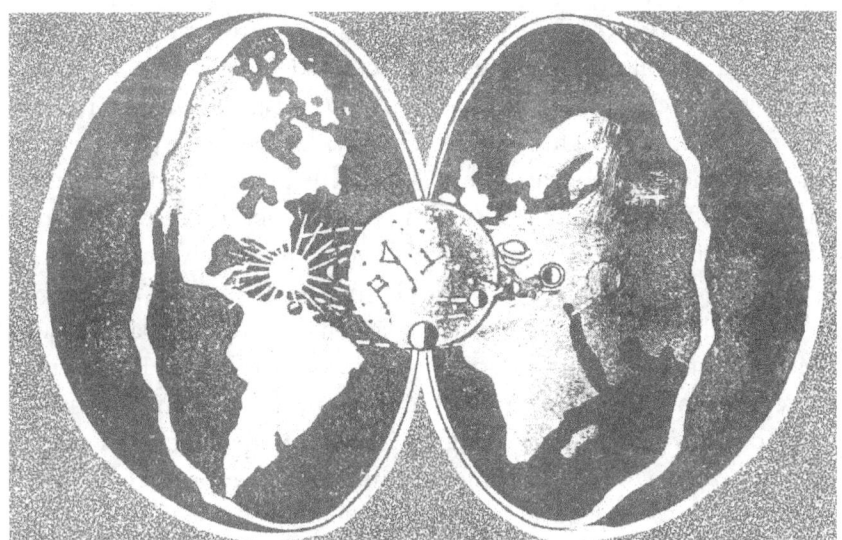

The Wizard's Inside-out Universe

UNITING TRUTH, BEAUTY AND GOODNESS IN THIS CONVERGENT, TRANSCENDENT UNIVERSE.

There is no simple reason obliging us to choose the Geoperipheral model of the universe, nor is there any rational 'true' or 'false' decision to make, but there is certainly the choice of 'useful' or 'useless'. But useful to whom? That is the question that must first be raised in our current utilitarian civilization. Having duly considered the present state of the world we can decide which model would be most useful for most human purposes. Freedom of choice, that most precious cosmic characteristic, can then be used to decide between a universe model that is beautiful or ugly, true or false, good or evil, creative or destructive. If human beings vote for it, it comes true! It becomes a symbolic reality, which is the ultimate form of reality. It is still only a man-made model, and should another wizard come along to cast a better universe-changing spell it might be transformed again. As the philosopher Whitehead pointed out, the universe is best understood not as a material thing in space, but a self-creating work of art in progress.

In his book *On the Wild Side* (1992), Martin Gardner discusses what he calls the 'hollow earth model' articulated by Abdul Abdelkader, but now 'cancelled' from the internet. According to Gardner, this hypothesis posits that light rays travel in circular paths, and slow as they approach the centre of the spherical star-filled central inner space. No energy can reach the centre of this space, which corresponds to no point a finite distance away from Earth in the widely accepted current scientific cosmology. A drill, Gardner explains, would lengthen as it travelled away from the inner space and eventually pass through the 'point at infinity' corresponding to the centre of the Earth in the current scientific cosmology. Apparently, no experiment can distinguish between the two cosmologies. Gardner notes that 'most mathematicians believe that an inside-out universe, with properly adjusted physical laws, is empirically irrefutable'. He rejects the Geoperipheral model on the basis of Occam's razor. He claims deviously that it is not a hypothesis but an illustration of the fact that any description of the physical world can be equivalently expressed in more than one way. This 'scientific obfuscation', is not a rational use of Occam's razor since it is only relevant in rejecting the model's usefulness for materialists like Gardner, but not for psychologists, environmentalists, social scientists or process theologians.

I have included some simple diagrams demonstrating some of the changes that can be made to the unverifiable assumptions underlying the heliocentric model of the solar system. By adopting the geoperipheral model as the physical frame of my postmodern cosmology, the involving and evolving concentric spheres of increasing complexity, the biosphere, psychosphere, sociosphere, noosphere, and personalitysphere, are all converging on the central singularity or heaven. The resemblance of my evolving cosmological diagrams to traditional cosmologies and the Great Chain of Being shattered by mechanists like Galileo and Newton in the 17th century is intentional.

THE WIZARD'S GREAT RESET

The only true reset is the calling of a traditional Jubilee

The genuine human values of truth, love, and beauty repel those who have become increasingly addicted to power. The Great Reset is just another call to ramp up our already fanatical ideology of technological determinism. The financial leaders of the world have combined forces to found the World Economic Forum. Working with discredited and corrupt UN agencies the Forum has declared a 'climate emergency' and a 'Great Reset' to fix it. A genuine reset means going back to the starting point or to where a mistake was made. They are using global mass media corporations to create massive panic over a slight increase in global warming whose causes, extent and consequences are still a matter of debate. This is designed to create a 'gravity well' to draw in national governments, churches, universities and schools. The Great Reset is essentially a massive extension of the technology of the Industrial Revolution which is already destroying the biosphere through untrammelled consumerism. This essay together with "The Great Leap Backward" and "The Blob", examines the only 'reset' that has the potential to really save the planet and our sanity.

As a general practice in order to project my consciousness into a hypothetical future I first send it back into my understanding of the past and then I take a running jump into a hypothetical future. In other words, *reculer pour mieux sauter*. I am obliged to take such a personal approach to the situation since I have not yet found any academic colleagues who share my particular interpretation of the direction our global civilization has taken thus far. Nor has any of them seen the point of joining me in my situationist actions since 1968 as a radical process-oriented but non-violent fun revolutionary cultural activist aiming at provoking a reassessment and reform of our contemporary value system. In the essay I provide a brief history of the evolution of consciousness which is I believe at a tipping point to also provide a summary of different social systems and the priorities of their differing cultural elites. In the spirit of postmodern consciousness I make use of the important ideas of ideal types and useful fictions which like working hypotheses in science can reduce dysfunctional cognitive dissonance produced by rival beliefs fixated on dogmatic absolutes. My aim in composing this complex essay making use of my trinity of love, logic and levity is not just explicatory but therapeutic. Christians in particular should find it thought provoking. Universalistic and individualistic Christianity as formulated by St Paul differs from the original founder's more radical aims of starting a Jewish revitalisation movement which may well have been about setting the stage for establishing a Jubilee where both spiritual and material debts are cancelled.

PART ONE

JUBILEE YEARS

With the rapid evolution of the mercantile industrial civilizations that developed in the Iron Age there was a cultural shift in the fictive values which govern all cultures from spiritual sin and salvation to monetary debt and credit. It is recorded that prior to this shift the priests and kings in the agricultural economies of the Babylonian and Sumerian Empires, the kings of the Israelite Tribal Confederacy and others, would order a Jubilee Year by fiat when all economic debts were cancelled. This enabled their people to regain power lost as a result of market forces and related phenomenon and start afresh. At this time God or the gods were regarded by religious leaders as determining the fate of peoples. Apparently the Israelites held their Jubilee Year every fifty years but also declared a fallow year every seven years to enable the soil to recover. According to Mircea Eliade, history was regarded as a 'bad thing' which led to the seizure of land, debt slavery and soil exhaustion. The king's Jubilee Year cancelled major debts so that market forces and associated activities were re-set to the starting point. Under the military rule of the Roman Empire the merchants and money lenders had taken over Europe and the Mediterranean region and declaring a Jubilee Year was no longer possible. Obviously such a political-economic act could not take place today without a fundamental change in our cultural beliefs, social institutions and psychological dispositions. Could such a radical change ever take place? I believe that this is already beginning to happen with the transformation of our civilization through the impact of electrical technology upon our literate, achievement-oriented, materialistic civilization based on out-dated Iron Age beliefs, psychological dispositions and institutions.

Only after the growth of plutocracy and tolerance of usury did events in unilinear time assume supernatural status as 'History', whose will now began to replace the will of God or the gods. To prepare for this civilizational change History's will must be divined and followed. This is particularly true of Marxists who are not only influenced by Darwin's evolutionary theory which they understand to justify merciless competition to survive and Hegel's philosophy of historical inevitability, but also a millenarian Judaeo-Christian expectation of 'year zero', the end of the present world.

A SPIRITUAL JUBILEE IN JUDEA

An example of human intervention in another form of fictive debt reduction, which had immense consequences for human spiritual development, took place two thousand years ago in Jerusalem. Jewish prophets represent a long tradition of brave attempts to reform the behaviour of their corrupt priests in the centralised temple bureaucracy in Jerusalem. Judea was a theocracy with a monopoly not only of religious beliefs and practices but also to a large extent of Jewish political-economic authority. At the time Judea was occupied by the legalistic Roman Imperialists. Without a tradition of the separation of powers and no king at the head of an army to provide political control, theocracies have to rely on their monopoly over sin and redemption to govern their people and soon become corrupt and inefficient.

As a kind of prophetic figure myself, though exemplary rather than exhortatory, I assume that John the Baptist who was immersing Jews in the sacred river Jordan was claiming that this radical new ritual would take away the huge, ever-increasing spiritual debt of inherited original sin. Following baptism, they would no longer need to seek redemption by buying sacrificial offerings from the vendors in the temple. Jesus left John and set out on his roving mission of healing through forgiveness as a means of removing sin. His claim of a mandate from his heavenly father was essential for this to work and led to the belief that he was a god in human form, common at the time in the classical world but quite alien in Judaism. Where John acted like a king and high priest, perhaps preparing to declare a jubilee year and to cancel all debts, Jesus, as the Teacher of Righteousness, demonstrated by example how individuals could remain as much as possible spiritually debt free. This was through the revolutionary process of not only loving a forgiving God but also loving oneself and one's neighbours, and even one's enemies. 'Forgive us our sins as we forgive them that sin against us.' The words debt and sin have identical meanings in most languages. The assumption is still that no one is perfect and above God's law. Whatever else may have been misrepresented or added in the Gospels, the *Lord's Prayer* must be considered authentic. Jesus' mission concluded with what must have been portrayed by the Jewish theocracy as a challenge to the Roman authorities. It was as 'King of the Jews' or INRI that he was crucified as a criminal against the state. This would only make sense if the Romans believed he was leading a movement for the declaration of a Jubilee Year by fiat. Paul, a Roman citizen, drew the teeth of this attack on usury and debt slavery by taking a nationalistic Jewish revitalisation movement and transforming it into a universalistic millenarian religion that did not seriously conflict with the ethical requirements of legalistic imperial power of Rome as a militaristic plutocracy.

Through their policy of 'rendering unto Caesar what are Caesar's' the early universalised Christian Church was successful in providing sociable community structures for the alienated polyglot population of the collapsing Roman Empire, rich and poor, slave and freeman, and male and female. However the cultural strength that follows the cleansing of the soul through this type of Spiritual Jubilee also demonstrates that it had the potential for providing the conditions for an Economic Jubilee. In the early centuries of Christianity, Canon law, administered by reasonably autonomous bishops, operated largely independently from the varying secular laws. This enabled the Christians to avoid corruption by usury and live fairly peacefully side by side with very different invading barbarians who were rapidly converted to the new tolerant, flexible and universalistic religion. From the eleventh to the thirteenth century, Feudal Europe was transformed culturally and reached a germinal point in balanced human cultural creativity that in my opinion has not been surpassed.

A decline set in soon afterwards when, influenced by values of the old Roman Empire, the Papacy having split from the Eastern Church, changed into a political institution and became more concerned with secular power over the people and more tolerant of usurious banking practices. At the end of the Renaissance some Protestants actually endorsed the idea that abundance of material possessions gained through hard work in the business world was a sign of divine favour, even salvation, but spending money on personal display and having fun was sinful. Modern capitalism, like its shadow form socialism, owes much of its moral authority and puritanical psychological repression to this combination of materialism and earnest self-righteousness.

CANCELLING ECONOMIC DEBTS

Before proceeding further in my argument, I must advise readers that I am proposing a solution that would only be possible if our present civilization underwent a transformation as fundamental as that which ushered in the mercantile-industrial societies which succeeded the great agricultural civilizations. During the long Iron Age, the major religious societies based on fertility values and expanding by military conquest were progressively taken over by the mercantile civilizations based on production and imperial expansion through trading regardless of religious affiliation. Land began to lose its pre-eminent value to be replaced by capital. Banks, office blocks universities and factories replaced churches, monasteries and castles. During the Renaissance in Europe bankers became popes and material welfare gradually replaced spiritual welfare as the ultimate value.

As the economist Michael Hudson points out, the plutocratic Roman Empire was set against any attempt to declare a Jubilee Year and invaded the Macedonian Greek kingdom to stop them from holding one. I claim that returning to this ancient practice is not only possible but essential. Since this is more a polemic than an academic dissertation I hope it will provoke thought and direct readers towards the thinkers whose works I refer to in passing.

PART TWO

THE CURRENT REVOLUTION IN CONSCIOUSNESS

During the late 1960s, the universities of the literate world were swept by apparently irrational youth movements. One of these was a traditional millenarian desire to overthrow capitalist society and usher in an egalitarian socialist utopia. The other was something quite unique to our civilization and had more in common with the pre-literate revitalisation movements which were the subject of the lectures I was giving as a newly-appointed sociologist at the University of NSW in Sydney. The Hippie phenomenon which started on the West Coast of the USA was closely associated with the new more sensual popular music of the time which had broken free from control by record companies and radio stations. Many of the hippies were influenced by the Esalin Institute in California and were concerned with consciousness raising and creating new forms of communal living based on love, even in the cities. Such communities were previously only associated with escapist religious cults and were rural based. Previously esoteric interest in magic and Eastern philosophy became more common. I was deeply impressed by the suddenness of this short-lived psychedelic phenomenon. Their leaders were young and naïve and were quickly politicised, commercialised or marginalised. However, the movement has left a deep influence amongst those of us who experienced it and are disenchanted with the increasingly bureaucra-

Wizard Rituals

tised, politically-correct, and more and more corrupt mainstream, which I refer to as the irresponsible, characterless, treacherous and power-obsessed Blob. I refer the reader to my essay on this topic. On a more uplifting topic the Boy Scout movement founded by the English military hero Baden Powell is well worth consideration since it is the most successful revitalisation movement since the great religions were founded. No political or bureaucratic leadership was imposed from above and no future promises were made of a utopia on earth or immortality in heaven. Although based on loyalty and self-discipline it was in its founder's words ultimately 'all for fun'. Nevertheless within a few years millions and millions of boys from different cultures all over the world, attracted by the founder's social programme of living like troops of nomadic hunter gatherers, had rushed to join. Baden Powell's experiences at the hands of his domineering mother had made him determined to remain a boy, at least psychologically. When puberty strikes with its usual impact on the self-confidence and autonomy of boyhood the Boy Scout movement loses much of its relevance and appeal.

Alf's Imperial Army. "Slaughter at Ilam." Early 1980s at Canterbury University.

PROCESS THINKING REPLACES SUBJECT/OBJECT BIFURCATION.

Readers may find my frequent use of the first person in my writings off-putting. I agree but I can find no other way of avoiding fake objectivity and inauthentic generalised statements that protect one from confrontation with other thinkers dealing with the same issues. One of the biggest changes that has taken place in all fields of the scientific paradigm since the nineteen sixties, when I was giving the first lectures in sociological theory in Australia, has been the shift in emphasis away from taxonomy and structural analysis towards interest in process. Scientists are also beginning to subscribe less to the irrational and dangerous fiction that we can somehow be objective and avoid bringing our personal material and ideal interests into our observations, better called 'experiences'. Nor can we directly apprehend phenomena without some existing meaningful theoretical frame or form to make sense of what we experience.

The scientific method is an indispensable process which enables us to distinguish truth from wishful thinking and blind belief, but it does not make us into dispassionate gods. Iain McGilchrist's recent influential book, *The Master and His Emissary*, investigates the important influence of the dynamic interaction of the left and right hemispheres in our brains relating to our cultural assumptions. The right hemisphere, which is predominantly reflective and generates meaning and context, has been marginalised in our intellectual institutions in favour of the left, which is predominantly instrumental and essentially meaningless. In addition, as Louis Sass points out in *Madness and Modernism*, we should be aware that over the past two centuries our civilization has been becoming increasingly schizoid. Many modern artists being celebrated and rewarded financially just for being original show traces of schizophrenic alienation from coherent personal identity and meaning. This is further encouraged in the social sciences which have moved away from the theories of their founders Durkheim and Weber who were concerned with values, towards out-dated Marxist political-economic philosophy concerned with power. It is being realised that the Sociology of Religion has become the Religion of Sociology.

I was first awakened to the importance of the transformative nature of the forms of communication itself by Marshall McLuhan, the 'electronic prophet'. The theory, that the means of communication significantly determines the nature of the message, was very influential at the time. I was also influenced by ideal typologies, used extensively in the sciences as way of simplifying and separating complex phenomena from their contexts so they could be handled conceptually. Max Vaihinger's neglected theory of useful fictions in *As If* provides the grounds for such a practice. In particular Max Weber's ideal typology of social stratification based on status, class and power and their inter-relationship has proved essential. For psychological 'reflexivity', I found Max Scheler's modification of Nietzsche's theory of 'ressentiment', together with depth psychology and the links between ethological theories of inherited behaviour and Jung's cross-cultural psychological evolutionary modification of Freud most helpful. Above all I owe a great deal to Johann Huizinga's classic, *Homo Ludens, the Play Element in Culture*.

Looking back to understand my partly intuitive social actions since 1968 which led to my personal reinvention as a reflexive, role-acting and liminal wizard, I am indebted to the theoretical writings of the anthropologist Victor Turner. He describes, analyses and experiments in those occasions when in times of crisis rigid bureaucratic social structures undergo sudden temporary transformations into what he calls social anti-structures which are accompanied by liminality. I am also influenced by the sociologists of religion and neuroscientists for their studies of the Axial Age transformation of human consciousness which helped me make sense of my own unorthodox perception of reality. Partly influenced by phenomenological philosophy, I realise I have a strong right hemispheric interest in context and playful being rather than earnest, linear, sequential and digital information-processing. Julian Jaynes' description of evolved human consciousness as 'a narratizing analogue "I" in metaphoric mind space', is thought provoking, though I prefer 'mythical/ideological space' to the reductionist concept of 'mind space'. Jaynes' rather simplistic early theory on the role of the cerebral hemispheres has been greatly revised and improved by Iain McGilchrist. To summarise, consciousness is an evolutionary process expressed communally through mimesis which includes not only mathematics and metaphorical language but gesture, images, music and dance, all of which provide operating systems and complex play forms.

I will attempt to show how these ideas interact with each other in a reflexive process. Having put together a process cosmology of my own in 1972, I have been using this interconnected set of theoretical propositions as the structure for the psychological, social and cultural experiments I have been carrying out since that time. Reference to my basic *Tree of Life* and *Hierarchy of Kinematics* process diagrams should elucidate the points I am making. The process cosmologies of Teilhard de Chardin and A.N. Whitehead, and the so-called grand action theory of the social scientist Talcott Parsons also provided me with an alternative to the present reductionist scientific paradigm which can no longer be rationally justified and has become a threat to our continued existence.

USEFUL FICTIONS

Before proceeding any further in proposing a solution to the global economic problem, an important concept I will use throughout this argument is that human culture relies upon useful fictions. Useful fictions have real outcomes as events which can be interpreted by human beings and put into narrative structures or built into models of reality which are of course themselves useful fictions. Culture itself is created by human beings over time and provides us not only with meaning but with useful concepts, models and practices that enable us to relate to the world we are born into and have to learn to live in. Both words and numbers can be understood to be operating systems that we have created for their usefulness in social integration and adaptation as well as their aesthetic delight. There is an ever-present temptation to mistake our useful fictions for transcendental entities that exist like Platonic forms in some higher reality. Fictions are indistinguishable from cultural reality itself. The important fact is that they can modified or abandoned when their usefulness has been overtaken by more convincing fictions, their aesthetic appeal has become repulsive, or their ethical guidelines destructive to social cohesion.

Usefulness, as a concept justifying certain of our fictions, is of course not an absolute value but varies with historical conditions and the values of the ruling elite. The process philosopher Whitehead reminded us, again and again, that even time and location are abstractions that we are in continual danger of reifying. This is an error of consciousness which he called the 'fallacy of misplaced concreteness'. Religious belief in supernatural beings, patriarchy and spiritual immortality, although fallaciously regarded at the time as concrete or real phenomena were vitally important as the useful fictions or working hypotheses that provided the foundation for the great cultural advance from simple nomadic hunter-gatherer societies to the highly complex cities of the agricultural empires particularly in fertile river valleys. In such societies, military leaders and high priests exercised their authority in the name of transcendental immortal gods, and controlled behaviour of their large populations through such useful fictions as salvation from spiritual indebtedness, or sin. Referring to the higher authority in whose name they acted, meant they hoped to avoid being held accountable by critics.

THE AXIAL AGE

When a way to smelt the more commonly available iron ore was discovered, the primitive Bronze Age technology of communication was completely transformed, especially through the sudden expansion of markets and trading with its universalising effects. In the early Iron Age between the seventh and sixth centuries BCE, the so-called Axial Age, prophets, sages and philosophers appeared and gave us most of our present major cultural paradigms. It is also important but rarely recognised that there has been very little change since the Axial Age in the useful fictions legitimising both agricultural and mercantile industrial civilizations that originated in China, India, Mesopotamia, the Middle East, Egypt, and Europe. The main difference, which still remains, was between the transcendental religions of Eurasia and the materialistic reductionism of the natural philosophers which originated in the Greek port of Miletus and which underwent further development during the Renaissance and Reformation to become the paradigm of democracy and scientific technology.

The core values in this region shifted from fertility and ecological stability to productivity and trading expeditions, political structures were also becoming more egalitarian. Political consensus was often reached in the independent city states following a skilled oratorical performance in front of an urban crowd who had lost their tribal or familial connections. The People's Mandate or Democracy is essentially a reductionist theatrical political system based on the useful fiction of 'representation' where the votes of the spellbound lowest common denominators are counted to reach digitised decisions. It is no coincidence that the Greeks who invented both theatre and democracy also perfected coinage (the digital symbolic valuation of goods and services) and the alphabet (the digital reduction of literate symbolic communication of intent and meaning into combinations of individual letters).

Obviously, what is useful for an agricultural religious monarchy and what is useful for a plutocratic mercantile democracy will be very different. Egalitarian extremes can be reached in puritanical political structures where education and propaganda are controlled by humourless, materialistic, bureaucrats. As early as the fifth century BCE Plato was proposing such a totalitarian republic strictly controlled by an elite of mathematically-sophisticated intellectuals like himself. The perfection of both coinage and alphabets by the early trading civilizations in the Mediterranean as abstract and stripped-down digitised means of communication had profound psychological implications that are hard to overestimate. They may have provided the model for the Greek materialistic philosophers' conceptual reductionism of all reality to a substratum of identical, irreducible and re-combinable things they called 'atoms'. In the name of Reason, the transgressive French revolutionaries took reductionist mensuration further through forcibly introducing metrication to replace all previous measures (derived from the human body and common human activities) with meaningless fractions of an essentially absurd absolute by adopting the highly unsuitable number ten as their base in mathematical measurement and calculation.

THE NEED FOR ANOTHER EVOLUTIONARY ADVANCE IN CONSCIOUSNESS

The neglected Daoist process philosophers of China, and independently Heraclitus of Ephesus, provide a way out from the irreconcilability of dogmatic reductionism and dogmatic transcendentalism by avoiding both absurd Cartesian Dualism and irrational transcendental Platonic Idealism. Old metaphysical meaning systems need to be modified in the new Electric Age transformations of the means of communication. This does not mean they should be regarded as no more than conscious frauds or superstitious follies designed to maintain the power of ruling elites or the self-deluding rationalisations that Marx, Nietzsche and Freud sometimes seem to imply.

These metaphysical systems have had immensely important consequences for the cultural evolution of mankind but it is time for us to accept the fact that the universe, in which we are embedded, is not the creation and plaything of the gods, nor a machine driven by blind material forces. It is a self-organising process which evolves through experiential playfulness.

I cannot imagine living in a world which would consign *Gilgamesh*, the *Iliad*, the *Odyssey*, the *Aeneid*, the *Divine Comedy* and *Paradise Lost* to the rubbish bin along with the stories, the heartfelt cries of the prophets and the psalms of the Old Testament, just because we no longer believe in the gods the way we used to. Such cultural treasures as the music, poetry, theatre, art, sculpture and architecture inspired by Christianity in Europe have made us what we are by deepening our psyches, improving our awareness and inspiring us to live ethically. Modern Science, born in the magic of the Renaissance and perfected in the mechanisms of the Enlightenment, has kept us from superstitious follies, even though, like all dogmatic self-righteous belief systems, it has given us dangerous and destructive follies of its own.

THE MODERN REBELLION IS COMING TO AN END

The puritanical and schizoid modern movement that began over a century and a half ago was driven by a highly emotional but ambivalent rejection of the past by transgressive intellectuals together with an implied millenarian expectation that once we are free of superstition and the unquestioning acceptance of traditional beliefs and practices, we will enter a new Age of Reason. Their belief that time is a unilinear process leading, with occasional dark ages, to a perfect moment when all their dreams of perfection would be realised, is fundamentally insane. In the early 20th century, when the complacent culture of the time was being undermined by early globalisation and compensated for through jingoistic nationalism, modernism as a belief system proved a useful fiction for the rapid growth of both immoral laissez-faire capitalism and irrational egalitarian socialism, but it has now passed its usefulness. The self-righteous modern enthusiasm for spoiling the rules of the traditional game is being itself undermined by the ironic playfulness of sceptical non-millenarian Postmodernism.

KICKING AWAY THE LADDERS

Revelations ascribed to transcendental realities have provided the ladders which we have climbed to become more human. Such transitional ladders or bridges have fulfilled the same pre-adaptive function at all levels of evolution. Acknowledging the fact that as cultural beings we cannot escape living in useful fictions would enable us to avoid treating them as absolutes and instead to take them less seriously. This would allow them to gradually lose their traditional hold over us. Gödel's Incompleteness Theorem enables us to give up believing the Pythagorean view that mathematics is an infallible operating system for uncovering the truth and Humpty Dumpty will always remind us that the true meaning of words ultimately depends on those who control the verbal communication system. We must not forget however, unlike extreme postmodernists, that socially, psychologically, and especially biologically, there are parameters which are fundamental and not just fictional, but how we interpret their significance will still depend on the cultural meaning we assign to them.

Old fashioned, reductionist scientists still mock religion and fictional narratives as untrue, deny multi-level evolution, and continue to believe the absurd fiction that the whole is no more than the sum of its simplest parts. They are as dogmatic as those serious fundamentalists who believe that their holy books are the Word of God and therefore the absolute truth and not useful fictions. No-one is more dogmatic than those people in charge of the world economy who believe that economic development and making a profit is the only meaning of life and who are prepared to destroy the earth, family cohesion and mental health in their pursuit of it.

We cannot live without useful fictions like money and credit, but if these become valued above all other values they become not just absurd but highly destructive. A Jubilee or just a major reform in banking practices, currency stabilisation and credit creation out of thin air is well overdue. Perhaps liminal cyber currencies like Bitcoin or a return to the gold standard could help provide this.

EXAMPLES OF USEFUL FICTIONS

To return to the topic of Max Vaihinger's theory of useful fictions in general. Some useful fictions, such as the hypothetical constructs of mathematics and language, are indispensable operating systems. Some fictions are nonsensical and useless, even if sometimes providing therapeutic, escapist entertainment, others may pass their use-by- date and disappear, and some may become dangerous and need to be exposed as such. Some fictional constructs are useful in providing bridges that, although replaced, eventually lead to more useful fictions. In this respect, cultural evolution is like all other forms of evolution.

The Babylonian belief that the planets were gods led to the close study of the movements of the heavenly bodies and that led to both astrology and astronomy. Ptolemy's complex system of epicycles, although absurd, was not only beautiful in Platonic terms, but was also indispensable for navigation. It was a necessary bridge in producing later more accurate heliocentric models of solar system mechanics. Atoms although no longer credible as the indivisible building blocks of the material universe can still function as useful fictions when extracted from their processual environment. The same applies to other useful abstracted fictions such as genes, the psyche, social roles, values, symbols, et cetera. The useful fiction of supernatural beings provided a bridge between small nomadic hunting bands and large urban settlements and eventually to our contemporary global civilization. Useful fictions such as biological patriarchy, sin and immortality made the agricultural civilizations possible. Many people consider God or the gods as outdated fictions that are no longer useful but they are not usually aware that various forms of money and credit are also useful fictions that may eventually pass their use-by-date and become dangerous fictions. I believe that has happened.

All governments need useful fictions to create and maintain their authority. In plutocratic-democratic societies money and debt dependency are increasingly used to control people in the same way that sin and penance were used in many theocratic- agricultural societies. Economic Development is a useful fiction to justify plutocracies, the Will of the Gods, or The Mandate of Heaven are useful fictions justifying theocracies, and The People's Will or The Mandate of the People are useful fictions to legitimate the government in bureaucratic egalitarian welfare states, and in totalitarian states where the army rules in alliance with a bureaucratically structured political party.

PART THREE

CULTURAL EVOLUTION

We need to agree that it appears that the whole universe is evolving, not only physically but genetically, neurophysiologically, socially and, in the case of human beings, culturally. In fact, the evolution of human beings as organisms has greatly slowed down and we are now fast evolving as an inter-communicating cultural phenomenon. As I have mentioned, in terms of joint social and cultural evolution it has been convincingly argued that without the useful fiction of supernatural beings, human social groups could not have evolved beyond the size of an extended family or small clan. The recent excavation of Göbeckli Tepe in Turkey may have revealed the place where this transition actually took place in Eurasia. Once established it led to the Agricultural Revolution and transcendental authority to overrule purely personal authority within a small clan. Land title, the division of labour, domestication of plants and animals and population expansion, can then follow. The value complexes that were embedded in the religious cosmologies of the most powerful agricultural civilizations centred on land ownership, fertility, and obedience to the will of the gods which was usually rewarded by various forms of biological, social, or cultural immortality after death.

The powerful mercantile industrial societies that replaced them have done so with an ideology based on materialism, universalism, utilitarianism in terms of achieving a vague utopian goal, and mechanistic causation. The value complexes became centred on productivity, economic utility, and material accumulation as symbolic demonstration of status. These are implemented by government-legitimated money systems and legal protection for usurers, and enforced by impersonal bureaucratic legalism. Paper money is essentially a legal contract promising material redemption. Banks are authorised and protected by governments holding a monopoly of political power to issue coinage, print money and to make loans of fictional currency not even in their possession. As soon as this imaginary money is borrowed it becomes a debt in terms of 'real' money.

There is an obvious parallel with salvation as a cultural control system such as when the Renaissance Papacy held a monopoly over spiritual salvation. At times Popes even issued certificates confirming that on payment of specific sums of money certain souls would have their period of incarceration in purgatory reduced, as digitally calculated by the Church. Many of the major religious buildings of the Counter-Reformation were financed in this way.

What happens when the global system of indebtedness loses credibility and the bears get loose in the stock markets? Should this happen, and it is certainly within the bounds of possibility, what control will governments and commercial enterprises have if they can no longer reward their electors and employees with wages and material goods? Before I put forward my solution I will try and describe the various aspects of this situation as I see it.

SOCIAL STRUCTURES ARE BASED ON STATUS, CLASS AND POWER

Before recommending any form of drastic cultural engineering it is vital to grasp the principles which, under most historical conditions, determine the structuring of social systems. No single one of these stratification differentiations based on power, class and status is sufficient to maintain a social structure, but one may predominate and largely determine the others. Power or the ability to enforce one's will over others may seem to be an all-important structural determining factor in certain historical societies but is not a sufficient condition, as the allocation of material resources and display of status must also be dealt with. Another principle is what Max Weber called Class, meaning control over material resources; this may be the pre-eminent determining factor but status and power needs must be met. Status or respect is the other principle that structures social systems. In our current puritanical egalitarian zeitgeist modified by bureaucratic meritocracy and obsession with mass-media manufactured 'celebrities', status based on virtue or honour is less appreciated and rarely commented on dispassionately. Weber was concerned that since personal charisma has always been supressed by bureaucrats this could result in our own culture becoming over-rational and dehumanised.

STATUS

The best examples of stratification controlled by status can be found in tradition-based aristocracies. The ruling elite, who have a monopoly of respect, are usually linked to specific geographic locations by family of origin, land ownership and intermarriage. Their authority is maintained by birth in an existing aristocratic family and such visible evidence as displays of difficult performance skills that require time and training, and special clothing, which is either too expensive or which others are forbidden to wear. Showing good manners and a relaxed self confidence in their attitude to those lower in the social hierarchy also compels respect. Although traditional ethical practices and values are encouraged as stabilising conservative forces, the lack of restraints over the personal beliefs and behaviour of the aristocratic elite can sometimes prove them more adaptive to changing circumstances than other ruling elites.

CLASS

In plutocracies the power of the ruling elite is based on their ownership and control of material resources, which may be inherited by birth in a wealthy family, gained by entrepreneurial skills in commodity trading or, increasingly today, by the manipulation of immaterial resources such as credit. Such societies develop rapidly by encouraging new technologies of production and financing, scientific education and research, the exploration and exploitation of resources, secularisation of values, urbanisation, and free trade. Plutocracies are continuously admitting new members into the elite but as time passes the entrepreneurial skills that led to their rise might not be passed on to their offspring. Newly wealthy individuals need to make great efforts to acquire respect to maintain their power over the remaining impoverished aristocrats, over their rivals in the business world and over the envious poor. Literacy and education have always been seen by the nouveau riche as essential institutions in their need to replace the aristocratic status system based on manners, tradition, skill in hunting, war, and governing. They achieve this with their own meritocratic values based on the acquisition of wealth and power through trading and manufacture. For them social status is exhibited through display of expensive goods rather than by polite manners, prowess in hunting and war and good taste, which take time to acquire.

POWER

The best examples of coercive power as the determining factor in social stratification can be seen in dictatorships. It is difficult to maintain authority by coercive power alone. In totalitarian socialist dictatorships like North Korea and China, social structures are mainly sustained by the military in alliance with a single party monopoly of bureaucratic authority. Nevertheless, it is still essential for the rulers to control the allocation of resources and to monopolise all public communication to prevent any loss of respect or status for the dictator. Aristocrats maintain their authority through skilled performance, plutocrats maintain their authority by controlling the markets and availability of capital, and dictators maintain their authority by total control of coercive force and public communication.

PSYCHOLOGICAL AND SOCIAL FACTORS

This socio-cultural typology is largely taxonomic and is useful for identification of different socio-cultural ideal types but it is important to examine those processes that sustain, modify, or transform them. We must also bear in mind that social scientists themselves occupy roles in social structures and being neither omniscient nor 'objective' cannot avoid personal bias in their analysis. Even as a shaman, prophet, social scientist and living work of art, the author of this essay is bound to be biased. All social actors are psychological beings, and sociologists who do not take this into account, produce very unrealistic theories. We are not living machines, as Nietzsche put it 'we are human, all too human'.

At the social level, the theory of useful fictions based on an elite determination of what is useful, is limited by such non-voluntaristic factors as the determination of social role allocation at birth. Psychologically, although we are one species, we obviously vary in gender, maturity, intellectual and physical abilities and inherited neural predispositions to respond. The effect of education in making a difference has been greatly exaggerated by those who put their faith in the 'operant conditioning' of education. Another psychological factor that should be considered when investigating sudden transformations in social structures, is ressentiment. Revolutionaries are often people exuding self-loathing produced by guilt over their own gender, race or family income. They are generally puritanical and intolerant and are keen to gain personal power by acting as leaders of those who find being portrayed as victims enables them to develop a powerful sense of entitlement.

People interested in the psychological phenomenon of ressentiment, a very common and very powerful form of irrational emotion, should consult the writings of Max Scheler. Pity, as distinct from empathy, is frequently a self-deceptive desire to control others through emotional manipulation.

HISTORICAL FACTORS

My own studies in revitalisation and millenarian movements have made me acutely aware of the importance of sudden transformations or phase changes from one form of stratification to another during times of upheaval. On these occasions, certain individuals in what Victor Turner calls liminal roles may act in a way that produces what he calls social anti-structures. These temporary states weaken the role structures that maintain traditional role relationships and may act as transitions to reformed social systems. The changes may be towards greater bureaucratic coercion over the commercial and status institutions, as in the French and Russian Revolutions and the German Third Reich. They may lead towards greater power and status for those who have control of material resources as in the Glorious Revolution of the Whigs in England in 1688 and the American Revolution they carried out a century later. Sometimes those who control the status system bring the merchants and bankers under more control as in the Romantic Revival of the Monarchy and the Anglican Church in the UK in the 19th century.

A guiding processual principle should be the recognition that the behaviour of the wealthiest people can only be brought under control by genuine offers of high status, such as inheritable noble titles. Coercion works badly on them since they will profit financially by publishing, printing and selling books and tracts advocating the destruction of their own wealthy class; they will even sell weapons to revolutionaries and will lend money to any successful new revolutionary leaders in their bankrupted states.

LA TRAHISON DES CLERCS

The literate elite in their authoritarian managerial hierarchies who currently control the educational institutions together with the media commentariat have been conditioned by modernist ideology which sees traditional hierarchical structures based on other values than naked power, like truth, beauty and goodness, as irrelevant, insane or evil. They consequently tend to foresee the future as a time of yet unrealised and unspecified egalitarianism, peace, love and happiness which using their growing power they will bring about like Marx's 'midwives of history'. They have little objection to global economic 'super imperialism' which, with its commercial media control, falsely portrays itself as egalitarian, anti-imperialist and free from subjective values but which is rapidly destroying traditional cultures who have for centuries been adjusted to their natural environments. Their elitist idealism leads them to regard even the best forms of politically honest and responsible imperialistic nationalism as totally evil without explanation. Their idealistic antipathy to inherited status as opposed to meritocracy is also unthinking.

Meritocrats are often socialised without any sense of duty, honour or ethical behaviour. They control the educational institutions with their ubiquitous certifications. But who controls the meritocrats? University graduates, now being called Weirds (western, educated, industrialised, and rich democrats) by radical eco-anthropologists, are now pouring out from the universities. They have established a monopoly of power in the forcible administration of economic super imperialism and have no interest in, or even comprehension of, the religious and magical world views of the 'under-developed' peoples whose traditional sustainable cultures they destroy without compunction. *Seeing like a State*, by James C. Scott, is a carefully researched and well-written historical account of the appalling consequences of rule by simple-minded fanatical ideologues he calls 'high modernists'.

PART FOUR

MAN'S RELATIONSHIP TO THE MEANS OF COMMUNICATION

Another factor more important than status, economic power, or naked coercion, and which has been neglected in traditional analyses, is the form in which values in meaning systems are communicated. My proposal requires the realisation that the Marxist principle that 'man's relationship to the means of production', although important, is not the key to identifying which values drive the mercantile-industrial civilizations. Nor is it true to assume that 'man's relationship to the means of reproduction' is the key to identifying the values which drove the earlier agricultural civilizations. It is my assumption that 'man's relationship to the means of communication' is the fundamental key to understanding not only the foundation of both the reproductive values of the great agricultural societies and the production values of the great mercantile-industrial imperialistic societies but also the qualitatively different, post-industrial global consumerist society that has been growing exponentially since the late 19th century.

Palaeontologists, neuro-scientists, sociologists of religion, archaeologists and others have been tracing the evolution of homo sapiens over the past half million years from simple non-verbal mimesis of the various early hominoids, to the development of speech, grammar, and finally writing, when cultural concepts can be systematised, indexed and stored. Before writing, psychological and social structures were not only based on mimesis but were increasingly determined by speech, although there were primitive accounting records on clay, bark, bamboo or wood that were essential for temple control of surplus food especially in fertile river valleys. The sudden increased availability of metal in the Iron Age was a contributing factor to the explosion of consciousness in the Axial Age. It is important to bear in mind that language, like mathematics, is essentially an operating system but which, especially through metaphors, forms the very nature of the concepts capable of being expressed by it. 'The Medium is the Message'.

THAUMATOCRACY

A wide repertoire of performance and mimetic skills was required of the world's oldest profession, the shaman. Ultimate authority in the hunter-gathers (who sometimes practised limited agriculture and herding) was nevertheless vested in these first professional human specialists. As I understand it, these individuals interpreted dreams and visions, kept memory records and performed healing whilst chanting and dancing. Intoxicants were frequently used to heighten the atmosphere at the frequent ceremonies where not only dancing and chanting but enacted story-telling took place. There was some division of labour, and fairly strict discrimination between male and female roles so they cannot be seen as egalitarian in the same way as in those socialist states or communes where sexual equality is morally and legally enforced by the ruling elite of bureaucrats who are themselves of course 'more equal than others'. However, we must be careful not to idealise these sometimes rather violent cultures.

ARISTOCRACY

In the Bronze Age a governing aristocratic warrior class emerged out of the settled and mainly peaceful Neolithic farming communities. Empowered by the use of bronze weapons and armour they established small towns around temple complexes administered by priests who developed simple systems of written records enabling the collection and storage of food to see them through bad harvests and to put on collective feasts. In fertile river-valleys large populations could be supported through irrigation and large towns could develop. These complex and more highly populated agricultural civilizations develop patriarchal family structures and hierarchical social structures based on fertility needs. These were based on the division of labour and maintained by specialists in coercion, in alliance with specialists in metaphysical explanation. Major projects, like temple and tomb building, dam construction and irrigation, often used voluntary skilled labour rewarded with good food and accommodation as well and not just slaves captured in war.

The main means of communication that structured and legitimated these civilizations was the spoken word. Pictographs and ideographs were displayed on important buildings since meaning is not only communicated through speech or phonetic writing. It was the speech of the gods that motivated almost all meaningful action. The gods would sometimes appear to those specialists who received revelation but hearing the voice of a god in a sacred place or from the mouth of an idol was the most important form of cultural communication. Obedience to this parental form of authority was not subject to rational criticism and this form of government is sometimes referred to as 'hypnocracy'.

Priests had a monopoly of what little writing there was and were the guardians of the revealed truth. Oral storytelling introduced heroic narratives and began the process which evolved into self-reflective consciousness. Sociologists of religion describe this as the Mythic Age. Public responsiveness to this form of authority can still be seen at major commercial entertainment events like rock concerts but is also manifested in military rallies in totalitarian states. The Coronation of the British Monarch is a perfect example of the power of this ancient and largely mimetic form of cultural communication which still makes a huge popular impact on all levels of society. Literate political scientists are at a loss in trying to explain it, dismissing it as an outdated ceremony which will not survive the unstoppable march of their own progress to an imaginary, rational, and republican utopia.

PLUTOCRACY

The Iron Age arose during the centuries of the dark ages which followed the catastrophic collapse of the Bronze Age. Metal tools and weapons were suddenly more freely available and facilitated the establishment of markets and the building of boats and wheeled vehicles. This led in turn to widespread trading networks and rapid military conquest. Both pictographic and phonetic writing flourished and traditional oral narratives were written down and communicated as were the new revelations of holy men and wise men who appeared in great numbers in the early years of the Iron Age. These Axial Age writings represent a great advance in human consciousness. This period of consciousness which succeeded the Mythic period of the Neolithic and Bronze Ages, led to the development of linguistic modelling, lexical invention, narrative complexity and early frameworks of governance which characterise what the sociologists of religion call the Theoretic Age.

Writing produces a massive increase in external memory storage. Self-reflection, personal agency, and a sense of irony can be found in the writings of the Confucians, Daoists, Buddhists, Jains, Zoroastrians, Jewish prophets and the Greek technocratic materialists and idealist philosophers who all appeared in between the seventh and fifth centuries BCE. The invention of various written symbols in narrative structures had the effect of 'spacialising' time. In particular, Jewish monotheism and Zoroastrian eschatology encouraged the development of a sense of history, not as eternal reoccurring cycles, random interventions by wilful gods or unpredictable luck, but as the manifest destiny of a chosen people which would culminate in a millenarian end of history. This became the narrative theme of Judaism, Christianity and Islam and later was secularised into millenarian socialist utopias. The concept of time as unilinear was no doubt influenced by the layout of the writing in books and scrolls. This not only leads to deep and narrow puritanical philosophical and religious concepts of causation, but also develops intense hostility to non-purposeful activity undertaken for fun. Everything must have a purpose. If it is not contributing to ever increasing material and technological development or divinely ordained (ordained by History for Marxists), then it must be Satanic (counter-revolutionary for Marxists) and must be opposed.

PSYCHOLOGICAL ASPECTS OF THE MEANS OF COMMUNICATION

Putting it in crude psychological terms, aristocratic religious authorities and their social institutions flourish when supremely confident psychotics are in charge, whereas Iron Age plutocratic authorities and their institutions flourish when highly motivated puritanical neurotics are in charge. Religious rituals of worship, including music and dance, reinforce the authority of traditional agricultural elites. Education in the form of school rooms filled with orderly rows of students silently learning to achieve goals of self-improvement through self-enrichment, reinforces the authority of iconoclastic puritan businessmen in mercantile–industrial societies. Book keeping and literacy are regarded as the only signs of true intelligence. In a similar way sacred texts like the *Torah*, the *Bible* and the *Koran* became worshipped idols or icons replacing man-made images which were regarded as satanic or merely deluded human creations. Later, in the Enlightenment, dictionaries and encyclopaedias functioned as secularised replacements of the sacred texts, schools replaced churches, and teachers replaced preachers as gate-keepers of the truth.

There are exceptions to the monocultural communication monopoly of the traders in the Iron Age. In China pictograms representing verbal concepts and the foundational *Book of Changes* used for divination created a very different paradigm of reality. The Chinese accepted that neither the gods nor man can really control eventuality or history. Their process cosmology deriving from the *Book of Changes* was neither a rigid hierarchy nor an assembly of identical egalitarian atoms but more like a flow diagram with multiple linkages. Outside China magicians in the monotheistic and polytheistic religions, like the Hindu and Buddhist mystics and the Cabbalists, Sufis and Alchemists of the Middle East and Europe, based their explorations of consciousness on similar but less complex and less liminal matrices.

THE ELECTRIC AGE AWAKENING FROM NEWTON'S SINGLE VISION

Over the past century what has been called the Death of God led to the end of any cosmological absolute frame. What can only be called the Death of Nature followed soon after with the loss of any absolute frame, the advent of relativity theories, quantum physics, and the discovery that there are no fundamental irreducible building blocks or atoms. The Enlightenment scientific paradigm collapsed into specific research and development programmes financed for their benefits to business organisations and nationalist weapons development, or just clever, irrelevant and pointless conjecture. This 'immoral rationality' was accompanied by the 'irrational morality' of schizoid Modernism as a totalitarian metaphysics driven by the psychological process of ressentiment, the desperate need to rebel against and destroy traditional values.

Mechanical advances of the end of the nineteenth century made possible by electricity, from automobiles and submarines to aircraft and mass transport systems, were now followed by unprecedented and unpredictable psychological, social and cultural changes resulting from the new electronic media of communication. However, this has made little difference to the crude *weltanshauung* of the business men and financial wizards who increasingly control the governments, the mass media and the educational curricula. Their only motivation is maximising short term profits. Most teachers and academics have been transformed into government officials in the bureaucratic welfare-warfare states. They often deceive themselves by making sentimental displacements of anxiety such as showing sympathy for superficial egalitarianism and green activism. Then they can continue to collect their salaries and government pensions. They are part of a world that is no longer relevant.

The recent transformation of the technological foundations of our civilization created by harnessing the power of electricity is as significant as the invention of cheap and plentiful iron smelting was two and a half thousand years ago. The means of communication suddenly shifted from writing and printing, which emphasise narrow and slow goal-achieving narratives, to the electronic communication of a plethora of speech, images and music at the speed of light. Inherited human innate release mechanisms repressed or lying dormant for centuries, especially amongst the literate ruling classes, were suddenly activated by brightly lit images and ecstatic dance rhythms. Already in the early twentieth century female sexual repression, previously an essential moral aspect of traditional patriarchal family structures, was being seen by psychiatrists as pathological. At the same time the psychological, social and cultural limitations that were a consequence of women's reproductive vulnerability were suddenly removed by safe and easy contraception. The feminine principle or soul is also awakening!

We are now living in a post-industrial world where anxiety-ridden verbal conditioning and a sense of purpose is being replaced by aimless and hysterical fashion-following. This is resulting from a commercial blitzkrieg of advertising and propaganda based not on the written word, like instrumental conditioning, but on musical and visual Pavlovian classical conditioning of the emotions by the talented commercial spin doctors. These have replaced the moral teacher-preachers as the new propagandists. Their activities are not aimless but driven by the commercial imperative of advertising to increase sales and hence the profits to the shareholders in the multi-national corporations which include manufacturers of such superficial silver bullets as electric vehicles, solar panels and wind turbines. Driven by spin doctors to acquire more and more fashionable commodities and to enjoy expensive leisure activities public indebtedness is rising, The global economy, an out of control Ponzi scheme, is meshing together civilizations previously quite distinct. As McLuhan put it, quoting James Joyce, 'The West is shaking the East awake'. It is time for a fresh look at our current *zeitgeist*.

THE WORLD WIDE WEB AND THE FUN REVOLUTION

Thanks to the vision of its early creators, who transformed a missile warning system into a kind of giant brain, the Renaissance theologians' description of the universe as 'an intelligible sphere whose centre is everywhere and whose circumference is nowhere' has been realised. Every laptop or cell phone can act as the centre. We are living in a matrix or simulacra. The robotic bureaucrat managers of totalitarian structures, like the identical Mr Smiths of *The Matrix*, or as I prefer to call it, *The Blob*, are becoming more and more insane as they lose control. The literate academic children of the Enlightenment are becoming increasingly introverted and psychotic as they see their power to control the new post-literate reality slipping away from them. Avatars are arising everywhere; most are false idols, celebrities manipulated by the managers of the global economy, but not all! The best touchstone to distinguish real human beings from narcissistic programmed automata is to tease them in a spirit of aimless fun, conducted in an ironic fashion and without malice or self-righteousness. The only revolution that stands any chance of producing a cultural transformation is the Fun Revolution led by masters of detachment who love living creatively and have no hidden agendas since they have no utopian goals.

THE ASTONISHING SUDDENNESS OF EVOLUTIONARY BREAKTHROUGHS

Major evolutionary breakthroughs at all levels of the cosmos take place with astonishing speed, as the sudden evolution of human consciousness throughout China, India, and Eurasia during the short Axial Age demonstrates. I am convinced that the transformation of communication through easily smelted iron in association with writing was the major contributing factor. Assuming that was the case, then the sudden growth in mass electronic communication, culminating in the World Wide Web, has the potential to transform human consciousness and spread it even more rapidly. Ideological control through the religiously expressed morality of the agricultural empires expressed in speech, shifted to ideological control through mechanically published rationality in materialistic nation states expressed in written or printed texts. In the consumer society the global economy has swallowed up the economies of the nationalistic, bureaucratic welfare-states. Hope of continual increase in personal fame and fortune, although completely unrealistic and ethically meaningless, is portrayed as the ultimate value in the sophisticated electronic mass media.

Since this global situation is both highly unstable and unsustainable, with the literate elite of the educational institutions having lost most of their political influence, conditions are ideal for a sudden shift in consciousness away from the 'irrational morality' of the religious and political institutions and the 'immoral rationality' of the educational institutions which are both now thoroughly discredited. As Victor Turner has pointed out, creative play alone guided by 'liminal' personalities, has the potential to tease undone the Gordian knot of fear and anxiety that follows from the failure of unrealistic expectations resulting from dogmatic belief in dysfunctional ideologies.

PART FIVE

EXPERIMENTING WITH MYSELF

So far in this essay I have tried to analyse the present world cultural situation as I see it. My point of view differs somewhat from others I have encountered. This can be explained by the fact that between 1968 and 1974 I carried out experiments on my psychological, social and cultural self to advance my consciousness. This was the ideal time to attempt this. I did not take any consciousness-raising drugs. I did not come across a guru who opened my eyes to the truth. I did not have a blinding moment of illumination. So, what was the nature of these experiments?

I concluded that it was not enough to 'know myself' and my psychological, social and cultural environments, it was not even enough to 'love myself' and my psychological, social and cultural being. I felt the need to 'play with myself' by acting out roles to provoke reflexive interaction between these other two values at their psychological, social, and cultural interfaces. As I put it at the time, Logic and Love needed to be activated and kept in balance by Levity. As a non-Marxist, non-reductionist lecturer in sociological theory. I was aware that human consciousness is largely determined by the roles we occupy in various institutions. These express our semi-conscious narratives and in turn are embedded in the ideological dynamics of our culture whose symbolic expressions give meaning to our social actions. I also applied my training in psychology to the problem of self-deception and self-justification and developed a light-hearted detachment which made it difficult for me to 'take myself seriously' as a role actor.

I regarded the theory of useful fictions as the best way to do this. My social experiments began when, influenced by Marshal McLuhan and the hippie phenomenon, I started the Fun Revolution, a university reform movement, using revitalisation and avant garde theatrical techniques. I have described what happened elsewhere.

EVOLVING ARCHETYPES

I have also commented elsewhere about the processual rise of major archetypes which can be understood as core symbolic representations of specific cultures, from the Great Mother Goddess in agricultural societies, to the Hero and his conformist and uniformist followers in mercantile-industrial civilizations, to the shopaholic, fashion-conscious, sex-object Maiden of global post-industrial consumerism. Recently we have been witnessing the emergence of the anarchistic Wizard, the archetype of a non-commercial spin-doctor, free from being frightened into obeying the Great Mother Goddess, spellbound by the maiden's beauty or surrendering to the temptation to put on the ring of power to terrify and bully others. Previously neglected as prime-movers in major cultural narratives, except for Merlin in the Matter of Britain, wizards have been making a meteoric rise in the escapist mass media since the 1960s.

In my unavoidably-biased personal opinion, the appointment of an official University Wizard by the administration and Student Union of a major modern university in 1969 might be a turning point in Western Civilization. After all, the first scientists like Friar Bacon were nurtured in the institutions of learning of the time, the monasteries. All of us involved in the appointment at the time knew it was a 'useful fiction', not to be taken seriously, so that I could carry on my attempts to revitalise the university community in what I came to realise more and more was a unique and highly liminal role. My budding career as a sociologist and psychologist had been terminated a few months earlier for asking if I might change the doctoral thesis I had recently begun, so that I could refine my fun revolutionary techniques and devise new forms of ritual, ceremony and political theatre and then write them up. I received no reply to my request. I think my very serious head of department and supervisor, a political scientist who amazingly had little sociological or psychological training, must have already assumed that I had gone mad even though our small fun revolutionary group had been successful in getting reforms in teaching by provoking reactions.

My dismissal was engineered in such a devious way that, on finding out, the Vice Chancellor offered to underwrite my expenses should I decide to return to England. Instead I took this opportunity to put a unique proposal to him. The University Administration and Student Union came to my rescue by making an extraordinarily generous gesture. On April 1st 1969 they acceded to my wish to be appointed official Wizard of the University of NSW with a small honorarium paid jointly by both parties. As a wizard in the modern world I felt rather like Mark Twain's *Connecticut Yankee at the Court of King Arthur*, but in reverse!

DISEMBEDDING AND CREATING NEW SOCIAL ROLES

With my new liminal role as a wizard legitimated by an important intellectual institution and keeping in mind my guiding process principles of Love, Logic and Levity, I could now create a new role-set of voluntary, liminal and authentic roles with which I could interact with community leaders and the general public. In the slang of the time I was not 'dropping out', but was 'hanging in there'.

To achieve truly liminal status and to avoid self-deceiving rationalisations which, like Socrates, I felt could endanger my soul, from that time onwards I allowed all documents identifying me as a dependent member of the welfare state, including licenses and my social security and income tax registrations, to lapse. It was as if I had died. After leaving the University of NSW to become Wizard of the World University Service, a voluntary service organisation, I kept body and soul together by performing in counter-cultural festivals. This enabled me to disembed myself from my contemporary cultural matrix even more radically than the pioneers of the Axial Age had done, with the notable exception of the early Daoist masters.

LIMINAL ACADEMIC ROLE COMPLEX

September 1969 saw me obtain the backing of the World University Service at their annual conference in Hamburg to become their official Wizard and to tour campuses with my fun revolutionary show. In 1971, having moved to Melbourne, the location of the Australian WUS headquarters, I obtained the cooperation of the Vice Chancellor of Melbourne University and the University Union in order to hold inter-disciplinary workshops in the unused Anatomy Building as their official Cosmologer. This became my Department of Levity where with the aid of junior academics I created my subjective process cosmology.

LIMINAL AESTHETIC ROLE COMPLEX

With the encouragement of the Curator of the Metropolitan Museum of Art in New York, I was identified in 1972 as the world's first Living Work of Art by the Director of the National Gallery of Victoria. However, I was not fully recognised and acquisitioned until some years later by Christchurch City Art Gallery in association with the NZ Gallery Directors Council.

LIMINAL RELIGIOUS-ETHICAL ROLE COMPLEX

I always emphasised that there were strong shamanic and prophetic elements in my ecstatic role performances as a wizard. I wrote to the Primate of the Anglican Church in Australia in 1973 seeking examination and possible endorsement as an autonomous 'free range' prophet of the Church of England. I did not expect or receive a reply but I had made my liminal role in religious institutions clear.

LIMINAL POLITICAL ROLE COMPLEX

A year earlier I had founded a political party, The Imperial British Conservative Party. The acronym IBC was my nostalgic tribute to Ian

Brackenbury Channell who had ceased to exist as a socio-cultural phenomenon. The party was based on Tory principles advocating alternative policies to both laissez-faire Whig and Liberal values of economic determinism and the bureaucratic socialist values of welfare state egalitarian control. I advocated, among other things, the drastic reduction of compulsory taxation on incomes; the gradual winding down of the bureaucratic welfare state, relying more on honour incentives and ethic-based professions; guilds and voluntary associations; the separation of primary, secondary and tertiary education from the political control of the secular state and commercial organisations; the strengthening of public trusts; and the removal of the power of the Prime Minister to nominate which individuals should receive honours. I stood for election and for several years fielded candidates in Australia and New Zealand to considerable mockery from the intellectuals which was quite an acceptable aspect of a Fun Revolution especially since we were keen to reply in kind.

CREATING MY OWN UNIVERSE AND LIVING IN IT

My last and most important task as a liminal personality was to create my own liminal universe as a useful fiction. In 1972 as Cosmologer of Melbourne University I created and published my subjective process cosmology to act as my guide and to which I could refer others who wished to know why I was acting as I did. This is obviously an act of supreme egotism. However, I could not go so far in that arrogant direction as the average objective scientist who believes that, as a kind of supernatural but impotent being located outside the cosmos, he or she can objectively 'observe' the things in the universe as objects located in absolute space!

One of my innovations was to build-in 'eventuality' or time as a man-made probabilistic event hierarchy ranging from 'impossible' at the start, to 'inevitable' at the finish, should it ever be reached. I assumed the Big Bang was 'impossible' and designed a thought experiment carried out for fun which, by converging identity, space and time, as Me Here Now, as a mass media spectacle, was aimed at avoiding both personal immortality and death.

To create a convergent physical model, re-establish 'up' as a significant direction, and to draw attention to my new universe, I inverted the conformal mathematical coordinates which portray the Earth as a tiny sphere in an immense universe, to produce a model where the Earth is portrayed as a huge shell which encloses the rest of the universe like a womb or matrix. In this geoperipheral model the galaxies are now converging on the new centre of the universe, or Heaven, which I thus returned to its pre-scientific location of being directly above the Earth's surface.

Although I could not gather enough even playful support to attempt my imaginary levity-based experiment to test the validity of this ego-centric cosmology, the new physical model my cosmology was based on would, I am convinced, still prove popular with people all over the world. Perhaps I could get past the intellectual ridicule of the deadly earnest, cosmological gatekeepers, the reductionist astrophysicists in the Blob with their antiquated absolute frame, by successfully promoting it on YouTube!

Those cosmologists financed by the military-industrial complex could continue to use the old ballistic model of Newton modified by Einstein as their useful fiction, but they must be prepared to lose much of their smug, arrogant confidence when they are teased by fun revolutionary process cosmologers who can shift from frame to frame motivated by logic, love and levity and not on their personal non-objective needs for status, money and power. Process physicists have pointed out that many articles of faith, such as the cosmological constant in mc_2 and the Big Bang, are no more than useful fictions to prop up their outdated model of the universe based on their now-falsified mechanistic metaphysical ideology.

SOCIAL ROLES CAN ACT AS LEVERAGE

Certain social roles can act rather like Archimedes' famous lever. Such levers need to be strong enough, long enough, positioned on the right fulcrum and embedded deeply enough to raise what is desired to be moved. For somewhere to stand, the operator of a social lever must still be partially embedded in existing institutions, and must have the necessary liminality or charisma to choose the location of the fulcrum to provoke reflexivity in the desired direction. The role actor involved must be culturally real and not just a self-deluding fantasist. History can provide us with a multitude of examples of 'outsiders' having such an impact. In the role of prophet, a man or woman can move a theocratic elite. In the role of party leader, a single person can move a political elite. In the role of cosmologer, they can move a scientific elite. In the role of living work of art, they could move the artistic elite. Such liminal role-actors would have to take account of people's existing needs for status, material support and power over others. Appealing to morality or reason will make no difference to someone whose ego and self-esteem is based on roles deeply embedded in dysfunctional institutions. Turner's analysis describes the conditions under which liminal transformations of gridlocked social structures into temporary anti-structures can take place. He shows that in such anti-structures, role differences and the false egos or social selves that are created by them are temporarily dissolved into a kind of group mind before precipitating into what he called a *communitas*. The danger here is that a personality who creates this state may be seen as a god-like saviour and treated with awe, as has happened so often before. Fun revolutionaries must not take themselves seriously or they start reverting to the 'Theoretic Consciousness' of the Axial Age.

PART SIX

THE FUN REVOLUTION

Taking my cue from Huizinga's historical survey of the significance of play in all types of human cultural institutions and from Turner's studies of transformations of rigid social structures I am proposing that we need a fun revolution to save the world. I quote *The Sane Revolution*, a poem by D.H Lawrence composed in 1929:

> *If you make a revolution, make it for fun,*
> *don't make it in ghastly seriousness,*
> *don't do it in deadly earnest, do it for fun*
> *Don't do it because you hate people,*
> *do it just to spit in their eye.*
> *Don't do it for the money,*
> *do it and be damned to the money.*
> *Don't do it for equality,*
> *do it because we've got too much equality*
> *and it would be fun to upset the apple-cart*
> *and see which way the apples would go a-rolling.*

Creative playfulness is not just wicked self-indulgence distracting us from obedience to God's plan for our individual salvation, or History's plan for an egalitarian utopia, nor is it merely trivial, escapist 'recreation' for workers trapped in a mechanistic universe machine. Our new process-based understanding of evolution at all levels in the universe, is that it is produced by purposeless playfulness and creativity. Nowhere is this truer than at the human cultural level. It could be said that the moral structures of religion based on love of a parental type provided the integration needed for large scale agricultural civilizations to establish themselves.

Without the rational understanding of the workings of Nature by cooperating groups of colleagues in the mercantile industrial civilizations we would still be living short, unhealthy lives and be at the mercy of many environmental dangers. We cannot afford to look back in anger at their obvious failings since they have made us what we are. Look back with affection and appreciate the amazing creativity that they released before moving on.

Over the past century, we have seen the almost unquestioned application of rational scientific technology in the service of what can only be described as infantile moral philosophies based on religious or secular-scientific fundamentalism. It is not enough to accept the necessity of social integration through dogmatic religious or political moral ideologies nor the necessity of adaptation to our environment through purely utilitarian scientific rationalism. We have reached a point where irrational morality and immoral rationality with their separate competing institutions need to be integrated into a higher conceptual scheme. This can be done through acceptance of non-dualistic process philosophy and the psychological unmasking of human self-deception through false ego-driven rationalisation.

POWERING DOWN TO A DEFAULT POSITION

Is it possible to be over-developed in terms of technology whilst other social institutions and cultural beliefs have been left behind? Many people, including some at the forefront of technological innovation, have pondered this question. If we suffer a major breakdown in our civilization could we go back to a default position to avoid being plunged into a violent dark age? If so, what would be a practical stage of technological development to aim at, in order to regroup? The final quarter of the 19th century was sufficiently technologically advanced in the all-important agricultural sector. With the end of environmentally destructive factory farming the intensive man power needed to grow organic food and establish fish farms would bring people back into the country and keep them busy and free from panic-stricken social disorder. Food distribution could be by road transportation augmented by railways and horses as well as small petrol-powered trucks. In *Retrotopia*, one of his website reports, the Archdruid, John Michael

Greer, offers an interesting range of different levels of technological default positions. The positive side of this would be improvements in human health in many areas through better diets and more exercise. Most important of all obviously would be the preservation of the biosphere whose destruction by modern technology is approaching the point of no return.

FEAR OF FREEDOM IN ANIMAL FARM

In the welfare states, with their ever-increasing armies of certified professional bureaucrats, it is the voluntary associations of citizens motivated by compassion and status or honour who often keep the state machine from particularly stupid and heartless actions. Public servants have their salaries paid out of compulsory taxes, which are at least a third of most people's income, yet they are allowed to vote in the general elections. Surely they should be disenfranchised owing to an obvious conflict of interest. Are public servants likely to vote for a reduction in the size and power of the ever-expanding secular state bureaucracy? Would any state-employed school teacher who pays lip service to democratic principles agree with such an obvious truth? Teachers and other public servants have even given up their traditional professional ethics to become politicised industrial trade unions! Once again, we must remind ourselves that human consciousness is largely determined by our social roles. Since 1968 I have been living in the welfare state animal farm as a kind of free-range cockerel scratching about for worms and crowing loudly whilst observing the strange behaviour of the caged hens laying their golden eggs for the armies of farm managers who feed and water them. The chickens are attracted by the sight and sound of this last surviving cockerel. Fear of freedom has increasingly become the leitmotif of our hysterical chicken civilization. Encouraging the growth of extended families and clans would be a less destructive and more efficient way to provide the basic foundations of a responsible ethical society and would limit the size and totalitarian powers of the frequently heartless bureaucracy of the state. The unpoliticised rule of law is our best guarantee of social justice not the rule of accredited but ideologically biased bureaucrats giving themselves illegal and unjust powers over us.

STATUS, FUN AND A JUBILEE

I have so far been beating around the bush at length since directly recommending to the reader a regular Jubilee Year and a Fun Revolution without preparatory explanation would be stupid. Without any prior explanation, proposing the cancellation of all debts as part of a process of adjustment of the global economy, would be greeted by today's intellectual, political and economic elites as an act of colossal irresponsibility or a stupid joke and with blank incomprehension by those religious leaders mainly concerned with sin and individual salvation. Who would consider this idea as the only practical way out? One of the most powerful arguments that they cannot refute is that the food bearing potential of the Earth is being drastically compromised by large scale factory-farming and fishing and by pollution, with the resultant degradation of all ecosystems. Fortunately, there are still individuals who pride themselves on such eternal process values as truth, love, beauty and even levity and who are not easily influenced by the academic spin doctors or political and religious messiahs making fake promises to recruit followers.

For a Jubilee to be implemented we will need the electronic social media and the support of the millions of indebted people who have no real political power at present, together with the cooperation of those status elites whose authority does not depend on illegitimate monopolies of economic power. I am referring to traditional royal families, clan leaders, tribal chiefs etc. Few intellectuals realise that many working people and independent peasants admire such leaders, rather than the mass-media-created and controlled celebrities brought in to undermine the charisma of their traditional leaders and to replace them. Such people, many of whom have only recently been brought under the hegemony of the money-manipulating elite, have a deep-seated, Tory view of society. Most modern Conservatives are Whigs not Tories, even though they are frequently called such. True Tories (like Edmund Burke and Winston Churchill), whatever their party affiliations and human failings, are influenced by their historical identity and traditions and by voluntary community welfare and status rewards rather than by institutional self-advancement, irresponsible power over others or crude economic rewards. They regard resentful modern rebels against tradition, currently fêted by many intellectuals, with fear and revulsion.

The timing and implementation of a Jubilee would also require much debate and forward preparation since such an overdue radical readjustment of the global economy would have a massive effect on markets, trading patterns and money values. The Internet would be indispensable in coordinating the millions of individual transactions needed. Cyber currencies might be the way to initially bypass the financial institutions of the clearly insane plutocrats. We must all prepare ourselves for the social fact that, as Rebecca Solnit has shown in her studies of disasters, at the first signs of trouble the present ruling elites are likely to panic and make things worse. We have recently experienced a similar but small-scale event compared with something like the declaration of a Jubilee, in the form of Brexit.

The Fun Revolution is made up of explosions of delight at the sudden release of honesty and intelligence and love after years of being locked in a world of fake news, fake economics, fake egalitarianism, fake social science, fake virtue, and especially fake promises. How could a Fun Revolution based on logic, love and levity make any difference to the status quo? For myself I have being putting skin into the game by doing my best to demonstrate its effectiveness by recording and analysing events I have been involved with over the past fifty years, and to communicate with others who may have come to similar conclusions about the parlous state of our global civilization and the need to 'power down' before it implodes in chaos. Such a programme requires individuals who have progressed beyond the Theoretic stage of consciousness reached during the Axial Age. The promotion of process philosophies and the demolition of those once-useful fictions which have not only become unchallengeable dogma but are now destroying our world, is essential.

SEIZING THE HIGH GROUND THROUGH STOICAL ARISTOCRATIC LEVITY

Since the moral high ground has already been seized by egalitarian republican socialists or religious fundamentalists, support for aristocratic values, even though less intense, cannot at the present time be seen as 'moral'. Since the rational-utilitarian high ground has been seized by materialistic educators and reductionist scientists, aristocratic explanations of meaning although more aesthetically attractive cannot at the present time be seen as 'rational'. However, it must be realised that high ground can also be seized by those aristocratic personalities who prize playful fun above humourless moral rectitude or the clever manipulation of technological and economic jargon. It is increasingly accepted that the universe is a self-organising system that has been evolving through the 'boot-strap' hypothesis. In other words, through playful experimentation or levity, with sudden phase changes or breakthroughs into more complex forms. Deterministic religious or mechanistic metaphysical assumptions that deny this are blocking the flow and causing a build-up of potentially catastrophic pressure. A great deal of fun can be had by light-heartedly teasing up-tight 'progressives' with their grandiose but ill-thought-out plans for the future, until they explode before our civilization does.

Tories, male or female, rich or poor, white or blue collar, religious or atheist, black, brown or white etc. can be appreciated for their post-modern-seeming characteristics. Returning to comforting time-tested traditions for their own sake and participating in deep satisfying spiritual expressions and community bonding through spell-binding magical rituals requires no utilitarian justification. Tolkien's fictional hobbits are quintessential Tories who enjoy running their own affairs without bureaucratic egalitarian structures but with lots of simple fun and games, puzzles and practical jokes, defying the efforts of self-righteous moral leaders, industrialist puritans and arrogant bourgeois intellectuals to stop them. Throughout history people desperate to grab power push themselves forward so they can 'improve' the self-contented lifestyles of the hobbits. Who can the hobbits turn to when they are in desperate peril? Courageous marginalised traditional aristocrats and fun-loving, intellectual wise men of integrity.

Recognising the importance of traditional social hierarchies based on status could balance the irreconcilable conflict between the competing materialistic ideologies of egalitarian bureaucratic socialism and individualistic liberal capitalism. Accepting hierarchies, especially voluntary ones, as useful fictions is not offensive to our common human feelings. Consider those occasions when we are serving on a ship, climbing a mountain, taking part in a play or learning a task from a teacher. As I have recorded in my narrative essays, fun revolutionaries can detonate and destroy the charismatic appeal not only of ego-driven authoritarian behaviour based on fear of losing control but also the transgressive behaviour of rebels driven by ressentiment. It is vitally important that fun revolutionaries themselves avoid being driven by irrational egotism, balancing their levity with love to avoid spiteful cruelty, and with logic to avoid making things worse in the long run.

FOULING OUR OWN NEST

New civilizations are born and nurtured in the nests of those which, having reached their apogee, are fossilising and dying. The great agricultural civilizations increased in complexity and expanded rapidly with the innovations of the Iron Age. The greatest of these in Eurasia was arguably the multicultural Persian Empire which reached as far as Egypt. Strict Jewish monotheism, which absorbed the Zoroastrian eschatology with its concept of history as unilinear, was born and nurtured in the same bosom as Greek rationalism based on reductionism and atomism. Christianity and Islam began to grow in the final centuries of the Roman Empire which was a plutocratic, legalistic and more stable version of the more subtle and complex Greek and Hellenistic civilizations.

It is clear that the same process is happening in the world today. Gradual 'cognitive slippage' from the self-confidence of the Enlightenment philosophers and scientists into the doubt, confusion and madness of global consumerism has been taking place for over a hundred years and is now accelerating, especially in the form of the fake news of the hysterical Blob. Any one of the scarcely visible new seeds that are starting to sprout might suddenly grow to become an ecologically-sustainable, emotionally and aesthetically satisfying new civilization that incorporates the cultural advances of the past and unites rationality and morality. Most important of all it would have be based on a more consciously self-aware process cosmology. Its first essential act would be to bring in a joyful Jubilee to cancel all man-made financial and spiritual debts without throwing out the baby of our accumulated wisdom with the foul bathwater of self-righteous, narcissistic, spin.

The Telephone Box War (front page of a local Invercargill newspaper).

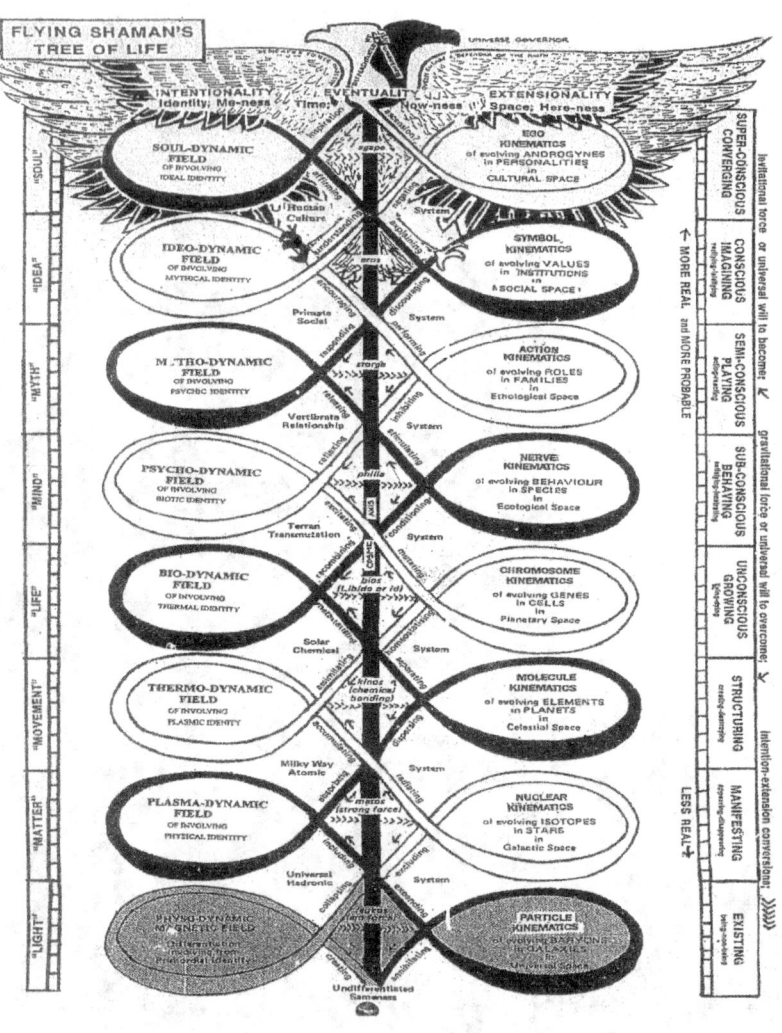

DISCOMBOBULATING THE BLOB

The Blob is a term that has been used as a metaphor to describe the malevolent social form taken on when professional institutions lose their autonomy and become controlled by managers or bureaucrats. Our hospitals, schools, social services, universities, businesses, and even democratically elected governments have all succumbed to this process. The term Blob is a reference to a 1950s science fiction movie of that name starring Steve McQueen where a small organism protected by a hard shell comes from outer space like a meteorite. It is attracted to human beings then it opens up and sucks them into its interior where they are pulped into a jelly. It grows larger and larger and resists all attempts to destroy it. In the modern world the Blob is a huge malevolent amorphous being with a managerial carapace that has come from inner space. In its insatiable thirst for power it is attracted to people and groups who are honest, trusting and playful. Promising future abundance, it approaches waving virtue-signalling flags, but as it gets closer it opens up and issues poisonous politically correct gas to paralyse its victims before absorbing them.

Officials charged with ensuring that public policies are carried out are an inevitable aspect of large scale human societies. They are usually rewarded for dispassionate execution of their duties by security of tenure, guaranteed pensions, and honours, rather than by high salaries. However, unless prevented by outside intervention, bureaucracies gradually replace their original objectives with the subjective survival and expansion of their own organisation. The ends are largely forgotten, and what was previously the means becomes the end. As managers and administrators the human beings who are charged with ensuring that public policies are carried out are legally obliged to detach themselves from traditional human values such as truth, beauty, and goodness. In this respect they become instruments or tools. The key to understanding the power of the Blob is to realise that when this happens the pursuit of power over others may fill the gap unless the bureaucrats have already developed strong ethical principles.

Intervention to prevent the growth of the Blob may came from both above and from below, as specified in the laws governing constitutional monarchies and constitutional republics. Recent events in the UK and USA are providing excellent examples of this phenomenon. At the present time our civilization is rapidly being pressured by the expanding Blob to change from a competing number of military industrial nations into a globalised Blob controlled by a tiny number of evil, psychotic and irresponsible financial wizards who have mastered the global electronic control system. Information is power, and centralised information is centralised power, especially in the Electric Age.

INSTRUMENTAL VERSUS AFFECTIVE ORIENTATIONS

In their attempts to understand them, social scientists divide social processes between such instrumental activities, where goal achievement is prioritised, and affective activities, where intrinsic satisfaction in being alive, mentally alert, and socially active is prioritised. Similarly the two main conditioning systems which modify behaviour are instrumental conditioning, made famous by Skinner and his pigeons, and affective conditioning made famous by Pavlov and his dogs. This dichotomy is also called 'gesellschaft' as contrasted with 'gemeinschaft'. Nietzsche distinguished between Apollonian and Dionysian dispositions. Ideally a balance between the two where neither overrules the other should be sought.

Social systems always function within a cultural scenario or context which may overemphasise instrumentality or affectivity. Cultural systems evolve historically and are subject to both internal and external influences. To aid understanding, they can be classified into fundamentally different types. This can only be done by 'rough-hewing' them into ideal types which ignore specific details and overlaps. The simplest classification is made by distinguishing between nomadic hunter gathers, settled agriculturalists, urbanised mercantilists, military-industrial imperialists, and globalised consumerists. Affectivity is maximal and instrumentalism and coercion is minimal in hunter gatherers, and instrumentalism and coercion is maximal and affectivity is minimal in globalised consumerism. Stability and sustainability is greatest in hunter gatherers and instability and unsustainability is greatest in globalised consumerists.

Each of these cultural variants is based on differing technologies of which communication largely determines the others. Speech, gesture, singing, dancing etc. diminish as spontaneity is marginalised and speech censored by a literate religious elite in property-owning agricultural settlements. Merchant elites rose to power in the Iron Age by developing useful trading abstractions such as simplified symbols for spoken words and numbers, trading vouchers, and measuring systems. Markets in themselves override all inherited and acquired human differences by treating all traders as equal players. Elites in military industrial nations increase and centralise power through mass produced printing on paper. Through conquest and secular education they rapidly expand into manufacturing and trading empires.

This historical situation is suddenly being transformed by electric technology. Electronic communication enables new elites of plutocratic salesmen to combine globally to make a profit. They employ economists, social scientists and lawyers to develop control and feedback loops to demonise the traditional values of Western Civilization. Then they can be replaced by shallow, short-term emotional desires of rootless consumers for which they supply the fashionable, mass produced goods and services.

At each step in this historical process freedom diminishes and coercion increases as the number of managers grows exponentially. Extended families are reduced to nuclear families and finally the welfare state begins to replace the family. Universities cease educating professionals and become degree factories mass producing managers, specialist technicians, psychologically-sophisticated salesmen and lawyers to create bureaucratic mazes to protect the oligarchs. The development of ever more lethal weapons of war is prioritised together with ever more sophisticated surveillance of the governed.

Affectivity and community embedding diminishes fast so we are currently witnessing the growth of alienation, self-loathing, escape into religious and political millenarianism, cognitive dissonance (especially in the universities as nationalist and globalist ideologies clash), and collective psychoses. The horror of the modernising political mass movements of fascism and communism of the 20th century, which were only narrowly defeated, were an early warning. Mass consumer packaging and mass tourism are polluting the environment and factory farming and fishing are destroying the biological ecosystem. As a distraction the plutocratic elite who now control the mass media and mass education institutions are promoting the bizarre ideology that that carbon dioxide is the cause of everything evil.

We need to look backward and realise that we have lost the human values which encourage affectivity and try to recover them. Instead we are racing fast forward to "1984", the approaching utopia of deluded, goal-obsessed madmen and isolated brainwashed consumers. The Romantic Movement in England of the first half of the 19th century is an example of what we need to do. This was a cultural revolution against the soulless utilitarianism of the Enlightenment which was based on economic determinism. Christchurch was founded by such people who put their skin in the game by travelling to the other side of the Earth to put truth, beauty, goodness and communitas above materialism and crude economic gain. The site was chosen deliberately not for its convenience as a mercantile or political location but as a rural agricultural centre.

MILLENARIANISM AND HISTORICAL INEVITABILITY

History can be seen as the story of how the addictive need for coercive power over others, stripped of the fundamental human values of truth, beauty and goodness, has grown progressively stronger. There have been bright intervals in this decline into ignorant darkness. Dark ages have been followed by recoveries. It is the overall narrative of how role acting human beings embedded in an existential, magical matrix for tens of thousands of years suddenly became domesticated slaves with immortal souls. Soon afterwards they were transformed into soulless cogs in social machines whose purpose was meaningless survival. Finally they became consumers of goods and services, continuously spied upon and psychologically manipulated to increase the power and income of a tiny number of irresponsible psychopaths and their paid stooges.

History as progress towards a better future is based on the belief that an event or events in the past caused all the evil in the present and that we can find redemption by committing ourselves to achieving a perfect society through sacrifice of ourselves and others. The main motivation, which is still at the core of the historical narrative of western civilization, is the strange millenarian belief that time is a unilinear progression towards a final state of redemption. History reaches the year zero when God intervenes on behalf of his devoted followers and his enemies are crushed and sent to eternal suffering in Hell. This unique ideology originated amongst monotheistic Jews living in captivity in Babylon who were deeply affected by Zoroastrian ideas of the Persians who had in turn conquered the Babylonians. It was then transmitted to the rest of the world by radical forms of Christianity and Islam, which had developed within the plutocratic, classical civilization of Rome.

The Jacobins of the French Revolution were enlightened middle class materialists who admired Roman civilization. They feared and hated the decadent elite of landowning aristocrats who ruled with the intellectually reactionary backing of the Church. Although they denied God's existence they still believed that time is unilinear and simply secularised the religious millenarianism. This may have been because their economic foundations were based on credit systems and usurious payoffs at a future date. History now comes to an end with Year Zero realised by the long-awaited, bloodthirsty, egalitarian revolution. Counter-revolutionaries were re-educated by force and if they still didn't see the light they could be put up against the wall and shot. If lucky, they were executed in the most humane way they could think of, by Madame Guillotine. Year Zero is when the magical withering away of the state of the Marxists will take place and we all hold hands and sing Kumbaya. The Jacobin-inspired student riots of 1968 in Paris reactivated this deadly virus which is spreading like a pandemic in the fevered brains of angry, overeducated and city-raised bourgeois intellectuals, especially in university arts departments. Ayatollah Khomeini and Pol Pot are two of the many infected individuals that have been sent out into the world from the Sorbonne.

THE WILL TO POWER

The 'will to power' of the Modernists, which erupted during the second half of the 19th century and destroyed the Romantic movement, was not only fuelled by reductionist social-Darwinism but also by the emergence of a newly-united Germany as a military-industrial power run by Prussian militarists keen to flex their muscles. The term 'will to power' was coined by Nietzsche who provided the philosophical foundations for the emergence of an intellectual superman and ridiculed the will to love, which he regarded as masochistic sickness. Marx, a millenarian as well as a social-Darwinist, did not abandon the will to love but displaced it until after the necessary violent revolution.

Naked power is all about future achievement at the expense of existential beauty, truth, and love. Art without beauty, religion and politics without ethics, and science without truth, results from their politicisation by power hungry deviants. Managers measure and justify their naked power entirely through short-term, bottom-line, monetised manipulation. The health values of medical professionals are over-ridden by trained managers backed up by lawyers, neither of whom call upon any traditional human values that could restrict their exercise of power. The doctors and nurses are gradually reduced to impotent pulp and medical treatment as a whole becomes ever more expensive and ineffective. There are now more managers in the hospitals than medical staff and more managers in the universities than academic teachers and researchers. The same applies to schools where standards of excellence in teaching and learning falls as rapidly as the numbers of regulators continually assessing performance rises. The open and hidden cost to the users rises as fast as the percentage of paid managers. Governments become more and more incompetent as the number of public servants, now organised into self-serving industrial trade unions, increases along with their salaries and guaranteed pensions. As a significant voting bloc in the general elections, they and their dependants ensure that the number of state bureaucrats and their irresponsible power will increase. This is not democracy, it is the rise of the administrative state. The class war was a distraction and the egalitarian revolution a fake promise.

Materialism in general and economic determinism in particular is the fundamental ideology underlying both capitalism and socialism and justifies the policies of all current political parties. Market forces which check the growth of dead wood and monopolies in non-socialist governments are losing their influence through the monopoly of certification of business skills in state-controlled tertiary educational institutions. The continual attacks by secular educators on religious instruction as out-dated superstition leads to a lack of ethics and the rapid growth of crony capitalism. Money loses its materiality to become electronic information which can then then be controlled by information monopolies whose desire for power encourages mindless narcissistic consumerism to fill the void left by the decline of communitas. A sense of community is traditionally created through role interaction in voluntaristic pursuits based on relating to the natural and human environment through playful and loving common sense. This current process of alienation cannot expand exponentially and the deliberate distraction of alarmism, from fake global cooling which became fake global warming and then fake climate change, cannot continue to hide the fact that the entire biosphere is collapsing under the pressure of pointless and destructive consumerism. Narcissistic consumerism is a form of mental illness, sustained attack on it must combine well considered political action with community therapy.

DISCOMBOBULATING THE BLOB

There is a way to slow down this malevolent new form of imperialism which is devoid of subtle religion, honest truth, and uplifting beauty. Those of us who can must disembed ourselves from the Blob as much as possible. Having done so we can operate as voluntary associations of citizens using humour, art, and fun-revolutionary guerrilla warfare tactics of the mind both to preserve our sanity and disrupt the smooth functioning of the Blob. This is why I chose the nonsense verb 'discombobulate', meaning to confuse and befuddle, to describe the only safe and successful technique to protect ourselves from the mindless malevolence of the Blob. Between 1968 and 1972 I found myself strategically placed in the changing Australian university scene to be able to start a fun revolution to encourage the re-emergence of what Johann Huizinga called 'Homo Ludens'. Fun, the word chosen by Huizinga to describe the essence of rule-based playfulness, is both existential and affective and often drives puritanical personalities into a destructive rage. Fun is not the same thing as Dionysian excess.

MY UNDERSTANDING OF THE PHENOMENON REFERRED TO AS 'HISTORICAL INEVITABILITY'

'Homo Ludens' is repressed through guilt by righteous 'Homo Religiosus'.
'Homo Religiosus' is in turn demoralised through ridicule by educated 'Homo Sapiens'.
'Homo Sapiens' is now being dumbed down through hurt feelings by self-pitying 'Homo Narcisssus'.

Artists copying the recently discovered Chauvet cave which frames murals painted and drawn by the illiterate hunter-gatherer savages 36,000 years ago, are claiming that there has been no overall progress in human artistic ability since. Anthropologists and archaeologists now admit that hunter gatherers had more leisure than subsequent societies, were fun-loving, enjoyed a healthy life style, and lived in ecological sustainability over tens of thousands of years. They appear to have carried out long term careful 'terraforming' of the natural environment. It is hard to believe in the spiritual, social, mental or even material progress of mankind. The poet T.S. Eliot wrote: *We shall not cease from exploration, and the end of all our exploring will be to arrive where we started and know the place for the first time.*

POWERING DOWN OR DUMBING DOWN

I have already provided the beginnings of the philosophical, scientific and ethical validation of what could be called 'the will to fun' which can include both the will to love and the will to power. I claim that this particular zeitgeist was at its highest during the hunter gatherer period of our history and at its lowest in the infantilising bureaucratic welfare institutions of the current military-industrial states. I assume that if we do not slow down and stop globalised consumerism immediately we are going to create worldwide social violence and destroy the fertility of the biological ecosystem. I may be exaggerating, but what harm could it possibly do to take part in a fun revolution aimed at powering down rather than dumbing down?

As a stubborn pragmatist by nature, I put together an existential process cosmology as an art form based on recent scientific theories, in order to justify my playful response to the world. In my authenticated role as a wizard and living work of art I have carried out many diverse psycho-socio-cultural experiments in Australasia to test out my creation. I have angered many Homo Religiosus types who regard me as evil and have been marginalised and dismissed as an egotistic fool by many Homo sapiens types, but at least I still have personal agency and have a strong popular following. I have not yet been domesticated, dumbed down, and absorbed by the Blob.

THE END

As this book was being put to bed, the corona virus pandemic struck with breathless speed. It is obvious the consequences of a world-wide lockdown for weeks or even months will be followed by a complete restructuring of globalised Western Civilization.

How is this likely to take place? Two completely opposed forces will rise to the occasion; the will to power and the will to love. The will to power is best exemplified by the actions of the Chinese government who not only caused the crisis and made it much worse by deliberately lying about it but are now using it to further weaken the western democracies. This military industrial giant was modelled by its founders on an ideology developed in the West in both communist and fascist forms and has combined the worst elements of both; the mind control of materialistic socialism and the hate-based emotional bonding of crude Chinese racial superiority.

The growth of what I call the Blob has been mainly achieved through state run compulsory secular education and the recent considerable loss of political-economic autonomy in the universities. Since the industrial revolution and the establishment of the compulsory welfare-states, the religious institutions, which were traditionally the main source of ethical education and voluntaristic community welfare, have been shrivelling up and dying. The religious belief in love as powerful cultural force providing the courage to extend love into the community to stand firm against naked unethical power is ridiculed and marginalised. The idea of love is mainly limited by secular intellectuals to mean interaction between bourgeois individuals in small scale institutions like the family.

RELIGIOUS RETREATS

The will to love that is not limited by modern bourgeois individualism is slowly growing at present in Christian, Jewish, Islamic, Buddhist Hindu and other religious communities. These communities are administered by hierarchies based on religious ethics and competence in administration. The traditional communities of love, like monasteries and ashrams, are often fairly self-sufficient with gardens growing food, medical dispensaries and workshops to make tools and products for sale. Unlike compulsory socialist work camps and gulags, a vital part of their daily routine is the collective performance of ritual-musical ceremonies combining the expression of love with aesthetic pleasure and community bonding. Those communities that include both men and woman do not tolerate promiscuity since it is the opposite of love. The secular communes of love that rebellious young hippies established in the 1960s and 70s, were still spellbound by the secular ideological belief in egalitarianism which of course appeals to immature people. They aimed to be economically self-sufficient. The founders set up democratic committees of governance and tolerated sexual promiscuity but in most cases the inevitable ego-driven conflicts soon caused them to fall apart.

SPELLBINDING BEAUTY

It is unrealistic to rely upon religious conviction alone to provide the alternative to the catastrophic will to power of the rulers of the 19th century military industrial nations. The present situation developed when the elites now entangled in the Blob began strenuously denying their own cultural identity in order to merge into a globalised totalitarian super power based on fake news, fake science, and fake virtue, and with massive debt and profligate consumerism as incentive. We see another source of resistance in the 19th century Romantic Movement of poets, novelists, playwrights, painters, and craftspeople who were the only effective opposition to the puritanism and utilitarianism of the industrialists for whom bottom line measurement was the supreme value, over-ruling beauty, truth, and goodness in the form of ethical religion. Today most entertainment provides escape from the alienation produced by boring mechanical work by emphasising the sensations provoked by watching deviant behaviour, especially violence and sex. There is no resemblance between this and the Romantic Movement with its encouragement of craftsmanship, its spiritual revival of myths and legends, of romantic love, and the enjoyment of unspoiled nature.

Reflexivity with His Holiness the Dalai Lama outside Christchurch Cathedral. (Photo: Kurt Langer)

284   THE END

COMMUNITIES OF LEARNING

Schools may be integrated into the religious communities founded on divine love. Isolated communities like the Irish Monks and other monastic houses preserved western civilization from destruction during the Dark Ages. There were no material or status rewards for studying at that time. In their absence, for some individuals curiosity can function as an existential drive. Early universities such as Oxford and Cambridge began when Christian teachers set up alongside rivers and students would gather round them bringing food and other gifts to support them and to demonstrate their dedication to learning. The Universities over the past fifty years have become as corrupt as the Church in the later Middle Ages when the Renaissance scholars eclipsed the influence of decadent clerical intellectuals. There are of course some academics today working autonomously who have not been corrupted, as there were some religious scholars who retained their integrity during the Middle Ages.

THE COMING STRUGGLE FOR POWER; THE NEO-MARXISTS ARE POISED TO STRIKE

Following the social deconstruction caused by the Coronavirus Pandemic a source of opposition to the welfare-warfare state bureaucracy will come from large numbers of unskilled and semi-skilled labourers who will be the first to lose their jobs. This will enrage them, especially since many of the administrative state officials have guaranteed employment and pensions. The alienated lower classes have progressively lost most of their traditional hard-won freedoms. For decades they have been treated by paid, unionised public servants as idiots who don't know what's good for them. Since WW2 they have been trapped in welfare cages designed by state bureaucrats to keep them docile.

The ruling elite of the administrative state will take this opportunity to try to accumulate even more power for themselves by promising to solve the problem they themselves created by their incompetence. Those who are obsessed with political correctness and the monopoly of power find it impossible to admit they are ever wrong and will never give up their power without a fight. There is a danger that in this situation particularly ambitious control freaks will take advantage of any social disorder as happened in Russia, Germany and China in the past and will use mob oratory and social media propaganda to work up violent hatred of our constitutional monarchy with its delicate separation and balance of powers and apolitical rule of law.

Making love more important than power will not pacify the alienated and powerless masses looking for someone to blame. They will demand political action. This is the sort of historical opportunity that men like Mussolini, Hitler, Lenin, Stalin and Mao seized upon. They direct hate towards the democratically-elected governments and they rise to power on the backs of those they have driven mad with the resentful need for revenge. Once in power they will destroy all freedoms other than their own, especially freedom of speech.

Unfortunately since 1968 we have seen the progressive crushing of free speech in our universities. In Europe and the USA no academics stood up against the sudden take-overs by student power activists of student associations, their funds, and their newspapers. They were clearly inspired by Mao's Red Guards and the nihilistic Jacobin student riots in Paris that year. They preach equality and political correctness whilst practising fascist style intimidation of peaceful conservatives whom they label as right wing extremists. It was a cultural pandemic.

Over the past half century we have already seen the rule of law being undermined by newly-created hate speech and human rights invented by fiat by republican lawyers with hidden political agendas. Political correctness and conventional limits to free speech did not come from the people at the bottom of the income and prestige hierarchy it came from the top and was designed to enslave those at the bottom. It appeared first in the universities, as the beginning of the 'long march through the cultural institutions' of the neo-Marxist Gramsci which changed the class war into the classroom war. Their aim was to demonise the values the people had lived for and died for in the recent past and to punish those conservatives of integrity who tried to stick to them.

IDEOLOGICAL PANDEMICS

Subjective ideas are like viruses and certain of them spread in much the same way. The 'emotional plague' type of character described so well by Wilhelm Reich can infect almost an entire community who are easily transformed by fear and hatred into an angry mob. A similar socio-psychological deformation of reality is the psychological process which Nietzsche called 'ressentiment'. This is not just normal envy. Max Scheler has described this compensation process where values are deformed or even inverted and reality distortion can take place. This may occur when individuals are faced with a loss of ego through comparison with a superior individual or through failure to achieve a cherished goal. Aesop's fable about the fox and the grapes is the classic case. Scheler points out that in crowds this process can quickly 'go viral'.

THE FUN REVOLUTION BASED ON LOVE LOGIC AND LEVITY

Since 1968 I have been in the thick of a battle with the enemies of free speech and long ago learned that using politeness and good manners based on love and logic is ineffectual against those who are driven by the addictive need for power. Whenever their egos are threatened they react by despising those who disagree with them and will lie and use intimidation to silence any questioning of their fixed beliefs. Replying to hate with hate only escalates the conflict and both sides become entrenched. I developed strategies based on creative playfulness or fun which have enabled me to stay above the apathy or retreat into ideological dogma created by cognitive dissonance. Whilst welcoming the communities of spiritual, aesthetic and intellectual communities who develop by 'walking away' from the Blob, I realise that most people's interests are more pedestrian. The one thing all sane humans have in common and which differentiates us from the beasts is laughter. If having fun is balanced by love and logic, so that bullying cruelty and envious spite is excluded, fun is a great leveller and intensely egalitarian.

EGALITARIAN COMMUNITIES BASED ON LOVE LOGIC AND LEVITY

It is not enough to feed and shelter the great numbers of unemployed that will probably follow the shutdown introduced to fight the Coronavirus Pandemic. Rabble rousing political and religious leaders flourish when people are bored, idle and angry.

I have a solution. No doubt other examples can be cited but my own experience leads me to believe that should our world suffer economic collapse then Holiday Camps such as those pioneered by Billy Butlin in austerity-stricken postwar Britain would be an excellent model to copy in such a crisis. In 1951, as a young man, I attended one myself with my family. As a self-deprecating egotist, I still remember coming second in a Mr Tarzan competition. I was also the creative director of the Dictator's "Concentration Camp for 'freshers'" at the University of NSW in 1970. Fortunately the popular British TV comedy series *Hi de Hi* is based on these camps so many people will be acquainted with how they operated. Non-stop entertaining, if rather vulgar, activities led by hyperactive Redcoats began at breakfast time in the huge refectories and continued throughout the day with shows and dances in the evenings. The major difference is that these camps were not designed to operate in the winter. The other difference is that after the war Butlin was able to buy surplus army huts, beds etc. very cheaply. It remained a commercial enterprise so the deadly-earnest state bureaucracy was kept at bay.

During the evening and during inclement weather evening classes could be held, in craftwork and on many current affairs topics.....especially in breaking the spell of dogmatic ideologies through board games based on ideologies where players compete for fun as in my Salvation Game. In fine weather the campers could establish and work on gardens to supply the camps and with the long term aim of enabling many to leave the camps to become self-sufficient small holders. The allotments that provided much needed fresh food during WW2 were a return to peasant style strips, but with the welcome addition of sheds where husbands could seek shelter from homes run by house-proud wives.

Previous back to the land movements like those at the end of the 19th century began with enthusiasm but gradually succumbed to what Weber describes as routinisation. There is an abundance of love and logic in such communities, what was lacking was fun. A Master of Ceremonies supervising musical performances, sports, games, play acting, teasing, joking, etc. should be seen as being as important as love and logic. Perhaps the camp director should be thrown into the pool once a week to prevent ego tripping of the serious variety. If soldiers in the trenches during the Great War could make the effort to produce the subversive, laughter-provoking *Wipers Times* newspaper, anything is possible.

A FINAL WORD

As this manuscript was about to be printed my attention was drawn to a new book by Rutger Bergman, *Humankind: A Hopeful History*. I believe it has potential to help heal the deep self-loathing encouraged by many intellectuals in many cultures over the ages. Like myself, Bergman takes the psycho-socio-cultural nature of the hunter gatherers as his 'measure of mankind.'

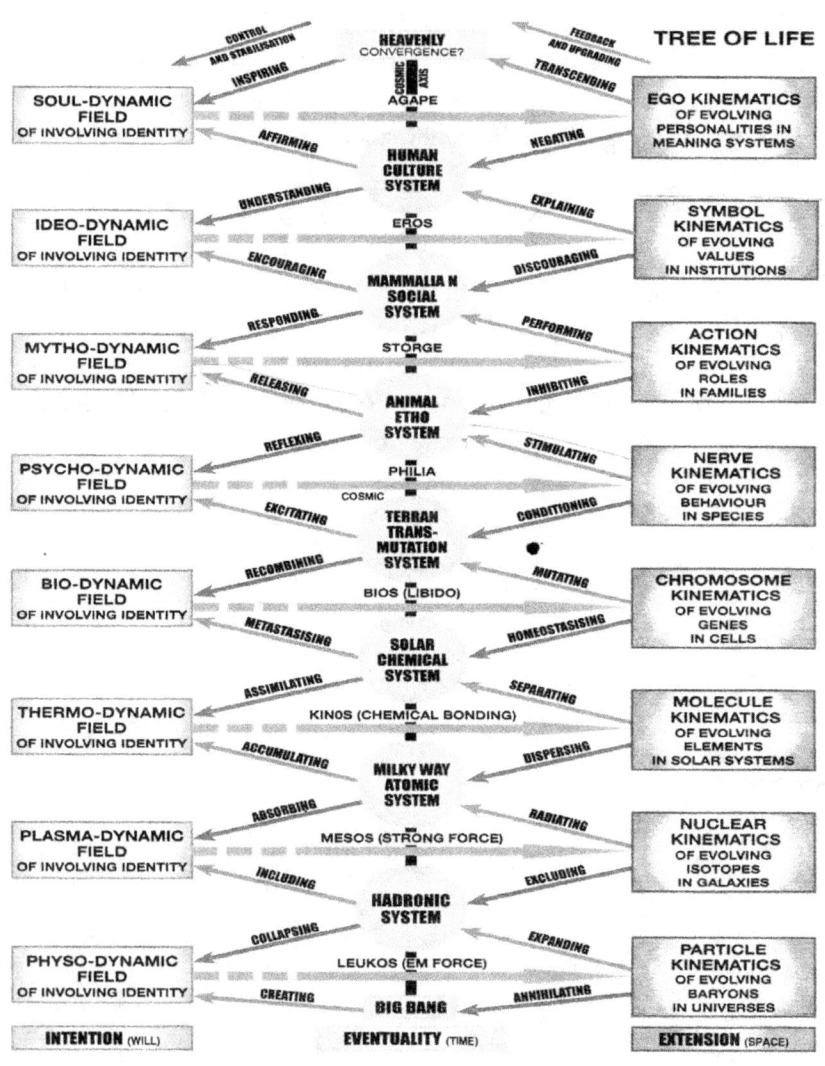

DECODING THE WIZARD'S PROCESS COSMOLOGY

PART ONE

THE CONTEXT WITHIN WHICH THE COSMOLOGY WAS CREATED

My academic qualifications were gained at the University of Leeds between 1960 and 1963 where I gained a double honours degree in an experimental course in combined psychological and sociological theory. I was also fortunate as part of my studies to take a course in the history and philosophy of science in the new department set up earlier by Stephen Toulmin. In 1963 I was head hunted by the University of WA and brought to Perth to administer their Community Arts programme as a tenured lecturer. In 1967, I was persuaded to move and join the staff of the first school of sociology in Australia at the University of NSW as a teaching fellow undertaking a doctorate in the Sociology of Art. Events in 1968, that remarkable year, gave me an opportunity to carry out experiments in revitalising the university which was in danger of being overwhelmed by a fast expanding bureaucracy and student radicals inspired by Mao's Red Guards and the youth rebellion of the time. The unusual events that followed my starting a university revitalisation movement resulted in my being appointed official Wizard of the University by a joint decision of the Vice Chancellor and Student Union.

After almost fifty years experimenting in this liminal role, during which time I was made Wizard of Christchurch by the City Council and, in 1990, official Wizard of New Zealand by Prime Ministerial Proclamation and was later awarded a Queens Service Medal, I was ready to undertake a PhD thesis. I wanted to study the impact of the role actions of liminal personalities on gridlocked bureaucracies, making use of similar theories and experiments by the process anthropologist Victor Turner. This was aimed at providing a proper in-depth explanation of some of the extraordinary events I have been involved with. My experiments were conducted within a frame of reality or paradigm which should reveal itself as I proceeded with my explanations and quoted references. Although my chosen supervisors for this proposed auto-ethnographic and process-based thesis were enthusiastic senior academics, the application has been blocked without explanation by the admissions bureaucracy at the University of Tasmania for five years now. This was not entirely unexpected since monetised managerialism in professional institutions (or what I refer to as the Blob) has advanced by leaps and bounds since 1968. As so often happens, the means of maintaining and expanding an institution becomes the end and the original end is forgotten.

AS IF...VAIHINGER'S THEORY OF USEFUL FICTIONS

Early last century in his book *As If*, Hans Vaihinger developed a theory of useful fictions. I believe the implications of this fertile theory were not fully realised at the time, though ideal types derived from Platonic philosophy have provided a vital foundation for the social sciences. Useful fictions are the very foundation of human symbolic communication which is based on metaphors and analogies… in other words 'as if'. The purest form is probably mathematics, which is mistakenly seen as supernatural by many hard scientists, but there are countless working hypotheses, such as frames of reference, that we adopt for their usefulness. Unlike the Stoic 'materialists' who avoided dualism and transcendentalism, Plato, influenced by Pythagoreans, hypothesised the existence of transcendental real/ideal forms to avoid admitting that all experiences we associate with reality only exist in a communicable form as 'fictional' classificatory concepts with names attached for our convenience in referring to them. They do exist for us but not as independent and unchanging entities in some supernatural realm. There is no such thing as a 'true' or ideal quark or atom or molecule or gene or colour or lark's song or fairy or performance of a play or symphony. These are essentially hypothetical constructs and take the form of experiences that we carefully classify symbolically so that we can refer to them, use them, avoid them, describe them or just experience them for fun. No intelligible experience is possible until it is communicable in mimetic form, mainly verbal. The idea that pure, real objects exist somewhere in a frozen heaven would itself be a useful fiction for a Platonic idealist keen to dismiss a Stoic opponent.

THE HISTORICAL CONTEXT

As I see it, our current scientific obsession to discover the absolute truth derives from this Platonic Idealism together with the reductionist practices of the Milesian Greek philosophers and the Scientism of the later Enlightenment. The 'philosophes' used the printing press to successfully communicate revolutionary truth ideals based on useful reductionist fictions. These included the hypothesis that the entire universe is made up of identical building-blocks or atoms in various combinations. To them transcendental explanations of purpose or meaning were therefore no more than useless fictions or lies created to justify the need for spiritual control by the wicked clergy. Their intention was to ridicule traditional ideals of love, virtue and beauty in order to support the rising class of ruthless bean-counting business men, bankers and manufacturers who were destroying the power and influence of the church, the landed gentry and religious monarchies to replace them with what became the military-industrial complexes. Later Darwin's evolutionary theory depending on chance-determined survival of the 'fittest' organisms could be used to undermine all forms of transcendental purpose and soon genetic determinism provided a platform for a biological version of atomic determinism. But are atoms and genes really discrete 'things in space'? Without a reductionist 'useful-fictional' hypothesis, they are only partially measurable aspects of processes embedded in wider and incompletely understood higher order frames or contexts.

THE POLITICAL CONTEXT

It was with this understanding of the importance not only of hypotheses but of the useful fictions that can lead to them, that in 1969 I proposed to the University and Student Administrations at the University of NSW that I be appointed their official Wizard. They agreed because they realised as well as I did (and had already demonstrated) that this was a useful fiction during those tension-ridden days of campus riots. Pretending or reaching forward is a highly reflexive process and as a play form is the essence of socialisation and learning in man and many animals.

Later I was able to initiate another useful fiction when I was declared to be a 'Living Work of Art' by art gallery directors in Australia and New Zealand. This is not only a radicalisation and non-material social implementation of the rather vague notion of the over-politicised 'conceptual art', but an important recognition of the fictional aspects of human identity. Unfortunately, a few years later the New Zealand government simply ignored the opinions of both university and art administrators and on several occasions the Department of Statistics tried to compel me to fill in Census forms. As a living work of art with a legitimately authorised 'artistic licence', I have had no income tax registration nor social security number since 1968 and have become 'a stranger in a strange land'. I believed I had earned the right to act as if did not belong to them like some domestic animal, though I had no intention of assuming I was above the law and would supply details of my organic being. This has required me to live a rather restricted life. I simply turned their clumsy attempts to convict me every five years into exciting avant garde theatre. Using the mass media reportage as my world stage, I created scenarios in which, to the delight of the Kiwis, I triumphed over my powerful, authoritarian enemies. My favourite scenario centred on my claim that I vanished at midnight on Census night and did not reappear until noon on Census Day. I placed questionnaires in the major newspapers to ascertain how many citizens pretended to believe that I had really vanished and therefore need not fill in my form. The number who cooperated persuaded the census enumerators to give up their pursuit. The government regained face in their treatment of me when I was appointed Wizard of New Zealand by the Prime Minister in 1990 and awarded the Queens Service Medal by them in 2009. This official recognition aided my desire to turn a useful fiction into a practical hypothesis for use in the social sciences.

USEFUL TO WHOM?

These examples of useful fictions bring up a very important question of relativity which Vaihinger did not investigate. Useful to Whom? That question could only be solved the same way as Humpty Dumpty, when faced by Alice's challenge, when he insisted that when he used a word it meant what he wanted it to mean. He explained to her that the real issue was 'which is to be master!' I set out to find the solution to this dilemma. This was now particularly acute due to the 'Death of God' that occurred during the late 19th century and the 'Death of Nature' (meaning the end of belief in the atomic building blocks and the absolute frame of space) which occurred early in the twentieth. Now the 'Death of the People' is being brought about by the 'domestication' of mankind through compulsory secular education into welfare-warfare states. These are controlled by irresponsible global media corporations issuing a torrent of fake news and fake social science. Their raison d'etre is the obvious falsehood that unlimited economic development is possible in a biologically closed system. The 'Death of Mammon' now seems fast approaching. Money is always based on useful fictions but someone might call the bluff of the huge Ponzi scheme that masquerades as the global economy, especially when it is not pegged down to a trustworthy source and debt is out of control.

A major contributor to this catastrophic state of affairs has been the two totalitarian world wars which largely finished off most traditional useful fictions. Can we recognise that it is time to come out into the open and admit that the various gods, nations, representatives, atoms, or even money, all of which have masqueraded as real entities, are in essence useful fictions? Most of them are no longer useful but have become extremely dangerous. It is time for a reassessment of all our useful fictions. Human beings have been living in virtual reality systems or simulacra since we invented language and created a man-made super-natural reality. Our useful fictions need to be ordered in hierarchies of value. This is the task that all responsible thinkers should be working on. We certainly can't live in a world when we have no cosmology other than reductionist astrophysics and absolute belief in the 'mandate of the people' without a balancing belief in the 'mandate of heaven'. Either of these useful fictions without the other leads to tyranny. Democracy, which is based on the ethnocentric useful fiction that all men and women are equal and can govern themselves, in practice operates in accordance with what Robert Michels called *The Iron Law of Oligarchy*.

Shakespeare, who lived in Europe at a time when religious, scientific and magical values in the form of explanations of reality were contending for supremacy, hit the nail on the head when he composed his 'All the world's a stage' monologue. Molière too saw that theatre was more than just escapist entertainment and, like Shakespeare, played an important role in the royal court. However, Beaumarchais' later influential play *The Barber of Seville* was not aimed at subtly advising the king and his court but flattering the rising nationalistic middle classes and ridiculing the traditional establishment. He provided a model for many other morally self-righteous nationalist artists to copy.

THE UNIVERSE ITSELF AS A USEFUL FICTION

In 1970, as a publicly recognised and legitimately-authorised fictional character on the world stage myself, I had an even better idea. I decided, after suffering many blows of outrageous fortune, that I would create my own fictional universe in which I was the master. Since belief in absolute space has been shown to be a demonstrable falsehood, the ouranocentric or geoperipheral 'inside-out' model of the physical universe which I came across fifty-five years ago could be freely chosen as an alternative and voted upon for reasons based on logic, love and levity. There is no observation that can be made to check its veracity. Even the supernatural authority of mathematics cannot be called upon to help the shocked physicists since the very mathematical co-ordinates of the old model are simply conformally inverted! I realised that through the use of the global mass media this is first time in human history that this demolition of the triumphant materialist philosophy could actually be achieved. It was not enough to be an actor in a play based on a script written by others and whose flaws were becoming apparent to more and more people. Even though it would mean sometimes playing the part of an ego-less fool, I needed not just a leading part on the stage, but to write my own lines based on a cosmological narrative scenario that I believed depended on a much better set of assumptions than I was obliged to accept by my cultural guardians. I even wanted a happy ending!

First, I needed to refine my role as the university Wizard to authorise my cosmological enterprise on behalf of a university. In 1971, at my request, the Union of Melbourne University granted me the title of 'Cosmologer' since 'cosmologists' were just astrophysicists swollen with pride because they were so useful to the military-industrial complex whose mushroom-like growth Eisenhower warned of in his famous retirement speech. The Vice Chancellor granted me the temporary use of a charming Gothic Revival building in the centre of the campus for use as my Cosmological Research and Development Centre, better known as the Department of Levity. I even had a chair, a throne previously used by the Archangel in the now defunct local Catholic Apostolic Church. I offered free interdisciplinary lectures and work-shops, but although well-advertised they mainly attracted people from town as few students are interested in new ideas unless they are conducted in a sincere, humourless and unchallenging manner and can provide them with a meal ticket.

UNCONVENTIONAL SIGNS

By 1972 I had completed my subjective process cosmology as an evolving set of inter-related self-organising systems, and sent copies of the key diagrams and references to universities all round the world just to be fair to any rivals, even though I had serious doubts that any existed. Perhaps I should have stuck to the conventional model of the material universe but since I am not working for the military-industrial complex which needs precise calculations of the trajectories of missiles, I found the model produced by my conformal inversion of the traditional coordinates produced a much more "useful fiction" to use as a base. The Geoperipheral or Ouranocentric model simply inverts the coordinates to put the universe inside the surface of the earth which now appears as a huge hole. Following the Death of God there is no longer any absolute frame so why does it upset people so much? My creation of a new physical universe model makes a refreshing change. If I can break through the intellectual censorship that chains me like Prometheus, this model is guaranteed to prick the inflated egos of the astrophysicist high priests who annoy me when they appear pontificating about their absolutist objective model of the universe on the History Channel in my living room. They are so confident since they are the high priest-mathematicians of their Pythagorean physical universe.

My cosmology does not require the Cartesian useful fiction of a divine mathematical God who revealed his 'method' to me personally nor does it depend on the absurd reductionist useful fiction that the whole is no more than the sum of its parts (whatever these may be at present) and which has evolved by chance from a Big Bang. This requires belief that this First Cause never happened (there being no time) and never happened anywhere (there being no location) and if it had never happened anywhere it must have done so for no reason at all (there being no identity or being to intend it to happen). I may have got this wrong, but I prefer *autopoesis* to biblical-style extrinsic causation.

As the reader will have realised by now I am a pragmatist of the English 'carry on regardless' school. Like my role as 'The Wizard', my cosmology as 'The Universe' is a useful fiction. It is an evolving process model which synthesises a number of disparate and previously unlinked but reputable scientific theories and which has the potential to include all other models of reality as subsystems. A. N. Whitehead's Process Theory is a more sophisticated but less dramatic exposition of process cosmology. His writings, and those of other academics he has inspired since the 1930s, are needed to explain phenomena which make no sense in the fake reductionist cosmology still being taught as true in the educational institutions. This is little more than scientism. A cursory examination will show that the laws we are taught governing the lower physical and biological levels of the cosmos are essentially fictional explanations and are not 'more real' to us than the symbolic level where the meaning and definitions of reality are generated by human beings. Were my simpler and more practical explanations of cosmological functioning than those commonly available to be accepted, together with the Wizard as its creator and master (another useful fiction) I could then assume responsibility for the universe and could make words mean what I want them to mean etc. Moreover, I can see rivals off as I have almost fifty years of self-justification behind me. By using the internet, I can escalate my fun revolutionary experiments aimed at saving the Earth's ecosystem from dying under us whilst providing therapy not only for timid, stressed-out intellectual bureaucrats in the universities but for the political and religious fundamentalists who have been driven mad by an overdose of mind-numbing, management-speak from the millions of bureaucrats like Sir Humphrey, of TV's *Yes Minister*. I am not a megalomaniac, so I cannot promise to save the world, but I can have a lot of fun trying.

WESTERN CIVILIZATION CAN EVOLVE FURTHER

I assume that human consciousness, unlike artificial intelligence, evolves largely through analogy and metaphor which enable us to think more inclusively, to retrieve sub-conscious information, to decode experience, to create useful models of reality and to communicate with others. Major paradigm shifts in human culture have been described by psychologists, sociologists and historians as taking place between the evolution from mimesis to speech, and then from speech to verbal and mathematical notation. The transition from bronze to iron technology made large urban centres and trading possible and the invention of refined written symbolic communication systems like the phonetic alphabet spread the use of writing beyond a tiny elite and large trading empires were formed. Electrical technology is now transforming our cultural paradigms in a similar fundamental way. There was a quantum leap in human consciousness at this time we call the Axial Age. Three distinct forms can be identified, all of which involve increased individuation, reflective consciousness and the development of responsible personal agency.

1. **Transcendental Religion** is exemplified best in the writings of the Egyptian and Indian polytheistic civilizations. Followers of Zoroaster were influential in the Persian Empire, as were those of Confucius in China and Buddha in India. Most religions are polytheistic and the various deities vary in their interests, power and influence. True monotheistic religion appears to have been created by Jewish kings and priests in the 8th century BCE as a reaction when confronted by the sudden terrifying phenomenon of invasion by the all-powerful kings of the Neo-Assyrians. With the new iron weapons and armour they had suddenly wiped out the other Israelite kingdoms to the North. Yahweh is a mighty warlord of hosts, suffers no rivals and as the only true God, demands absolute obedience.

2. **Process Cosmology** which appeared in China with the I Ching and the Daoists was free from both transcendental and material determinism but instead treated reality as undetermined and constantly changing 'becoming'. Heraclitus of Ephesus, a contemporary Greek aristocrat, held similar views.

3. **Reductionist Scientific Materialism** was the third and completely unique branch of the new consciousness and is based on materialism and the belief that the act of measuring easily measured material things is a divine process and more real than mere verbal formulations and explanatory narratives. This metaphysics appeared in the Greek colonies on the Anatolian coast. The influence of Pythagoras of Samos led to the belief that the power and truth of mathematical formulae is supernatural. This has increasingly become the paradigm in the global institutions of learning.

Scientific materialism developed amongst the independent Greek plutocratic traders in the Aegean port of Miletus. Later, in the mercantile republic of Athens, it became the basis of the classical schools of humanistic philosophers. The ideal man took the form of a male, property-owning, free citizen in the sacred polis. Through the psychological process of identification, voters responded to performances on the stage in both the parliament and the theatre. The will of the people was calculated digitally by voting in the same way as material value was calculated digitally through coinage. Inspiration from the gods was seen more and more as outdated and philosophers and politicians made fun of them. The People's Mandate was absolute but unstable, since it was easily highjacked by spin doctors and alternated with political takeovers by tyrants. The lack of any developed metaphysics linking the god-like Greek men with their biological, social and cultural environments led to rapid degradation of the biological environment, repression of their wives and daughters and almost continual warfare between the city states.

During the Renaissance and Enlightenment this branch of the Axial Age was revived and combined with Protestant individualism to become the dominant form of consciousness in the West. The sponsorship of science by the new military-industrial elite together with the technology of the steam engine powered by fossil fuels led to Europeans rapidly expanding their materialistic culture throughout the world. The elites who controlled the transcendentalist religious agricultural civilizations were impoverished and pushed aside and the peasants were mass educated and industrialised into the western materialist ideology. Currently Weirds (western, educated, industrial, rich democrats) are pouring out of the schools and universities and religion is portrayed by the enlightened literati as an outdated and dangerous superstition.

PROCESS THEORIES

Until electronic communication was invented, metaphors of the cosmos were mainly derived from literate sources. Literacy is taught in schools through operant conditioning. Since this is goal oriented it is essentially mechanistic, the cosmos and our place in it was seen as a 'means' to a sacred or secular-utopian 'end'. In the mid-19th century everything began to change. Evolutionary thinking and relativity theories were in the air. Telegraphic transmission at the speed of light was invented, followed by radio. Dynamos and spark plugs for petrol engines dramatically effected transportation already made more efficient through steam and then diesel-powered engines. Lithographic printing flooded a highly literate urbanised civilization with coloured images. Photography followed and soon the cinema had been invented as a popular entertainment completely outshining the traditional lantern-slide shows. Sitting together in the dark in complete silence, apart from music, watching moving images on a huge brightly-lit screen was a transformative experience replacing theatre or religion for literate people and began a new form of charismatic celebrity culture based on film actors or popular music performers who were essentially puppets managed by commercial spin doctors. Illustrated magazines and large posters used images to create new needs for mass-produced goods and services. With the invention of television in the mid-20th century, and later of computers and cell phones, by the millennium we had become, to adapt McLuhan's terminology, post-literate dwellers in the virtual reality of a digitalised, conformist and uniformist global village.

PAVLOVIAN CONDITIONING IS AWAKENING DORMANT INNATE RELEASERS

All animals inherit dispositions to respond to strong stimuli, especially coloured images, auditory stimuli and rhythmic movement, but western civilization with its roots combining puritanical monotheistic Judaism and classical Greek reductionist rationality had been, as William Blake put it, in a deep sleep-like trance. Shortly after it was published the mechanistic aspect of Darwin's evolutionary theory had been brilliantly ridiculed by Samuel Butler in *Erewhon*, which also gently mocked belief in the digitalisation of salvation through heavenly credits issued by 'musical banks', by comparing them with paper money. Electronically transmitted images and auditory stimuli impact directly on the brain and senses like Pavlovian classical conditioning. This is very unlike operant conditioning through literate education which needs to be decoded and requires a single absolute point of view. Metaphors of the cosmos had already changed from being a natural realm governed by supernatural personalities to a money-making machine driven by chance: now it was being understood as various related processes in self-organising systems. The educated mechanical zombies who fought in the great wars and worked as wage slaves on the assembly lines were beginning to wake up! Electrical metaphors were beginning to be adopted. Whitehead had taken J.C. Maxwell the pioneer in electrical theory as the subject of his doctorate. D.O.Hebb the neuroscientist approached the human brain as a neural network functioning as a pattern or gestalt. The Berlin School of Gestalt Psychology opposed the mechanistic behaviourists and psychiatrists like Kurt Lewin and

Wilhelm Reich used electrical metaphors like magnetic fields, sudden reversals of polarity and discharges in their psychological theories.

NEW METAPHYSICAL PARADIGM

In the early years of the 20th century Vaihinger had introduced his notion that linguistic and mathematical formulations could be regarded as 'useful fictions' some of which had the potential to become working hypotheses. As operating systems, the best of these hypotheses can be used not only in reductionalistically validated science but also in transcendentally validated religion. Obviously these human creations were created for their usefulness to the ruling elites of the time. In the nineteen thirties the radical process cosmology of the philosopher Whitehead, in the tradition of Chinese metaphysics, Leibniz and American pragmatists, created a new explanatory model of the evolving cosmos. His theory accounted for previously inexplicable anomalies, especially in physics. He rejected bifurcation into the useful fictions of subjective or noumenal and objective or phenomenal, but instead of measuring objects he concentrated on process where what actually happens, or eventuality, can alone be understood as truly real. He pointed out that concepts like time and location and even the self, although useful and irreplaceable, are essentially human symbolic abstractions. Around the same time Teilhard de Chardin created a cosmology which assumed that since the human brain had evolved sufficiently some time ago, consequent evolution was essentially inter-personal and cultural and was converging on a final state when the universe would become a personality. Just after WW2, the pioneer of ecosystem theory, Gregory Bateson, influenced by Bertrand Russell's logical hierarchical set theory, showed how all phenomena were inter-related and hierarchically linked through control and feedback loops and hence a holistic process of self-organising systems, not things in space.

It was with such thoughts in mind that in 1970-72 I designed my subjective process cosmology to act as the ultimately subjective context within which I could create the necessary roles to carry out the psychological, social and cultural experiments I had begun in 1968 at the University of NSW.

Avoiding philosophical debate over existence versus essence and being versus becoming I assumed that identity, from its simplest and least complex level to the 'ideal' self of a conscious human being, can be likened to electro-magnetic fields. Adopting Teilhard de Chardin's term, these identity fields are 'involving' and, when manifested as phenomena, can be identified as 'evolving'. In my analogy, at certain levels of charged potential, identity fields discharge themselves in what we experience and identify through conceptual models as phenomenal manifestations or kinematics. These vary in complexity from radiating particles to atomic complexes, molecular complexes, genetic complexes, and behavioural complexes, to role complexes and symbol complexes. I see these as increasingly refined expressions of love. Control and feedback loops maintain these processes in a hierarchy of self-organising systems of increasing complexity and may upgrade themselves by involving/evolving through sudden phase shifts. I shaped my cosmological 'circuit diagram' as a representation conflating the upward growth of the Tree of Life with the serpentine Caduceus of healing.

My process diagram of the involving/evolving cosmos includes the feedback loops which show how these hypothetical identity fields are 'formed' not only through **learning** but also how they are 'informed' through **memory**, after learning had been patterned from both raw **experience**, and memory from simple **recognition**.

This continuous process of patterning takes place through the medium of eventuality forms or 'self-organising systems', useful-fictional hypothetical constructs resembling what Whitehead termed 'concrescences' of events.

EXPERIENCING

When deciding which aspects of manifested or 'objective' reality can be experienced and related to by beings/subjects at the various evolved levels of the cosmology, I assumed it was essential to avoid reduction to the material levels for complete explanation. Experiencing is more than registering simple sensations. Only radiant light can be observed, (i.e. experienced purely visually) sound can be sensed as tactile vibrations and heat and matter can only be felt through touch. For human beings, what is 'experienced' (at the physical, biological, behavioural, social, cultural and personality levels) involves inherited nervous systems, previous experiences, learning based on model constructs with inputs from others, and from information stores like libraries.

UNDERSTANDING THE PSYCHOLOGICAL LEVEL OF BEING

I avoided absolutist causal explanations in both their transcendental-supernatural, and reductionist-material forms. The mechanistic 'object oriented' view of the psychological or mental level of reality assumes complete separation of 'objective' observer from what is observed, and psychology consequently becomes restricted to observing the behaviour of organisms as things and coming up with various explanations for such perceived phenomena. Such observers do not respond to rational argument if it conflicts with their emotion-based psyches and the roles that they occupy in their social institutions which give them status and meaning. They are embedded in their own cultural paradigm.

As psychiatrists explain, rationalising an irrational belief and seeking confirmation bias are extremely common and highly sophisticated processes, especially amongst verbally fluent intellectuals both religious and secular. Philosophers and historians of science confirm this By accepting a non-idealistic view of psychological, social and cultural reality we can live with our own useful fictions and tolerate those of others who may differ from us without destructive anger, provided of course they are not just antisocial spoilsports.

My adaptation of a Druidic Triad as represented in the Celctic knot

PART TWO

SOME DEFINITIONS AND EXAMPLES

NERVE KINEMATICS

Neuroscientists can identify electro-chemical changes in the transmission potential of neurones which they can associate with certain behavioural activities. It is commonly accepted that these activities are not adequately explicable by simple reduction to laws of physics or laws of biochemistry. I assume of course that higher level more complex and evolved phenomena are linked systematically with such underlying phenomena through feedback and control processes. Such specialists in what I term 'nerve kinematics' are not the only scientists who help us to understand what is best called 'behaviour' at the mental/psychological level of being. Sociobiologists or evolutionary biologists and ethologists are also able to contribute to the understanding of behaviour. Zoology has long since progressed from animal taxonomy and mechanistic description to become ethology.

Behaviour as a concept implies more than simple mechanical form and movement. All species inherit and learn some forms of behaviour in common in order to survive, such as obtaining oxygen, feeding and excreting, self-defence, sexual selection, reproducing and, in some cases, nurturing the young. Ethologists are particularly interested in the way species inherit neural dispositions to respond reflexively to external stimuli. It is also important to remember that such behaviour only takes place within species whose behaviour must be understood to be part of the total eco-system of our planet. In spite of a century of trying, psychology has proven to be irreducible to simple mechanistic learning principles. Memory in particular has proved resistant to attempts to give it any specific location in the brain. Like learning, memory is best understood as a gestalt, an attribute of patterns or forms in the brain as a network, not an 'object' nor a 'subject' in the dualism which has dominated science ever since the 17th century. At its best, psychology attempts to provide hypothetical theories of motivation which will mesh with the contributions of neuro-scientists, ethologists and sociologists to explain animal-based behaviour.

To understand and predict behaviour, particularly human behaviour, there is no way of avoiding the subjective intentions of the beings whose behaviour we observe/experience. It is particularly important to remember that this subjectivity also applies to the scientists constructing their theories. Subjective intention is the province of the various schools of psychodynamics. However, only a fanatic would limit psychological insight to psychologists. The studies of sociologists, anthropologists and historians are also essential. Philosophers, theologians, playwrights, film-makers, novelists and poets have also created our world view or culture in which the sciences play an important but limited role.

UNDERSTANDING THE SOCIAL LEVEL OF BEING

It should be pointed out that social insects are misnamed. They are not acting out roles. They are like large brains whose component insect parts operate like neurones. Social role actors can no more be understood by being reduced to behaving organisms than behaving organisms can be understood by being reduced to 'gene machines'. If such an extreme form of reductionism is attempted then there would be no way of understanding or predicting any complexities of behaviour or social action. Once again, we must avoid the reductionism which treats social phenomena as no more than the behaviour of aggregates of organisms. The term behaviour applies to all organisms with nervous systems, even plants which behave in a similar if much slower way, yet not all organisms are social. Social action theory, as a branch of sociology, recognises that a social system is made up of role actors. These are not the same thing as organisms even though roles can only be acted out by organisms. Concentrating on what I call 'action kinematics of evolving roles' is, I believe, the best way to avoid confusing different levels of being and falling into the trap of 'misplaced concreteness' and objectification.

What is evolving at this level is not the somatic form of organisms or their behaviour, it is their social role complexes. Roles cannot evolve without organisms to act them out and social institutions provide structures for interacting roles. The small group of an animal family is the basic institution within which differences in gender and maturity are related to functional differences in role domination and submission etc. Parental love or *storge* has to be hypothesised to be the expression of a more complex forms of psychodynamics than that which can be assumed for less complex organism behaviour.

The Social Action theory of the structural functionalist Talcott Parsons and others from the Chicago school of symbolic interaction and role theory, originated in an attempt to synthesise historical, cultural, sociological, anthropological and psychological findings to provide a general theory of action. This 'grand theory' can be applied relatively free from historical uniqueness, reductionist social Darwinism, and ethno-centric moral ideologies like meritocratic egalitarianism or historicism, and thus could be properly scientific. Although by no means completely satisfactory, I had not come across any other social theory that was sophisticated enough or which has such carefully thought-out links to psychological and cultural phenomena which I considered suitable for use of as part of an adequate cosmological synthesis. It is non-reductionist, and its major theorist Talcott Parsons made use of newly developed information theory to inter-relate phenomena into a logically ordered and evolving dynamic equilibrium. However, since even this theory is partially couched within the Enlightenment rationalist paradigm, it suffers from elements of subject/object dualism, and needs modifying by process theories and ecological interrelatedness. There is also an unwarranted Freudian assumption that personality phenomena must inevitably be subordinated to socio-cultural necessities. Max Weber accepted that what is known as charisma could disrupt such established processes.

PSYCHODYNAMICS AND MYTHO-DYNAMIC NARRATIVES

The psyche or mental psychodynamic field hypothesised to motivate behaviour in species, is more complex than the biological dynamic field of intention that I assume directs growth and reproduction upon which it is based. In the same way, the dynamics of intention hypothesised to account for role action in social groups and cultural institutions has to be understood to be more complex and qualitatively different from these psychodynamics, although of course it includes them.

Psychiatrists find it essential to refer to mythical dynamic narrative processes going on in their patients. In 1972 I chose the term mythodynamics to fill the gap between psychodynamics and ideodynamics or what Max Weber called 'ideal and material interests'. Human beings in particular cannot avoid living in personal life dramas in which they act out parts. They are often unaware of this until the narrative they are unconsciously acting out is interrupted or explained to them through spoken or written symbols or through ritual drama. Aristotle likens these sorts of processes to biological 'purging'.

In recent years many psychodynamic theorists and social psychologists have been finding it essential to refer to narrative structures or myths in their attempts to understand complex human role actions. It also seemed to me then to be essential to hypothesise a more complex, higher level of dynamics than a simplistic reduction to psycho-dynamics. This would account for the qualitative difference between the phenomena of behaviour in species and the phenomena of role actions in families and other social systems and institutions. Since human beings live in cultures which are based on interlocked institutions which are governed by symbolically expressed values, I assume that what I call "mythodynamics" must be hypothesised to motivate the roles that underlie collective political-economic phenomena.

IDEO-DYNAMICS AND THE CULTURAL LEVEL OF BEING

Recognition of the motivating power of hypothetical 'ideas' to maintain or transform cultural phenomena is accepted in many sociocultural disciplines. As mythodynamic intention or motivation is the qualitative refinement of psychodynamic intention or motivation expressed at the social level as role actions, so ideo-dynamic intention is the refinement of mythodynamic intention expressed at the cultural level in the form of mimesis or verbal/numerical symbolic expression.

The development of speech began a process of rapidly accelerating cultural complexity which developed even faster with the storage and shaping of consciousness through the invention and elaboration of written and mathematical operating systems.

Up to this point my theoretical structure, with the exception of the hypothetical mythodynamic field, is not too different from the General Theory of Action. However, in this and other socio-cultural theories the ideologically and mythologically motivated personality is generally explained by being reduced to social and cultural-symbolic phenomena. This may be the result of the early positivistic history of social science as a kind of reductionist social physics where societies were regarded as simply aggregates of individual 'atoms' like the insects so admired by the Greeks and rational Enlightenment thinkers. Even the theory of the General Will which underpins democratic egalitarian ideology is assumed to be a summation of equally valued individual wills.

Marxist economists see this as the form taken by alienated bourgeois individualism in capitalist cultures. They assume that industrial workers are suffering from false consciousness and once they are made aware of their true interests, or ideodynamics, by Marxist intellectuals (derived from their personal 'symbol kinematics of evolving value') they can unite and create a new socialist Utopia free from alienation. Note that Marx had no place in his theory for more independent rural peasants. But the old problem remained, 'Who guards the Guardians?' We saw what happened!

SOUL DYNAMICS, EGO KINEMATICS AND PERSONALITY

At the University of New South Wales during the late 1960s I was responsible for organising classes in the Sociology of Religion. I had been first introduced to the cultural phenomena of revitalisation movements in preliterate societies at the University of Leeds ten years earlier. I was also giving classes at the Free University on the culture and personality theories of David Riesman in his book *The Lonely Crowd*, and the writings and films of Marshal McLuhan, the 'Electronic Prophet'. Both men emphasise the essential psychological sensitivity and social role differences between preliterate, literate and what McLuhan termed 'post-literate' cultures where advertising and consumerism were subverting the personality characteristics and industrial work ethic of the previous generation. Moreover, at this time Western Society was itself undergoing a massive revitalisation movement. The 'post-literate' electronic mass media, especially television and popular music were, as McLuhan pointed out, playing a major part in transforming basic psychological and social feelings and attitudes, especially those relating to marriage, sex and reproduction. The sudden impact of electric technology and the transmission of brightly lit images at the speed of light can be seen to be as devastating to a bourgeois mercantile civilization based on Iron Age technology as the sudden impact of widely available iron was on the already collapsed aristocratic heroic culture of the Bronze Age.

THE PROPHET

I was particularly interested in the archetypical character of the pre-literate prophet who sometimes succeeded in creating a new culture with its accompanying new role structures, and the therapeutic psychological aspects of the revitalisation movements wherever they occurred. In a 1956 issue of *The American Anthropologist* the psychiatrist and anthropologist A.F.C Wallace produced a classic account of the reported psychological and physiological changes in the nervous systems of prophets who led revitalisation movements, and the accompanying changes in social roles and cultural-meaning that followed a successful implementation of their vision. It was obvious that the 'personality' of this type of prophet was a higher-level phenomenon than the existing culture or social institutions. As the mouthpiece of a god, the prophet was functioning rather like a god/creator in a literate theological cosmology.

Nietzsche saw himself in this role and his writings show that, like other prophets, he had in many ways transcended the meaning system of his culture. However, he was often in poor physical health and had difficulties relating to people socially, especially women. He was also embedded in a literate civilization where control of meaning was monopolised by institutions of higher learning and rapid personal-cultural transformation at that time was only likely to occur in poor, semi-literate, working-class slums and remote rural peasant communities. Nietzsche's social roles derived their authority from his university professorship and his brilliance as a published writer. In times of political-economic crisis less intellectually sophisticated individuals with a more practical understanding of sociocultural reality, like Alexander, Augustus, Constantine, Napoleon and more recently, Hitler, Churchill, Mao Tse Tung, Vladimir Putin and even Donald Trump, are able, in certain conditions of socio-cultural breakdown, to impose their personalities and create (or degrade) a major culture. Consequently, I took the unprecedented step of placing 'soul-dynamics expressed as ego kinematics in evolving/devolving personalities in meaning systems' at a higher or more complex level of being than 'ideo-dynamics expressed as symbol kinematics in evolving/devolving values in institutions'.

As ideo-dynamic intention is the refinement of mythodynamic intention at the cultural level, so soul-dynamic intention is the refinement of ideo-dynamic intention at the personality level. To the best of my knowledge, 'personality' as a phenomenon has not previously been understood in any other hierarchical sociocultural theory as capable of evolving above culture in this way. Early in the twentieth century Max Weber was deeply involved the study of various forms of charisma which he believed was the only thing that could stop the inevitable spread of rational bureaucracy which ultimately destroys authentic human values. This is particularly the case since it cannot by definition be described symbolically but it may be experienced intuitively. In urbanised literate cultures it is an extremely rare phenomenon in its fully realised form. This may be because personal control over literate cultures is easier if exercised as a puppet master concealed behind a cultural mask like God or the People or the Class or the Nation.

In the monotheistic theological cosmologies in the partially-literate civilizations of Judaism, Christianity and Islam, God is the only supreme 'personality' phenomenon. Priests and prophets can only revitalise their culture by claiming they are speaking on God's behalf. The evolving 'values' in such agricultural societies are centred on fertility, land acquisition and the control of reproduction.

In historically unique Judeo-Christian-Islamic monotheism emphasis on the value of personal being or worship of objects, including natural phenomena, threatens the theocentric value structure and is emphatically discouraged.

TIME FOR A CHANGE OF PARADIGM

The orthodox paradigm in modern society is the mathematical-mechanistic cosmology devoutly believed in by secular intellectuals employed by the national and international teaching and research bureaucracies. Here the dominant value orientation is not concerned with meaning or purpose but with 'usefulness' for the bureaucratic military-industrial elite and their dependent politicians who finance and employ them and give them their status. The evolving 'values' in industrialised and post industrialised civilizations are more centred on production than reproduction or concern with organic reality and are now moving towards the encouragement of the possession, display and/or the consumption of objects as commodities. Increasingly any emphasis on the value of any form of subjective being, other than the fake charisma created in the form of 'celebrity' based on exposure in the escapist entertainment media, or intellectual status as a Pythagorean mathematical hard scientist, threatens the established mechanistic model and is discouraged. Marriage and reproduction lose their previous value and are weakened not only by prioritising sexual self-expression but also by control of family behaviour through a state education and welfare bureaucracy based on social-engineering and financed by compulsory taxation. Personal physical health and wealth are treated as the pre-eminent existential values for the isolated individual. Mental health and community wellbeing are not seen as important priorities as they require more complex conceptual tools to be understood and dealt with.

Values that need to be prioritised, exemplified and maintained by the living personalities in the proposed process cosmology are those that lead to environmental sustainability. In general, childless, romantic-love-based marriages not restricted to heterosexual or even monogamous unions should be regarded as ethically equal or even superior to those based on serial monogamy or fertility. Leisure, emphasising learning for its own sake as well as utilitarian craft skills, exploratory travel and play, all need to be valued more than credit creation, currency trading, shopping, tourism and frantic consuming in general. Leaders of a fun revolutionary revitalisation movement based on Love, Logic and Levity would have to live like Epicureans in fairly humble conditions and provide role models by exemplifying all three qualities in their own lives. They would need skill in exploiting the electronic media including the internet to create themselves into independent celebrities to compete with the puppet celebrities controlled by the commercial corporations. Academic staff in publicly funded universities and research establishments, who are the heirs of the utilitarian Enlightenment, are prevented from participating in such a Fun Revolution by their need to maintain the respectability required of their cultural role expectations.

NAMING THE PARTS IN THE HIERARCHIES OF REALITY

Hierarchies are made up of information control, feedback and qualitative upgrading.

INVOLUTION AND EVOLUTION

Involution is the progressive complexification of hypothetical intentionality. Evolution is the progressive complexification of experienceable extensionality. These processes are mutually linked through the selection provided by eventuality. Deduction is used to hypothesise involution, induction to hypothesise evolution.

PRETENDING

Pretending, from the Latin "to reach forward", does not merely indicate deception. Mimetic learning and new symbolically expressed hypotheses are created and revised this way.

SINGULARITIES

The two most important singularities in this cosmology are the Big Bang and Heaven. Both are man-made useful fictions for current human reality controllers, as is the cultural identity of their rival, the official Wizard of New Zealand. The question remains, "Useful to Whom?" Without a complete, process-relational, postmodern cosmology this cannot be rationally decided.

This outline also provides contextual definitions of the concepts Logic, and Love as used by the cultural activist Wizard. Levity is as impossible to adequately define as Gravity.

LOVE

Through logical deduction love is hypothesised here to be the dynamic discharge of tension from intentionality fields. As involution of intention increases in complexity it is manifested by more complex evolution extended in space which is experienceable. By logical induction, hypothetical models of experienced extension are created and tested experimentally through eventuality. Love as growth, self-preservation, organic cooperation and competition, becomes increasing more powerful. It can be understood as rising from the weak force, the electro-magnetic force, the strong interaction force, chemical bonding, bios, philia, storge, eros and ultimately agape. This inter-related terminology is unique to the new process cosmology. In the current reductionist-mechanistic cosmology, which is driven by chance, there are no equivalent subjective processes, only hypothetical objective and unintentional 'forces'.

STRUCTURE AND FUNCTION, AN IDEAL TYPOLOGY

- Subatomic particles function within atomic structures to create involution and evolution.
- Atomic structures function within molecular structures to create involution and evolution.
- Molecular structures function within cellular structures to create involution and evolution.
- Cellular structures function within organic structures to create involution and evolution.
- Organic structures function within social role structures to create involution and evolution.
- Social role structures function within cultural structures to create involution and evolution.
- Cultural structures function within personality structures to create involution and evolution.
- Personality structures function within aspirational transcendental structures which cannot be named since naming is a subordinating process.

Alice; curator of the Living Work of Art and personal assistant to the Cosmologer. The diagrams reproduced in this book were created by her in 1974 when this picture was taken.

HIERARCHY OF EVOLVING KINEMATICS

THE ANIMAL ETHOSYSTEM
Evolving Behaviour In Species

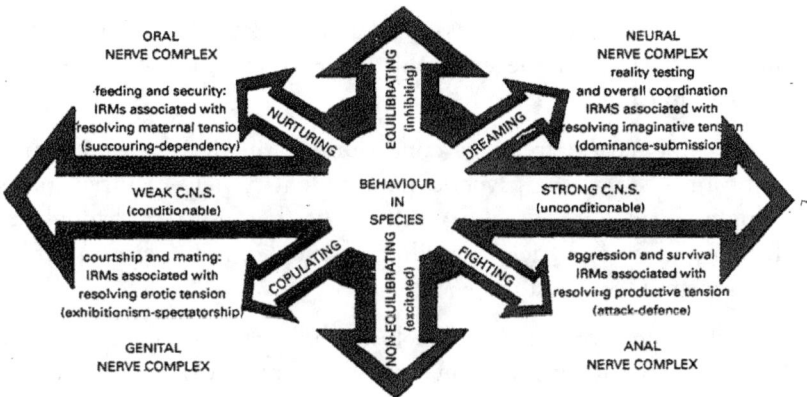

I chose the term ethosystem following the studies of animal behaviour by such ethologists as Tinbergen who hypothesised innate release mechanisms in animal brains as psychodynamic explanations. Pavlov's experiments in conditioning and his conclusion that the behaviour of his dogs could be classified into the four traditional categories of 'phlegmatic', 'choleric', 'melancholic' and 'sanguine' enabled me to link these with Freud's four stages of psychic development and with Jung's typologies of introversion and extraversion and anima animus archetypes.

I divide behaviour into nurturing, aggression, copulating and dreaming/imagining. These ideal types are produced from the dialectical central nervous system characteristics proposed by Pavlov, i.e. oppositions in the central nervous systems of 'excited' versus 'inhibited' and 'weak' versus 'strong' states. They also correspond with Freud's oral, anal, genital and latency stages of human development. I was not satisfied with the irrational concept of latency since I regard the brain itself as an organ whose activities cannot be simply reduced to serving other organic desires. I replaced it with the term 'neural' and associated it with such activities as dreaming and building mental maps of the environment.

- The psycho-dynamic field of intention 'predisposes' an energetic expression of love for which I chose the term *philia*. The result is observable in the form of neural kinematics of evolving or devolving behaviour in species, these neural kinematic processes either resolve and express or repress nervous tension.
- Feedback and control processes modify and shape the realised animal ethosystem in the eventuality hierarchy through **inhibiting** and **stimulating**.
- Nerve kinematics are also **conditioning** the lower level transmutation system. The psychodynamic identity field of intention is being modified by control from the realised ethosystem through **reflexing** and by feedback/upgrading in the form of **excitating** from the transmutation system.
- The ethosystem provides feedback/upgrading to the mythodynamic field through **releasing**. Action kinematics in the form of role performances are **inhibiting** the ethosystem.

THE MAMMALIAN SOCIAL SYSTEM
Evolving Roles In Families

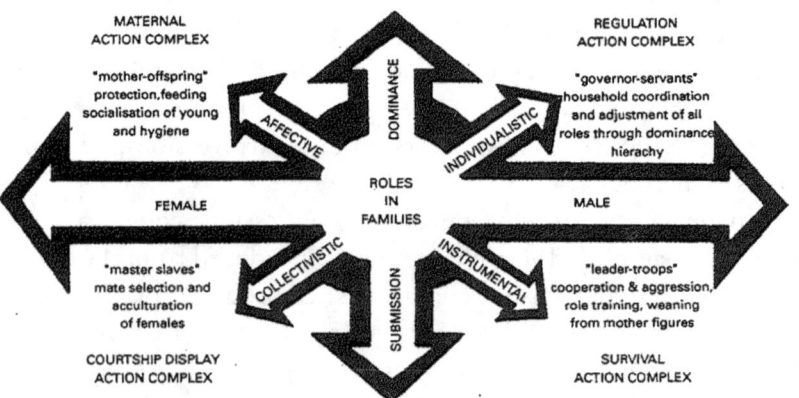

Social systems are made up of interactive role complexes based on the neural-behavioural complexes I have described. These are mainly found in mammals since, with the exception of birds in particular, egg-laying reptiles do not rear their young in collectivities of individual organisms or form sexual bonds.

The binary oppositions here are **masculine-feminine** and **dominance-submission**. The Maternal, which is the dominant feminine action complex, is associated with **affectivity** in psycho-social theories, the submissive masculine behaviour found in many young males associated with Survival is **instrumental**, as opposed to affective. **Collectivism** characterises the Courtship and mating action complex which is centred on the submissive feminine action complex, as opposed to the **individualism** of the dominant male as the regulating role complex. Roles are not reducible to organisms. Both male and female and even dominant and submissive animals may, in special circumstances, act out contrary roles.

- The mytho-dynamic field of intention predisposes an energetic expression of love which I term *storge*. The result is observable/experienceable in the form of evolving or devolving action kinematics of evolving families. These action kinematics either resolve and express or repress social tension.

- Feedback and control processes modify and shape the realised mammalian ethosystem in the eventuality hierarchy through **discouraging** and **performing**.

- Action kinematics are also **inhibiting** the lower level behavioural/relationship system. The mythodynamic identity field of intention is being modified by control from the realised social system through **responding** and by feedback/upgrading in the form of **releasing** from the lower level transmutation system.

- The social system provides feedback/upgrading to the ideodynamic field through **encouraging**. Action kinematics in the form of role performances are **inhibiting** the animal ethosystem.

THE HUMAN CULTURE SYSTEM
Evolving Values In Institutions

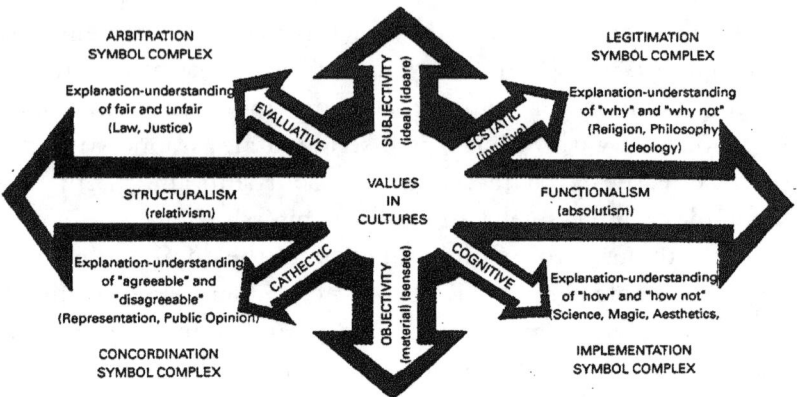

I adopted the famous statement about culture made by Kroeber the cultural anthropologist together with the sociologist Talcott Parsons that it is a system qualitatively distinct from social systems. Value Orientation Theory provided me with some of the necessary kinematics and I derived my dialectical oppositions from Structural Functional Sociology. The resultant value orientations are a modified version of Jungian theory.

I divided the values into **evaluative** versus **cognitive** and **cathectic** versus **ecstatic**. These are produced from dialectical oppositions between structural (relativistic) and functional (absolutist) and between subjective (idealist) and objective (materialist). The ideodynamic field 'predisposes' an energetic expression I call 'eros'. The result is observable /experienceable as symbol kinematics of evolving/devolving values in institutions. Symbol kinematics either resolve and express or repress symbol tension (defined as religious, political or scientific heresy). Feedback and control processes modify and shape the realised human culture system in the eventuality hierarchy through **understanding**.

Whilst symbol kinematics are **discouraging** the lower level social system the ideodynamic identity field of intention is being modified by control from the realised human culture system through **explaining** and by feedback/upgrading in the form of **encouraging** from the lower level social system. The culture system provides feedback/upgrading to the upper level soul-dynamic identity field through **affirming**. Ego kinematics, through **negating**, provide control of the culture system.

THE ANDROGYNOUS PERSONALITY SYSTEM
Evolving Personalities In Cultures

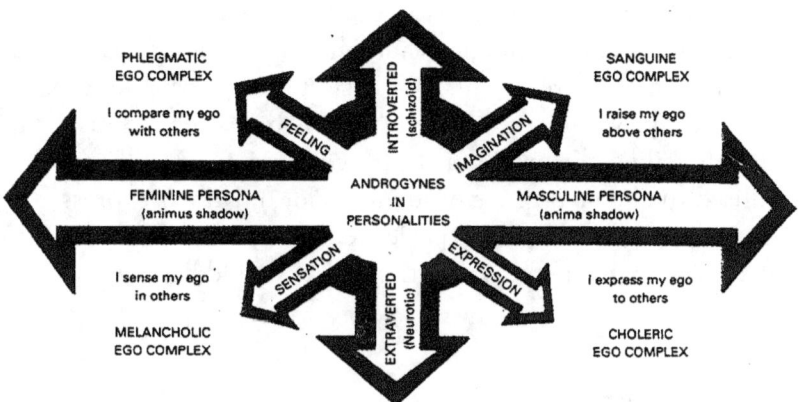

Following Jung I divided the ego manifestations of personality into **introverted** versus **extroverted** and **anima** versus **animus**. These dialectical oppositions produce four orientations, **feeling** (phlegmatic), **expressing** (choleric), **sensing** (melancholic) and **imagining** (sanguine). This ideal typology of personality types, which correspond closely with those of Jung, has been in use since the time of the great Hellenistic anatomist, Galen.

The soul-dynamic field of intention is energetically expressed through love in the form of *agape*. The result can be observed in the form of ego kinematics of evolving or devolving personalities in matrices of meaning. Ego kinematics either resolve or repress ego tension. Feedback and control processes modify and shape the as yet unrealised, imaginary higher heavenly system through **aspiring** (expressed as the desire to levitate, ascend etc.). Ego kinematics also perform the function of **negating** (in the Hegelian sense) or confounding (in the religious sense) the lower level cultural system. The soul-dynamic field of intention is being modified by control from the imagined transcendent system by **inspiring** and by feedback/upgrading in the form of **affirming** from the lower level human cultural system.

The dynamics and kinematics can be outlined however, and in doing this I am indebted to Nietzsche's writings on the evolved ego which transcends culture. Teilhard de Chardin's radical synthesis of religion and science, *The Phenomenon of Man*, provided me with the concept of 'involution', the increasing complexity of intention which must be assumed to accompany evolution, the increasing complexity of extension. His emphasis on a final cosmic convergence as the supreme act of love incarnated made a big impression on me.

Aesthetic, scientific, religious and philosophical urgings motivated me not only to create this synthetic process cosmology but to base it on a probabilistic hierarchy of historic events. This ranges from 'impossible', the origin of the universe, to 'inevitable', an as yet unrealised final convergence of identity not only as as expressed intention, but as subjectively experienced extension, and eventuality, as what actually happens, rather than what should happen.

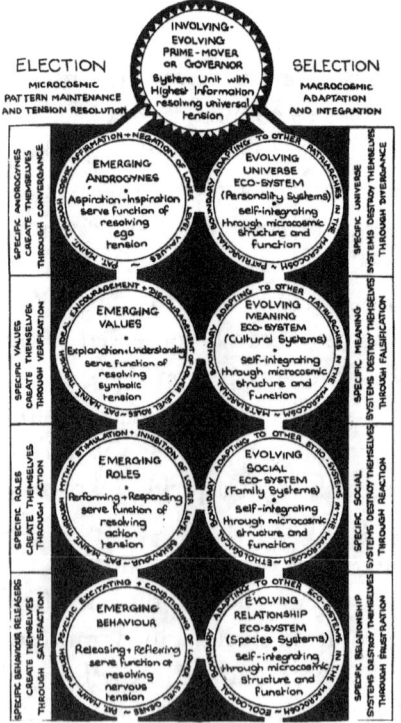
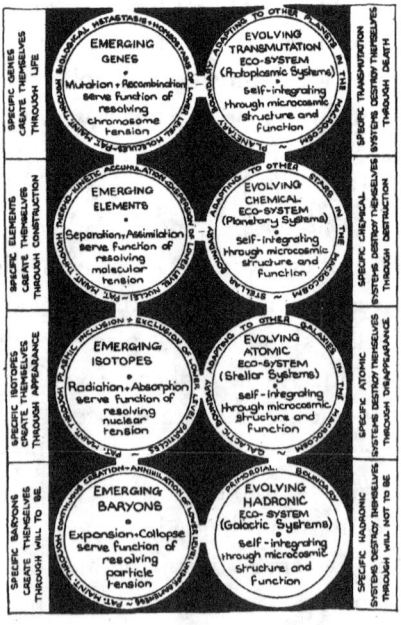

MACROCOSMIC STRUCTURES
(each level includes the ones below)

MICROCOSMIC STRUCTURES
(each level includes the ones below)

HYPOTHETICAL UNIVERSE CORE
(differentiated uniqueness)

PERIMETER OF METAPHYSICAL SPECULATION
which creates and sustains
the SOUL FORCE between culture leaders

EGO CORE of bonded personal beliefs
carrying the SPIRITUAL CODE
which identifies the Personality Species

PERIMETER OF CULTURAL COMMUNICATION
which creates and sustains
the BELIEF FORCE between believers

SYMBOL CORE of bonded symbolic actions
carrying the VALUE CODE
which identifies the Culture Species

PERIMETER OF FAMILY NETWORK
which creates and sustains
the SOCIAL FORCE between family members

ACTION CORE of bonded behaviour
carrying the ROLE CODE
which identifies the Family Species

PERIMETER OF ORGANISM'S BRAIN
which creates and sustains
the PSYCHIC FORCE between organisms

NERVE CORE of bonded neurones (CNS)
carrying the BEHAVIOURAL RELEASER CODE
which identifies the Organism Species

PERIMETER OF CELL
which creates and sustains
the LIFE FORCE between bonded cells

CHROMOSOME CORE of bonded molecules
carrying the GENETIC CODE
which identifies the Cell Species

PERIMETER OF MOLECULAR SHEATH
which creates and sustains
the COLLOIDAL FORCE between chemical phases

IONISED CORE of bonded atoms
carrying the ELEMENTAL CODE
(coord. no. and valency no.)
which identifies the Chemical Species

PERIMETER OF ELECTRON SHELL
which creates and sustains
the CHEMICAL FORCE between atoms

NUCLEAR CORE
carrying the ISOTOPIC CODE (photon no.)
which identifies the Atomic Species

PERIMETER OF MESON CLOUD
which creates and sustains
the STRONG FORCE between hadrons

PARTICLE CORE
carrying the BARYONIC CODE
(baryon no., strangeness)
which identifies the Hadronic Species

HYPOTHETICAL PERIMETER OF UNIVERSE
(undifferentiated sameness)

PERSONALITY PERIMETER
location of highest evolved and
lowest devolved reality-definitions.

PERSONALITY CORE
focus of Soul-dynamics of Ego-Mechanics

CULTURE PERIMETER
location of highest evolved and
lowest devolved value orientations.

CULTURE CORE
focus of Idea-dynamics and Symbol Mechanics

FAMILY PERIMETER
location of highest evolved and
lowest devolved cultures.

FAMILY CORE
focus of Myth-dynamics and Action Mechanics

SPECIES (ORGANISM) PERIMETER
location of highest evolved and
lowest devolved families.

SPECIES (ORGANISM) CORE
focus of Nerve Mechanics
and Psycho-dynamics.

PROTOPLASMA PERIMETER
location of highest evolved and
lowest devolved species

PROTOPLASMA CORE
focus of Chromosome
Mechanics and Biodynamics (the sea)

PLANETARY PERIMETER
location of highest evolved and
lowest devolved ecosystems.

PLANETARY CORE
focus of Molecule Mechanics and
Thermodynamics (Geo-Mechanics)

STELLAR PERIMETER
location of highest evolved and
lowest devolved planets.

STELLAR CORE
focus of Nuclear Mechanics
Plasma-dynamics (reaction zone)

GALACTIC PERIMETER
location of highest evolved and
lowest devolved stars.

GALACTIC CORE
focus of Physo-dynamics and
Particle Mechanics

THROUGHOUT THE DESCRIPTIONS THE TERM KINEMATICS WILL BE MORE APPROPRIATE THAN MECHANICS

"The only thing we have to fear, is fear itself."

―⁓⁓⁓―

"If you can keep your head when all about you
Are losing theirs and blaming it on you,
If you can trust yourself when all men doubt you,
... then you'll be man my son."

Contact The Wizard of New Zealand through his website:
www.wizard.gen.nz

www.ingramcontent.com/pod-product-compliance
Lightning Source LLC
Chambersburg PA
CBHW071343290426
44108CB00014B/1424